D1523242

Studies in the English Renaissance

JOHN T. SHAWCROSS
Editor

The
Unfolding God
of Jung and Milton

JAMES P. DRISCOLL

THE UNIVERSITY PRESS OF KENTUCKY

Copyright © 1993 by The University Press of Kentucky

Scholarly publisher for the Commonwealth,
serving Bellarmine College, Berea College, Centre
College of Kentucky, Eastern Kentucky University,
The Filson Club, Georgetown College, Kentucky
Historical Society, Kentucky State University,
Morehead State University, Murray State University,
Northern Kentucky University, Transylvania University,
University of Kentucky, University of Louisville,
and Western Kentucky University.

Editorial and Sales Offices: Lexington, Kentucky 40508-4008

Library of Congress Cataloging-in-Publication Data

Driscoll, James P., 1946-
    The Unfolding God of Jung and Milton / James P. Driscoll.
      p. cm. — (Studies in the English Renaissance)
    Includes bibliographical references and index.
    ISBN 0-8131-1809-3
    1. Milton, John, 1608-1674—Religion. 2. Jung, C.G. (Carl
Gustav), 1875-1961. 3. Archetype (Psychology) in literature.
4. Psychoanalysis and literature. 5. God—History of doctrines.
6. God in literature. I. Title. II. Series.
PR3592.G6D75 1993
821'.4—dc20   92-21769

Dedicated to the memory of
my mother, PHYLLIS DRISCOLL,
and of my friend, DAVE OLSON

Contents

Preface

Books have for progenitors other books. *The Unfolding God of Jung and Milton* has for its dominant progenitor C.G. Jung's *Answer to Job*. *Answer to Job* mounted a challenge to orthodox dogmas about Godhead as radical as Freud's challenge to Victorian pieties about sex. Now commonplace, Freud's theories have lost their initial shock value. Not so Jung's ideas on Godhead: still profoundly unsettling, they are alternately disregarded, misconstrued, and opposed with fervor.

Approaching scriptural myth in an iconoclastic spirit, Jung ignored scholarly tact along with those historical backgrounds sectarian pedagogues use to obfuscate embarrassing problems. His objective was to uncover the psychological motives and philosophical ideas that power the basic myths ordinary Christians believe. A ready, easy, and safe Jungian treatment of Godhead in Milton's major poems would enumerate and tactfully comment upon archetypes and mythic patterns. But that would betray the spirit and objective of Jung and do nothing to account for the difficulties moderns experience with Milton. I shall avoid the ready, easy, and safe way. My interpretations will hold true to Jung even where a Jungian stance controverts established doctrine and disputes standard readings.

Accordingly, those ill-prepared to entertain fundamental rethinking of sacred verities may spare themselves some anguish by returning to the shelf unread both *Answer to Job* and *The Unfolding God of Jung and Milton*. Those ready to reject religious orthodoxy may nonetheless balk at Jung's rejecting science as a modern, secular orthodoxy. For Jung experimental science is a set of tools generated by the larger psyche whose study forms the task of psychology. We cannot, Jung held, explain all phenomena of the larger psyche with the limited tools of science. Something more encompassing is needed to deal with the engendering whole: Jung proposed the theory of archetypes.

While there is scientific evidence for the archetypes, those who seek it will have to look elsewhere. In support of using archetypes I offer two nonscientific arguments, one analogical, the other pragmatic. First, it can be observed that archetypes are like gravity: no one has ever isolated gravity, we only perceive that objects fall and planets follow their orbits—

the theory of gravity has been formulated to account for these patterns in natural phenomena. Similarly, the theory of archetypes has been formulated to account for patterns in psychic phenomena. The pragmatic argument is simply that, valid or not, Jungian psychology, like Freudianism, Marxian thought, and orthodox Christian doctrine, enjoys wide influence. Jungian psychology cannot match the sway of the others, but its influence is growing, nourished by cultural change and new discoveries in physics, biology, linguistics, anthropology, and psychology. Jung deserves to be understood. Whether and to what extent he deserves belief must remain a personal decision.

Some will acknowledge the impact of Jung's theories but object to applying modern theories to Milton. There is no reason to apply modern theories to Milton if we do not care whether Milton remains alive. However, if we wish him to be more than a historical artifact, we must do more than just study him against the background of his time. We must reinterpret him in light of the germane thought of our own age.

Among the influential thinkers of our century, Jung is the most significant one hailing from Protestant origins. Milton is undoubtedly the foremost Protestant poet. Both men began with an individualistic Protestant approach to certain fundamental questions: the relationship of man to God, the unfolding nature of Godhead, the meaning of the Trinity, the role of Satan and evil, and the function of the sexes. Both men's religious outlooks were shaped by personal responses to God the Father, albeit those responses stand quite opposed. Both developed their own views of the Son and of Adam and Eve, and both were fascinated by Satan in his protean manifestations. Moreover, since to be free is to be conscious and to be conscious for Jung is to be free, freedom and consciousness, the signal values of Milton and Jung, are entwined.

Thus, it would seem, among the greats of our age Jung has unique potential to illumine Milton. Illumination often works both ways. That is the case here where the light Jung sheds on Milton's religious concerns reflects back to illumine those same concerns in Jung. The result can be new insight into Christianity itself.

Not only do they come from the same general tradition with similar concerns, Jung and Milton the poet share a basic approach to those concerns: imaginative amplification. Jung held that we do not directly know archetypes; we apprehend them indirectly through images, myths, and symbols. He sought to enhance our awareness of the archetypes by imaginatively amplifying images, myths, and symbols. Visionary poets also amplify images, myths, and symbols. And, what is crucial, a culture's supreme visionary poets—the writer of Job, Homer, Dante, Shakespeare, and Milton for instance—amplify images, myths, and symbols to give us glimpses, or epiphanies, of their culture's prime archetypes or gods.

Let me turn to the critic's goal, archetypal meaning. Just as a Möbius strip has only one side, the archetype and its meaning are inseparable, one ever continuous with the other. Since archetypes cannot be directly known, archetypal meaning is less specific and more mysterious than intended meaning. In addition, it compensates for the imbalanced conscious values of the artist and his culture—such is the fundamental principle of authentic Jungian criticism. Conventional critics who make authorial intentions and cultural values their touchstones for meaning will find Jungian criticism often frustrating and at times downright maddening. "You're wrong," they'll cry, "Milton could never have intended that archetype to mean what you say it means." To which I must respond, "It wouldn't be an archetype if it obeyed Milton's conscious intentions." Visionary poetry is born of the strange, irregular interplay of intentions, archetypes, and imagination. And not only do archetypes and imagination go their own ways subtly defying intention, that is their proper function. Here many critics may wish to join their orthodox religious and scientific brethren returning this book to the shelf.

For those remaining readers, few but undaunted, I offer two additional caveats, the first about the book's peculiar structure. So autonomous are its four main chapters, the first written in draft ten years prior to the others, they often more resemble distinct treatises sharing common topics than parts of a unified whole. The loose structure, however, reflects an overall method. With Jung's principle of imaginative amplification of archetypes and the idea of process as my guides, I have found in the spiral an image for my method and structure. The opening chapter introduces the basic critical issues, philosophical concepts, and archetypal themes shaping what follows. The second and third chapters spiral up, like a widening gyre, each recapitulating, amplifying, and deepening what went before. Because these three chapters address two distinct concerns, archetypal theory and its critical application, I have separated them into distinct Jung and Milton parts. The two concerns are blended in the fourth chapter, which uses *Samson Agonistes* to wind out the spiral.

An extensive glossary defines concepts and nomenclature peculiar to Jung, Milton, and this work. The necessity of often referring to the glossary signals my final caveat: the theoretical aspects of *The Unfolding God of Jung and Milton* are notably difficult, making heavy demands on attention, knowledge, and imaginative insight with their challenges to accepted paradigms. The difficulty, like that of *Answer to Job* itself, reflects high ambitions.

The Unfolding God of Jung and Milton will synergize Jung and Milton to manifest Father, Son, Satan, and Holy Spirit in a widening gyre of consciousness of psyche and Godhead. Such is my paramount ambition; I no more limit myself to cataloging the archetypes in Milton's poems than Jung limited himself to cataloging the archetypes in the Book of Job. In *Answer to Job* Jung works from the startling premise that our perception of the psyche shapes our vision of God. Jung's premise implies that as we become more conscious of the psyche we simultaneously envision a more conscious God. We see this process in archetypal works treating man's encounter with divinity, for example, Job, Ezekiel's visions, the Gospels, and the Apocalypse. These works show man making Godhead conscious, but the process did not stop with Saint John the Divine. Powered by archetypes, it moves in a gyre, each spiral recapitulating, yet amplifying and deepening, what passed before.

To trace that gyre in subsequent ages we must focus upon literary works that, amidst their sophistication and complexity, give epiphanies of the primal archetypes of Godhead. Approaching Godhead in Milton we should seek not what is old, for that merely reiterates doctrine, but what, in his distinctive treatment of archetypes, evinces upward spiraling consciousness. The results may unnerve a final group of orthodox believers, those conventional Jungians who resist acknowledging that our supreme imaginative achievements, *King Lear* and *Paradise Lost*, constellate the archetypes of Godhead for our modern era even as the Book of Job, the Gospels, and the Apocalypse constellated these archetypes for their times. Despite all orthodox qualms, *The Unfolding God of Jung and Milton* will remain true to the spirit of Jung and follow Milton's visionary muse as it strives to unfold Godhead to consciousness.

1

Something
of Graver Import

Hence poetry is something more philosophic and of graver import
than history, since its statements are of the nature rather of univer-
sals, whereas those of history are singulars.

—*Aristotle*

With both the *Iliad* and more or less in all epic Poems where the
subjects are from History, they have no rounded conclusion—they
remain after all but a single chapter from the volume of History
tho' an ornamented Chapter. . . . The superiority of *Paradise Lost*
is obvious, . . . it comprehends . . . the origin of evil and the
combat of Evil and Good, a matter of such interest to all mankind
as to form the basis of all religions, and the true occasion of all
Philosophy.

—*Samuel Taylor Coleridge*

Paradise Lost is rich above all other epics in the graver import of the
universal or the archetypal. Critics, however, have left unexcavated some
of the richest veins of its graver import. Bringing them to light requires two
fundamental changes. First, we must give archetypal elements priority
over historical influences and Milton's conscious designs, those surface
veins of meaning critics commonly pursue. Second, we must supplement
standard critical methods with philosophical and psychological methods
designed to probe the archetypal. Implementing these changes, this
chapter will utilize the combined methods of modern philosophy and
Jungian psychology to explore the graver import in Milton's treatment of
Godhead.

I have divided the chapter into five parts. In the first section I
establish the need for new approaches by showing how the dominant
critical schools neglect or misconstrue Milton's graver import. In the
second section I apply a philosophic-psychological approach to the the-
odicy of *Paradise Lost*. In the third section I consider how archetypal
conflicts influence theological positions on free will. In the fourth section I

use Jung's analytical psychology to investigate the archetypes of Godhead. And in the final section I establish an archetypal perspective upon the ethical and philosophical outlooks that shape *Paradise Lost;* the chapter concludes with a critical overview. Like the book as a whole, this chapter has a twofold character: it is an original study of Milton informed by Jung and an original study of Jungian thought.

DOMINANT CRITICAL SCHOOLS

The philosophic-psychological approach I employ will incur resistance among traditional Milton critics and scholars.[1] Rather than try to gloss over differences between my approach and that of my more traditional colleagues, I will show the limitations of their basic assumptions. Once these limitations become apparent, it ought to be clear that a philosophic-psychological approach, such as the one I offer, is a legitimate, indeed a necessary, alternative.

Assumptions about the Reader.   Stanley Fish's *Surprised by Sin* remains a prime watershed of traditional assumptions about the reader. Cut to its essence, Fish's argument is that in *Paradise Lost* Milton orchestrates reader responses to the main drama through rhetoric functioning like metadrama. Milton's presumed intentions are (1) to entangle the wayward reader in Satan's rhetoric and Adam and Eve's errors thus inducing a guilt that can spur repentance and doctrinal purification or (2) to test the wary reader and thereby strengthen his faith. Objective understanding of *Paradise Lost,* Fish contends, comes only to those readers who respond to Milton's rhetoric the way Milton intended.

However, suppressing our modern responses to follow Milton's Christian rhetoric, as some traditionalists attempt to do, creates a problem of authenticity. Authentic reader responses are born of authentic personal values choices. Even orthodox Christians living in the twentieth century choose their values within a modern, not a seventeenth-century, context. Because moderns must reject or embrace important alternatives to orthodoxy (e.g., scientific philosophy, Freud, Jung, and Marx) that were unavailable in the seventeenth century, their value choices necessarily differ from those of Milton's original "fit" readers. The authentic choices and responses of Milton's "fit" readers are, therefore, as lost to us as Adam's unfallen state.

The problem of authenticity extends further. Twentieth-century readers of *Paradise Lost* themselves are an increasingly heterogenous lot. They include Jews, Moslems, Hindus, Buddhists, adherents of heterodox Western thought systems like Marxism, analytic philosophy, existentialism,

Freudianism, and Jungianism along with non-Protestant Christians and Protestants for whom Milton's scriptural literalism proves unpalatable. The most that can be expected of these "unfit" modern readers is to suspend disbelief temporarily in order to apprehend what the poet endeavored to say or do to his "fit" reader. Afterwards they must return to themselves and respond authentically from their personal values. If we prohibit the last step, the poem will become for them a dead artifact.

Supreme works of imagination, even those that are openly didactic, stimulate the minds and stir the spirits of readers committed to diverse value systems. However, didactic works that lack ecumenical appeal remain essentially propagandistic. To be sure, Milton the prose writer was an accomplished propagandist, but Milton the poet was much more than that. By reducing Milton to a Christian apologist, admiring critics diminish his achievement no less than those who disparage his work because they reject his theology. In either case Milton's poems dwindle to artful propaganda for a dated theology, their enduring value mere technical virtuosity.

Oblivious to these considerations, traditional critics often assume recalcitrant modern readers are like seventeenth-century Protestants in need of a heavy dose of repentance and reform. Repentance and reform, however, go beyond imaginative suspension of disbelief to promote theological and psychological credulity. Suspension of disbelief to achieve an overview of one's own values that allows appreciation of an alternative value system is a legitimate critical request.[2] But criticism cannot legitimately ask readers to drop their personal beliefs (that is, suspend belief, not disbelief) and embrace the beliefs of an earlier age. Such a betrayal of authenticity would yield atavism, not objectivity, nostalgia, not insight.

Assumptions about Meaning in Art.   Reevaluation, traditional critics often argue, does not give us the poem Milton wrote. This assumes that the only valid meanings in Milton's poems are the ones he intentionally put there. When we apply to Milton criticism Jungian scholar Rivkah S. Kluger's discerning advice to religious historians, it becomes evident why the critics' assumption is untenable:

To be sure, one must let one's ideas grow out of the material, not put them into it. But in the process of grasping the material, one cannot ignore all possibilities of understanding which have crystallized during subsequent cultural developments. For instance, to understand archaic thinking does not mean to think archaically oneself. Distance, not identification, is just what makes understanding possible. . . . our understanding of the material must necessarily go beyond the self-understanding of a past era, for, old material contains more meaning than was conscious at the time of its origin. . . . We must immerse ourselves in the material in as unprejudiced a manner as possible or better, with the greatest possible awareness of our own preconceptions. But we cannot avoid expressing the meanings we have grasped in the cognitive terms which our culture has created since. Concepts like "hypostasis," "manifestation," "identity," and the like can therefore be applied with full legitimacy to an Old Testament context, even though they are not Old Testament concepts themselves.[3]

Similarly, to understand Milton does not mean to think like Milton oneself. Understanding requires distance, not identification, which abdicates critical judgment. Milton's poems contain more meaning than their author or his contemporaries grasped, and it's our obligation to probe their total meaning. While we must always remain aware of our preconceptions, we cannot and should not avoid expressing meaning in cognitive terms that our culture offers or avoid posing questions Milton's beliefs or conceptual tools would not have allowed him to pose.

Because it was not possible for Milton to comprehend the entire meaning of all the ideas, symbols, and myths his vast subjects encompassed, his poems convey meanings different from and larger than what he intended. Moreover, in dealing with powerful, archetypal figures such as Adam and Eve, the Father, the Son, and Satan, and in following his muse, Milton the artist necessarily fell under the sway of unconscious forces that have their own intents and purposes that, however much he may have tried, Milton the apologist could never entirely suppress or control. Of the artist whose visions carry him beyond the constrictive dogmas of the cultural canon into the heart of our primal myths, C.G. Jung observes: "Being essentially the instrument of his work, he is subordinate to it, and we have no right to expect him to interpret it for us. He has done his utmost by giving it form, and must leave the interpretation to others and to the future. A great work of art is like a dream; for all its apparent obviousness it does not explain itself and is always ambiguous. A dream never says 'you ought' or 'this is the truth.' It presents an image in much the same way as nature allows a plant to grow, and it is up to us to draw conclusions."[4] Accordingly, the most significant meanings of *Paradise Lost* are not interpreted by Milton the Christian apologist through rhetoric. Milton the artist presents them through symbol, myth, and archetype and leaves their interpretation to us.[5] Moreover, when we learn to interpret the artist's meanings, we realize that they frequently subvert the conscious meanings of the apologist.

Assumptions about Milton's Logic and Methods.   But before we take up *Paradise Lost*'s most significant meanings, its graver import, we need to raise a mundane question: are modern critical disputes generated by flaws in the logic of the poem's theology? Milton's theology, I contend, at times violates logic. Those who lack the training to articulate the violations nevertheless sense them and register their protest in critical disputes.

Acknowledging violations of logic in *Paradise Lost,* Stanley Fish offers an explanation widely accepted by traditional critics. These violations, he insists, are deliberate on Milton's part, their object being to entangle the reader in sin and error in order to compel him to abandon his own reasonings for blind faith in absolute authority.

Milton doubtless aims to strengthen the reader's faith. The problem lies with the method attributed to him: it can be employed to strengthen radically opposed religious and political faiths. It works for the Catholics Milton hated (it is "jesuitical") no less than for the English Protestants he favored. A method that can with equal ease support opposing views can never provide convincing support for any single view.

To be surprised by sin is to be surprised by guilt. Hence, Milton must methodically use guilt to strengthen belief. Where in the poem can we find unambiguous evidence that the poet sought to induce guilt? What indeed proves surprising (and refreshing!) is how little Milton belabors sin and guilt and how much he relies on faith to lead men to God. The decisive evidence of Milton's predilection for faith over guilt is his choice in *Paradise Regained* to make the temptation, not the bloody, guilt-soaked crucifixion, the pivotal event in the Son of God's incarnation. Another Miltonic predilection was for truth, which he pursued with a genius's disdain for mere cleverness. Yet the sophisticated rhetorical methods Milton supposedly employs to entangle the reader in sin and guilt are just that, mere cleverness.[6]

Rather than ascribing to Milton rhetorical subterfuges and psychological manipulations like those of Satan, why not admit that Milton's knowledge and beliefs had their limitations? Why not acknowledge that in *Paradise Lost* he, in his apologist role, undertook the impossible task of offering a rational defense of Christian theology and myth? We will then be left free to examine the ways logical hiatuses in theology and refractory elements in myth affect argument, character, and drama and thereby give rise to critical difficulties.

Since these difficulties reflect profound psychological conflicts along with philosophical problems that have perplexed the best minds of two millennia, we will not expect definitive solutions from Milton. Understanding the conflicts and problems and Milton's treatment of them will become our critical goal.

Assumptions about Historical Causation. The assumption that historical causation moves monodirectionally from a fixed past to a distinct present to an unknown future is widely accepted by traditional critics. This assumption devalues the influence exerted by the artist's vision of the future and by his unconscious intuitions about both present and past. Jung and Erich Neumann provide a corrective.[7] The psyche of the visionary artist and seer, they maintain, follows unconscious, teleological causation as it remedies past and present imbalances in the cultural canon by activating compensatory archetypes.[8] Wherefore, a visionary opus like *Paradise Lost,* in addition to reflecting and reinforcing its cultural canon, manifests, despite the author's conscious designs, the unresolved tensions between past, present, and future. In Milton's case the unresolved tensions generate the most perplexing critical problems, and, far from detracting from his achievement, these tensions guarantee his work lasting interest by spurring each age to perceive it anew in its own lights.

A Revealing Anachronism.   Unresolved tensions, however, exist solely to be resolved for critics who insist their answers are the only correct ones. Their traditional Christian interpretations are often surprisingly well-tailored to quell doubts common in our skeptical age, indeed, surprisingly Kierkegaardean in tactics. The crucial similarity to the founder of modern religious existentialism is reliance on radical freedom and faith to smash through the paradoxes in which skeptical reasoning entangles man.[9]

In Milton's age skepticism had yet to expose the logical and psychological inconsistencies that mar Christian theodicy. Consequently, he had no pressing need to supplant reason with radical faith. While he did not believe that reason by itself could generate faith, he was optimistic enough to assume that reason directs men toward faith and naive enough to presume that though the ways of God transcend human understanding they never confute or defy human reason. God can do nothing, he intrepidly declares, that involves express contradiction.[10] His buoyant confidence in rational theology rendered unnecessary a faith founded on paradox and the absurd. Denis Saurat argues not without justification that philosophically Milton stands close to the nineteenth-century absolutism of Hegel (Kierkegaard's bête noire). From the early tracts to *Paradise Regained,* Milton stresses regeneration through reason.[11] Regeneration through reason precludes leaps of faith from the springboard of arbitrary freedom. "What obeys/Reason is free" (IX.351-52), Milton's God declares—a far cry from Christian existentialists whose radical freedom embraces irrational commitments.

Milton had no Enlightenment, Kant, Hegel, or post-Newtonian materialistic science to react against, struggle with, and learn from. Hence, he displays an apparent naïveté that in our century has cost him the facile assent earlier readers accorded his theology. One undeniably finds in

Milton a great and vital emphasis on faith. But one looks in vain for an avowal that faith cannot exist without prior recognition of "the impossible," for a call to transcend by radical faith reason's dead end in paradox, or for open recognition of Christianity's fundamentally paradoxical nature.[12]

Rejection of Unconscious Causation and Meaning Evaluated. Psychological meanings the artist did not consciously intend, traditional critics often argue, are not there because the artist did not intend them. This is a circular argument that assumes what it pretends to prove: all meanings are placed in a work with conscious intent.

Ironically, denial of unconscious meaning in Renaissance literature impoverishes literary understanding more than does its denial in modern literature. The richer unconscious meaning of Renaissance literature accounts for the difference.[13] What accounts for the richer unconscious meaning? Renaissance writers, I suspect, could more freely mine the deep unconscious precisely because they lacked our authoritative psychological theories. Modern writers, by contrast, tend to use in an intellectual manner those myths and archetypes mapped out by Freud and Jung. The unconscious, however, yields her treasures more readily to those who court her through imagination than to those who ply her with intellect.

The want of authoritative psychological theories also freed the artist's audience or freed him from his audience as the case may be. Because the audiences of Shakespeare and Milton lacked the theory and bent to anatomize psychological nuances, these poets were safe to imaginatively communicate subliminal meanings that profoundly challenged their culture's official dogmas. So long as meanings remained couched in myth, symbol, and nuance, they would escape the condemnation that befalls direct challenge. Seventeenth-century moralists were now and then disturbed by artists' subliminal challenges. The puritan attack on the theaters attests to such disturbance. But their contemporaries usually responded, as healthy spirits do, with what they felt not with what they ought to say.

If Milton's contemporaries had scrutinized psychologically and philosophically his portrayal of the Father and Son, they might have condemned him for the same reason Plato condemned Homer and other unruly, spirited poets: portraying deities filled with human flaws subverts belief. Yet conservative Athenian pillars of society, like Milton's contemporaries, executed no poet. The Athenian rulers evidently deemed poets harmless (unlike Socrates) because they did not directly challenge established values. These ancients and their counterparts in Milton's time were too literal-minded and psychologically unsophisticated to perceive a serious challenge in mere myth, images, symbols, and those vast, nebulous intuitions we call vision.

A Need for Alternatives. Whether a classic is religious or literary, it is precisely its ability to reveal new vistas of meaning to each new age that keeps it alive long after the age that nurtured it has expired. Not so for many traditional Milton critics for whom Milton's major poems often become vehicles for escaping the present age, and their criticism becomes an instrument for rebuking modernity.

These critics subscribe to a notion, originally made fashionable by T.S. Eliot, that the cosmopolitan, modern sensibility is decadent whereas the more narrowly Christian sensibility prevalent before the Enlightenment was healthy.[14] A corollary is their assumption that the most important thing we can learn about ourselves from Renaissance literature is how far we have fallen. For them paradise lost is not Eden but the lost paradise of secure belief.

Outside the confines of traditional criticism, however, many acknowledge that modern philosophy and psychology have enhanced our sensibility. Philosopher Walter Kaufmann observes: "We have developed a kind of second sight. To say we have become more perceptive in psychological matters would be an understatement, not because our age is so perceptive, which it is not, but rather because the psychological obtuseness that prevailed until quite recently is almost unbelievable."[15] Next, I shall probe with our second sight the theodicy of *Paradise Lost.* I hope to discern, thereby, what traditional criticism neglects, the epic's graver import.

THE THEODICY OF PARADISE LOST

If *Paradise Lost* has one overriding conscious purpose, it is theodicy, the vindication of God's justice in his allowing evil and suffering to exist.[16] The narrator proclaims that purpose at the outset invoking the heavenly muse: "That to the highth of this great Argument / I may assert Eternal Providence, / And justifie the wayes of God to men." (I.24-26). Much of the uneasiness *Paradise Lost* occasions modern readers stems from doubt that one can justify the ways of God to men (or to women or Satan for that matter) simply by asserting Eternal Providence as a means of salvation.[17] Certainly, it is difficult to believe God just when we recall that he chose to create a world full of evil and pointless suffering.

Where did the belief that God is just originate? Its mythological beginnings lie with the Old Testament prophets, but its theological source is the Platonic concept of *summum bonum.* By defining the God of Christian myth as the *Summum Bonum,* orthodoxy made his justice a facet of his overriding goodness and rendered both his justice and his goodness absolute. In the same movement toward absolutism, Christian orthodoxy also made God omnipotent and omniscient. Therewith the existence of evil became a problem of logic no less than of feeling. The problem of logic becomes apparent once we consider the following: (1) if God is perfectly just and all good, he will want to create only good things; (2) if God is omnipotent, he can create whatever he wants; (3) if he's omniscient, he knows what will befall everything he creates; (4) therefore, it is logically impossible for such a God to create Satan and man, beings whom he knows will become evil.[18]

To escape this troublesome conclusion, Milton and Christian orthodoxy bring in free will. Satan's and man's free will, they insist, requires the option of choosing good or evil, and freedom is a good that outweighs the resulting evils. But, comes the skeptical rejoinder, the God of Christian myth can create beings whom he knows are certain to freely choose only good—witness Christ the man, the angels who don't rebel, perhaps also, depending on your theology, the Virgin Mary and shadowy "righteous" figures like Enoch and Elijah. Why doesn't God create only good-willed beings and leave defects like Satan, Adam, and Eve in the realm of untried ideas?

There is no easy answer to these objections, and no answer at all for those not firmly committed to orthodoxy. In the void where the answer should be grows fear that the Christian God is either indifferent to human values or, worse, evil. The most compelling evidence for the Divinity's evil nature is his arrogant demand that we violate our integrity by worshipping him as absolutely just and good when we know his creation shows him otherwise.

Freedom is God's sole excuse for allowing the existence of evil, and over the centuries his only defense against responsibility for creating evil became free will. Hence, we are obliged to scrutinize the meaning of freedom and free will.[19] Freedom for Milton, many critics assume, means spontaneous action. "Spontaneous," however, has more than one meaning. The two meanings that apply to free acts are mutually exclusive, indeed contradictory. The first is action springing from the actor's best nature or, to be psychologically precise, action springing from the actor's whole, integrated self. Reason, Milton believed, tells man if an action accords with his best nature. Reason is deliberate, whence its synonym "deliberation." Yet what is deliberate cannot be spontaneous in the word's second meaning, which refers to action divorced from conscious planning or, in the sense used by extreme existentialists, action divorced from causal antecedents. This last sense I call radical spontaneity. It has a scientific analogue in randomness. Radical spontaneity precludes deliberate, rational action in the same way that randomness precludes predictable order.

Although Milton, more wary it appears than his critics, left that perilous word "spontaneity" to professional philosophers, Stanley Fish invokes it in its most radical sense.[20] It is a bold and, considering his aims, a shrewd move. He writes of man's primal sin and the transition from innocence to fall: "The unintelligibility, and hence freedom, of the transition is Milton's thesis. Making it intelligible, and hence excusable, either by compromising the efficiency of the will or forging a chain of causality, is the reader's temptation."[21] Should freedom be spontaneous in its first meaning, that is, springing from the actor's nature, the Divine Creator bears responsibility for creating in man a being who by nature chooses to do evil. Because God the Father insists that he created man good and innocent, traditional critics have reason to assume, even though Milton never employs the term "spontaneous," that radical spontaneity lies implicit in Milton's usage of "free will."[22] Thus, it appears, is God relieved of responsibility for man's fall.

But, and here all traditionalists close their eyes, radical spontaneity makes it logically impossible for God to foresee the fall. (It also makes the free agent a first cause along with God, therein setting up dualism or pluralism, a dilemma I shall explore later.) An event can be foreseen, assuming the universe is rationally constructed, only by grasping its causal antecedents. Accordingly, God's foreknowledge of man's fall entails its intelligibility and his responsibility.[23] God, as omniscient, omnipotent Creator, knowingly brings into being both his creatures and the circumstances of their choices. Their choices are, thus, an unfolding of his original creative act, an unfolding that reflects their natures and his.

It may be objected that if God's creatures choose with a radically spontaneous will and their choices exhibit true randomness, the Creator could foresee that some might choose evil and still be unable to specify which ones or when. Consequently, he'd not be responsible for any specific choice, although as creator he'd still bear a generalized responsibility. This approach cannot logically exonerate Milton's God because, since he can foresee who will defect to evil along with when and how, in his universe defection cannot result from radical spontaneity or randomness. Asserting radical spontaneity along with specific divine foresight asserts a logical contradiction: God can foresee spontaneous acts that by definition are impossible to foresee.

The presumed radical spontaneity of man's will entails something even more disturbing than contradiction: since we can foresee our choices only if their causal antecedents are intelligible, when choosing spontaneously we will be unable either to foresee our choices on the verge of making them or to account for them once they are made. Most disturbing of all, radical spontaneity entails that man's originally "good" nature can change (i.e., become corrupt) because of wills that can go berserk without warning! Such a condition, far from giving men freedom in Milton's sense of ability to obey right reason, subjects them to the anarchy of irrational will.

Will's power to alter identity spontaneously is a power Milton's God himself appears not to want, for he limits his divine freedom to the choice of sending forth his goodness or not. There is something suspicious, the astute modern reader will conclude, about a freedom God himself warily eschews. He will conclude further that radical spontaneity is a stratagem to shift responsibility for evil from the Creator to man.

A simple argument exposes the stratagem as a sham: a man cannot be held accountable for radically spontaneous choices because so choosing he would not remain the same person from choice to choice. Accountability requires stable identity. Thus, radical spontaneity in an attempt to relieve God of his responsibility for man's evil choices simultaneously relieves man of responsibility as well!

Not only does spontaneous free will fail to convincingly relieve the God of Christian myth of responsibility for creating evil, he compounds both the evil and his culpability with his harsh punishments. While Milton remains oblivious to the problems spontaneous free will creates, his concern over God's harsh punishments becomes evident in his efforts to soften, rationalize, and obfuscate divine harshness.

Punishment not condign to the transgression, Milton doubtless realized, is unjust. Philosophers have traditionally offered four justifications for punishment: (1) to protect the innocent by isolating evildoers; (2) to reform evildoers, i. e., alter their characters; (3) to let the evildoer's suffering warn and deter potential violators; and (4) to satisfy the psychological need of the wronged party for retribution. The fourth presupposes lack of mercy in the wronged party. Unfortunately for Milton the Christian apologist, the orthodox Christian God relies on the fourth justification: he punishes to satisfy his own need for retribution. The justification accounts for the harshness of his punishments—and for the negative conclusions about his character.

Divine retribution is absolutely crucial, for it determines the doctrine of atonement along with the entire scheme of human history. The Son shall overcome Satan, the archangel Michael assures Adam, simply by,

> fulfilling that which thou didst want,
> Obedience to the Law of God impos'd
> On penaltie of death, and suffering death,
> The penaltie of thy transgression due,
> And due to theirs which out of thine will grow:
> So onely can high Justice rest appaid.
> The Law of God exact he shall fulfill (XII.396-402).[24]

Thus, an inflexible (and unexplained) legalism lies behind God's insistance on strict retribution. Reform, isolation, and deterrence may apply incidentally to the punishment meted out to fallen man, but they do not in any way apply to that of Satan and his cohorts. Man, we must remember, would not have fallen had God tried to reform Satan or, barring that, isolated or effectively deterred him.

Inasmuch as God's punishments are chiefly retribution for disobedience to his rigid law, they are manifestly unjust if those he punishes lack stable, continuous identities. Since in *Paradise Lost* neither men nor devils are portrayed as insane, we can conclude that, despite theory, in practice they have the stable identity requisite to just punishment. Stable identity doesn't mean they are justly punished, only that they are responsible agents and therefore can be justly punished. More important, it doesn't relieve God of his responsibility for creating agents that he knows will choose evil. Creating them, God chooses evil by proxy. Punishing them, he punishes by proxy his own dark choice. At least that is how Jung would analyze it and how it's likely to appear to the second sight of astute modern readers.

Milton's own repressed misgivings about God's motives become apparent when we compare the claim that God will turn all Satan's and man's evil into greater good with the Father's assertion that it would have been better had man never chosen to know evil in the first place: "Happier, had it suffic'd him to have known / Good by itself, and Evil not at all." (XI.88-89). The Father's remark, one of Milton the artist's many quiet epiphanies of Godhead, allows us to conclude that man's fall was not fortunate and ours, therefore, is not the best possible universe.[25] Better than our universe where God busies himself turning Satan's and man's evil into good would be a universe where all freely choose good.[26]

The rationalizations for an omnipotent *Summum Bonum* creating a universe full of evil and suffering are limited only by human imagination and our will to delude ourselves. Although each of them can eventually be exposed, innumerable variants are there for the inventing. Hence, one can neither expose them all nor finally refute the claim that the Creator of a world where babes starve and children are tortured to death is omniscient, omnipotent, and perfectly good. No marvel that Christianity's proponents and opponents, alike reduced to despair in the end, take contrary versions of the Kierkegaardean leap to accept God's moral perfection or lack thereof on faith!

Not so for Milton the apologist, stranger to modern psychology's second sight; rather than offering impenetrable faith he offers denials and transparent rationalizations from the mouth of divinity! Consider these words, which, if interpreted as Jung in *Answer to Job* interpreted the pro-

nouncements of Yahweh—to draw out the inner conflicts of the deity—
reverberate with the mechanisms of defense:

> For man will heark'n to his glozing lyes,
> And easily transgress the sole Command,
> Sole pledge of his obedience: So will fall
> Hee and his faithless Progenie: whose fault?
> Whose but his own? ingrate, he had of mee
> All he could have; I made him just and right,
> Sufficient to have stood, though free to fall.
> Such I created all th' Ethereal Powers
> And Spirits, both them who stood, and them who faild;
> Freely they stood who stood, and fell who fell.
> Not free, what proof could they have givn sincere
> Of true allegiance, constant Faith or Love
> Where onely what they needs must do appeard,
> Not what they would? what praise could they receive?
> What pleasure I from such obedience paid,
> When Will and Reason (Reason also is choice)
> Useless and vain, of freedom dispoild,
> Made passive both, had serv'd necessitie,
> Not mee. They therefore as to right belong'd
> So were created, nor can justly accuse
> Thir maker, or thir making, or thir Fate;
> As if Predestination over-rul'd
> Thir will, dispos'd by absolute Decree
> Or high foreknowledge; they themselves decreed
> Thir own revolt, not I: if I foreknew,
> Foreknowledge had no influence on their fault,
> Which had no less prov'd certain unforeknown.
> So without least impulse or shadow of Fate
> Or aught by me immutablie foreseen,
> They trespass, Authors to themselves in all
> Both what they judge and what they choose; for so
> I formd them free, and free they must remain,
> Till they enthrall themselves (III.93-125).

From the outset the Father, seen in the light of *Answer to Job* rather than in
light of Christian theology, resembles a person unconsciously bent upon
undercutting his own conscious stances. The telling phrase here is
"glozing lies." Gloze commonly means either to flatter or to interpret
deceptively as in a smoothing of difficulties in a text. Instead of using an
unambiguous term, the Father chooses "gloze," which causes us to ponder
whether he means flattery or deceptive interpretation. By the end of the

speech the modern reader's second sight will notice that "deceptive inter-
pretation" perfectly fits the Father's self-vindicatory rationalizations. His
overt defensiveness, however, will strike the modern reader first and
indelibly. No one in the poem, not devil, angel, or man, blames him for
man's fall or raises philosophical objections to his conduct. Why in the
absence of criticism is the Divinity himself so quick to raise possible
objections and why the touchiness of his answers? (Some may protest that
Milton aims these remarks at Calvinistic predestination; however, follow-
ing Jung's example in *Answer to Job*, we shall not let speculations about
authorial intentions sidetrack us from depth analysis of the poetic phe-
nomena.) Is God trying to forestall accusations from his own conscience?
He certainly resembles a person at war with conscience. To the perceptive
modern reader, his defensiveness forms an epiphany of his awareness of
his arguments' deficiencies: therein Milton the artist subverts Milton the
apologist.[27]

The speech's crucial epiphany and its key rationalization, "What
pleasure I from such obedience paid, / When Will and Reason . . . had
serv'd necessitie / Not Mee," is its most subversive feature. Indirect obe-
dience paid to the necessity that he in his Omnipotence has decreed fails
to satisfy him. The clues to his ruling motives are those willful, feeling
tones that betray the power hunger (and insecurity) behind the pleasure he
takes in direct shows of obedience. Milton the Christian apologist failed to
note the subversive clues of Milton the artist because he, like other
seventeenth-century believers, lacked our modern second sight. The lack
did have one signal benefit: it eliminated our need for Kierkegaardean
leaps.

So far I have focused on orthodox Christian theodicy's convoluted attempt
to blame evil on a single, elusive feature of God's creation, that springboard
of Kierkegaardean leaps, man's free will. Let me turn to God's mode of
creation for alternative explanations of evil. Western philosophy offers
three primary theories about God's mode of creation: (1) creation out of
preexisting matter; (2) creation out of nothing; or (3) and creation out of
himself. Milton opts for the last alternative.[28] The first yields a straightfor-
ward if not altogether satisfactory explanation of evil by placing the source
of corruption in unformed matter separate from God's nature and good-
ness. God can then work within the temporal process to perfect matter and
the universe. However, if matter is not preexistent, God must create it
either from nothing or from his preexistent self. *Creatio ex nihilo* is illogical
(for which Milton rejected it) and shows, therefore, that God can do
whatever he wants. Nonetheless, it leaves open the possibility of matter's
having a neutral value and God's working to perfect it. The Augustinian

doctrine that evil is *privatio boni* accords with *creatio ex nihilo* because it implies a need to perfect whatever is deficient in goodness.

On the other hand, if, as Milton contended, an all-good God created the universe *de Deo*, it becomes difficult to explain why there should be any *privatio boni*. Indeed, only varying manifestations of divine goodness would seem possible. Milton's professorial angel, Raphael, appears to support this last point when he tells Adam that an angel can eat material food because all creation is good (V.469-504). Although Milton doesn't acknowledge it, creation *de Deo* discredits *privatio boni* and thereby lays the problem of evil in God's lap. If God omnipotent freely created out of himself a universe where depravity is possible, it must reflect his nature and his objectives. The pivotal questions, then, become: why did God choose to create at all and what does the world he created reveal about his moral nature?

Tillyard and Saurat, who were disturbed by what the existence of evil in God's creation indicates about his moral nature, argued that in creating out of himself Milton's God must be purging himself of evil.[29] To say that God created the universe out of himself certainly implies that it partakes of his Being and Nature, indeed that his Being and Nature, like the universe, must be at once good and evil. It implies, additionally, a kind of proto-Teilhardism wherein God's creation of the temporal universe becomes part of a transformative process the goal of which is full realization of his own divinity.[30] He must need to change his raw power to purposeful goodness, his chaos to order.[31]

What emerges from the process of creation is a universe structured through time by history to form a divine psychodrama wherein God develops his potentials and works out his problems and thereby becomes conscious of himself. To see the universe dramatically rather than morally, indeed to see God as an emerging, almost biological entity rather than as static perfection, renders unnecessary the contrived and defective argument that the mystery of free will explains why an all-good, all-powerful, and all-knowing God permits evil.

Milton doubtless glanced down this path that would have led him away from the *Summum Bonum* toward Teilhardian or Jungian heterodoxy or his time's equivalent, alchemical heresy, but Milton as conscious theologian never traveled it.[32] Had he so traveled, *Paradise Lost* might offer a more satisfying explanation of evil. Instead, Milton became the apologist giving us the orthodox Christian ruse that evil is an unfortunate side effect of the Omnipotent's choice to create the most perfect good: creatures who worship his Supreme Goodness of their own free will. Notwithstanding, *Paradise Lost* is more art than theology, and Milton the artist, as we shall eventually see, traveled a separate path.

For Milton the apologist all roads in the kingdom of theodicy led back to free will. How can one explain free will's proclivity to generate ugly side effects? Theologian Nelson Pike has developed a widely endorsed modern theory consonant with Milton's rationalistic God. The explanation, Pike contends, lies in the logic of the universe which entails that free will must take wrong turns.[33] Knowing that free will cannot explain evil so long as it is itself inexplicable, Pike chooses to push the mystery back another step to what he hopes will prove a more convincing absolute.

Pike's "logic of the universe," however, is not logic in its ordinary sense but a metaphor for either a metaphysical truth or a law of empirical nature.[34] By subjecting God to a metaphoric "logic" independent of his divine nature, Pike attempts to relieve him of responsibility for evil without denying him omnipotence. The denial, though very subtle, nevertheless remains real because Pike sets up a dualism between God and the universe's "logic." If, as Pike maintains, the "logic" is independent of God's nature, obeying it, he'd bow to external necessity, which would make him less than God. While Pike's metaphoric use of "logic" is consistent with Milton, it solves nothing. It's merely another apologist sleight of hand.

In addition, Pike's "logic" creates a moral problem he (along with Milton) ignores: it must be accepted on faith in a divine authority that, for all we know, is based solely on power. To worship any kind of power, divine or otherwise, seems an implicit renunciation of freedom. (More pernicious still, worshiping power elevates power over love and thereby sabotages the Christian ethic.) Kierkegaard made the renunciation explicit in teaching that freedom exists solely to be renounced for faith in divine power.[35] How far Milton is from renunciation of freedom becomes evident when we consider his almost Pelagian optimism about man's ability to reform himself through free will.

Even if, for argument's sake, we grant validity to the theory that by the logic of the universe free will requires the byproduct of evil, we cannot allow an all good, omnipotent God to permit a single particle of unnecessary or superfluous evil. Milton's God never denies superfluous evil, he claims only that evil happens because of free will and that he'll provide a means of salvation. His limited claim tacitly acknowledges superfluous evil and so calls into question his Supreme Goodness. Moreover, by letting Satan enter Eden, Milton's God explicitly permits an unnecessary evil. His dubious conduct remains true to the deity of scriptural lore who, in one of the most conclusive of the many instances where he permits unnecessary evils, unlooses Satan after a millennium of rule by Christ. Thereby, he once again allows the devil to deceive all nations and bring down fire and brimstone yet once more on himself and hapless mankind (Revelation

20:4-8). The Bible, like *Paradise Lost,* is not a book helpful to those who want to believe God the *Summum Bonum.*

Theodicies based on free will can never make either the Christian God or the superflux of evil He allows compatible with the ideal of *summum bonum.* They only add extra twists to the serpentine trail of responsibility that ends at the doorstep of a deity whose final justification is not goodness but power.[36] Explaining nothing, they are subtle ploys to conceal lack of explanation.

To escape the pitfalls of theodicy, Kierkegaard, as I have noted, used radical free will to assert radical faith in God's absolute power. To the selfsame end, Calvin choose an opposite strategy and used eternal predestination to uphold God's absolute power. Rigidly committed to logical consistency, he sacrificed both human freedom and the intelligibility of God's goodness to God's absolute power.[37] Thus, he eliminated theodicy by declining to make excuses for God's ways. In the same stroke Calvin deprived his deity of the humane qualities Milton gave his God.[38] The Calvinist God is a God more to be obeyed and feared than understood or loved. At his worst he resembles an oriental despot given immortality and omnipotence. Cast in a more favorable light, he may be likened to the voice from the whirlwind who offers Job not theodicy to persuade but power and magnificence to browbeat him into blind submission:

> Can you draw out Leviathan with a hook,
> Press down his tongue with a cord?
> Put a cord through his nose,
> Pierce his jaw with a hook?
> Will he make long pleas to you,
> Cajole you with tender words?
> Will he make a covenant with you,
> Will you take him as eternal slave?
> Play with him like a bird,
> Leash him for your girls? . . .
> Lo, any hope is false;
> Were not the gods cast down at sight of him?
> Is he not fierce when one arouses him?
> Who could stand before him?
> Who could confront him unscathed,
> Under the whole of heaven, who? . . .
> He seethes the deep like a caldron,
> Makes the sea like an ointment pan.
> Behind him glistens a wake;
> One would think the deep hoary

> On earth is not his equal,
> One formed without fear.
> He looks on all that is lofty,
> Monarch of all proud beings.[41]

To feel as well as see the difference between this Yahweh who flaunts his untrammelled power and Milton's theodicy-obsessed God, we need only contrast Yahweh's awesome poetry with God's niggling attempt to evade responsibility for loosing Satan on hapless man:

> When first this Tempter cross'd the Gulf from Hell.
> I told ye then he should prevail and speed
> On his bad Errand, Man should be seduc't
> And flatter'd out of all, believing lies
> Against his Maker; no Decree of mine
> Concurring to necessitate his Fall,
> Or touch with lightest moment of impulse
> His Free Will, to her own inclining left
> In eevn scale. [X.39-47]

The difference becomes plainer still when we ponder God's transparent scheming to insure that Adam takes the blame for the effects of God's decision to give Satan free rein in Eden:

> Raphael, said hee, . . .
> Converse with Adam . . .
>   whence warn him to beware . . .
>   this let him know,
> Lest wilfully transgressing he pretend
> Surprisal, unadmonisht, unforewarnd. [V.224-45]

For Yahweh and for Calvin's deity, power justifies all he does including loosing Satan on Adam and Job; man is too low and insignificant to demand explanations of the Creator. That Milton has God proffer explanations and contrive excuses reveals his conviction that God needs a rationale for suffering and evil beyond dismissal of the human accuser's right to accuse. Milton's humanity and breadth of feeling made Calvin's harsh, narrow God unacceptable to him. Indeed, as we have seen, a God whose ultimate justification is his power so troubled Milton's sense of justice that his anxiety undermined his attempts to rationalize divine power.

Milton's feelings wanted to give man a chance by having God lock up Satan forever, yet thought reminded him it's not in the orthodox Christian myth. Milton's thought bowed reluctantly to feeling and offered a defensive deity without the primitive Yahweh's sublimity, the Calvinist God's logical consistency, or the Gospel Jesus' insight and compassion. The summary effect is that *Paradise Lost*'s graver import resides not in its Christian theodicy but in its subversive revelations of the flaws in that theodicy.

FREE WILL AND THE DUALIST ARCHETYPE

Free will became the cornerstone of orthodox Christian theodicy as an outcome of the struggle with the Manichaeans. These ancient dualists, being feeling types, insisted that God must be all good but, bowing to the reality of evil, denied him omnipotence.[40] To compete, the Christians, led by erstwhile Manichaean Augustine, claimed that their God was both the *Summum Bonum* and omnipotent.[41] Christians could no longer admit any evil in God, yet evil remained an incontrovertible feature of the world and the human nature he in his omnipotence had created. That made urgent the need for an explanation of the genesis of evil that did not controvert the *summum bonum* doctrine. For Augustine man's alienation from God because of deficient love explained how evil came to be. But Augustine's psychological accounting did not satisfy many theologians who, seeking a metaphysical basis for their theodicies, elevated to dogma the primitive church's notion of free will.[42]

With evil explained by free will, the chief mystery became free will itself! As free will gained in mystery, significance, and power, a covert dualism entered the Christian world view. Therein, free will became in its own right a metaphysical reality rivaling God.

While free will waxed, the credibility of the omnipotent and benevolent Creator waned. God's waning credibility forced the orthodox custodians of his Truth to "prove" his existence. The primal mystery, that which stirs man's profoundest awe, is creation itself. The mystery of creation is the strongest argument for the existence of a Creator. Creation in all its sublime power and variety, as Job's Yahweh puts it in the aesthetically preferable if less accurate King James phrasing, "humbles all the children of pride."

Free will by contrast is neither sublime nor genuinely mysterious, and it never exhibits authentic creativity. It is a metaphysical notion derived from our sense of ego autonomy; whereas the mystery of creation is an immediate response to our primal experience of being alive in a world we did not make. Those not subject to Christian conditioning will find it odd for orthodoxy to declare free will unintelligible, indeed the ultimate mystery, while claiming that God's nature and creation, are explicable to reason and consonant with human values. The uninitiated might well conclude that Christians ought to worship free will instead of God; which, of course, is what Milton's Satan, archetypal patron of those who assert dualistic free will, in fact does.

In emphasizing free will more than Christian orthodoxy requires, Milton followed his Satan a step down the dualist path that ends with individual free will challenging God. The challenge, Jung's psychology tells us, does not originate principally in the formal doctrine of free will. Dualism and the notion of free will are latent in the very archetypes that comprise the Christian Godhead. Jung maintained that Godhead, or the psychological reality hidden behind the divine personae of orthodoxy, includes, along with the acknowledged Father and Holy Spirit, an un-acknowledged dualist pair. The pair comprise the archetype of the hostile, or rival, brothers manifest in the beloved, obedient Son and the black sheep, Lucifer-Satan.[43]

The hostile brothers archetype imposes its duality across the entire spectrum of Western culture. In the philosophical arena the duality ener-gizes two opposing metaphysical outlooks whose contention has pro-foundly influenced Western thought. Reduced to elementary formulas these outlooks hold: (1) the universe is fundamentally static, monistic, eternal, rational, and perfect—a position associated with the Son who embodies Hellenistic logos; (2) the universe is flux, pluralistic, temporal, irrational, and imperfect—a position linked to Satan-Lucifer and Prome-theus and increasingly dominant in the twentieth century.[44] The latter of these two outlooks, flux, nurtures the notion of free will.

Flux, if carried to its extreme, can make the free agent absolutely responsible for his evil by making him the creator of his own nature. Milton's Satan asserts self-creation when he tells Abdiel that they are: "self-begot, self-rais'd/ By our own quick'ning power" (V.860-62). Here is a viewpoint Christian existentialists furtively assume and atheistic existen-tialists openly espouse. Free will, then, becomes a nonderivative, self-created reality. The metaphysical implication is multiple first causes. These open the door to rampant pluralism, which, in fragmenting the unity of being, supplants God, seen as *Unus Mundus* or implicate order, with individual will to power.[45]

Although the Father and black sheep Satan talk much of free will, that subject is significantly absent from the Son's discourse. Because Satan becomes the apostle of flux, getting unintended support from the Father, the Son is left to champion stasis. Stasis's absolutism, in contrast to flux's relativism, renders God all powerful and, though the Son never acknowl-edges it, all responsible. Proclaiming his unconditional union with the Father, he declares:

O Father, O Supream of heav'nly Thrones,
First, Highest, Holiest, Best, thou alwayes seekst
To glorifie thy Son, I alwayes thee,
As is most just; this I my Glorie account,
My exaltation, and my whole delight,
That thou in me well pleas'd, declarst thy will
Fulfill'd, which to fulfil is all my bliss.
Scepter and Power, thy giving, I assume
And gladlier shall resign, when in the end
Thou shalt be All in all, and I in thee
For ever, [VI.723-33]

Those who take stasis to the extreme of absolutism, the Neo-Platonists, Calvin, and Spinoza for example, tend to emphasize the oneness of God and minimize free will. Often they dismiss evil as illusory. The Son doesn't minimize free will, though he loves to proclaim God's supreme power and make a show of subordinating his will to the Father's. Always, he seeks, like orthodox Christian theology, to obscure the Father's ultimate responsibility for man's and Satan's evil choices. To these ends he wars against Satan, driving him from Heaven, and later sacrifices himself to redeem man and, what is perhaps more important though unstated, to confirm man's sins and thereby vindicate the Father's "justice."

Despite identifying *Paradise Lost*'s supernal hero, the Son, with stasis, Milton knew he must steer his own theology between the Sylla of stasis and the Charybdis of flux.[46] Those who attempt to anchor divinity on the rock of stasis, as did Calvin with strict predestination, sacrifice human freedom along with credible divine goodness. The whirlpool of flux presents a more subtle but no less dangerous menace. Here the great example is Kierkegaard. Drawn to the primitive and arbitrary Yahweh, Kierkegaard embraces flux to assert the paradox of the absolute freedom (and power) of God the Father and the real freedom of man. At the same time Kierkegaard downplays logos and its creation of man. The repercussion of glorifying God's absolute freedom (and power) at the expense of his creative logos is to leave it up to man to create God's goodness in a free act of faith!

Kierkegaard's flux philosophy, based on paradox and the absurd, provides no moral ground for Christian faith, no rational basis for choosing the Christian God over rival deities, and no solid reason not to follow Heidegger and Sartre in their leap of faith to the opposite stance of atheism. Moreover, Kierkegaard's Yahwehistic God who demands absolute obedience (as he does of Abraham in *Fear and Trembling*) inspires dread rather than love. Without love, once men overcome fear of divine power, they pursue their own will to power. Consequently, Kierkegaard, by downplaying the limits logos imposes on divine freedom and power, supports that sect of egocentric individualists whose founder, Milton tells us, is Satan.[47]

Espousing stasis, Calvin formulated a theology that met the needs of his time for order but at the cost of freedom and justice. Embracing flux, Kierkegaard formulated a theology that, while seeming to meet the needs of his time for passionate commitment, validated untrammeled will to power in succeeding ages.[48] Milton too strove to meet the needs of his time. His was a time of war, fear, and chaos, and Milton, like Calvin, responded to the need for assurance by stressing reason. Rationalism prompts his distrust of radical breaks of order, like miracles, and his rejection of irrational *creatio ex nihilo* for creation out of God's Self. Nevertheless, Milton's love of individual freedom and dignity led him to emphasize free will and so bring in a strong element of flux. Hence, he denied predestination and refused to commit himself unconditionally to static rationalism.

Milton the seventeenth-century man believed free will an intelligible aspect of God's rationally ordered, hierarchical universe. Because Milton's notion of freedom relies on ratiocination no less than on faith, it is, unlike the more fashionable modern notions, cautious and qualified. Never does Milton stress freedom to the point of denying, as do radical existentialists, that rationality and hierarchy can define or limit our free will. Such denial he puts in the mouth of Satan who declares that all are:

> Equally free; for Orders and Degrees
> Jarr not with liberty, but well consist.
> Who can in reason then or right assume
> Monarchie over such as live by right
> His equals, in power and splendor less,
> In freedom equal? or can introduce
> Law and Edict on us, who without law
> Err not, [V.792-99].

Satan's contention makes good Sartre and has the surface appearance of good sense; it is at the same time rank heresy, for which cause Abdiel zealously denounces it:

> O argument blasphemous, false and proud!
> Words which no ear ever to hear in Heav'n
> Expected, least of all from thee, ingrate . . .
> Shalt thou give Law to God, shalt thou dispute
> With him the points of libertie, who made
> Thee what thou art, and formd the Pow'rs of Heav'n
> Such as he pleas'd, and circumscrib'd thir being? [V.809-25].

God, Abdiel insists, made Satan what he is and set the limits of his power and freedom. Considered together, Satan's and Abdiel's speeches suggest the dilemma Milton the apologist remains loathe to confront: a radically free Satan relieves God of responsibility for creating evil but limits his power; a God-formed Satan secures divine omnipotence but limits the divinity's goodness by making him responsible for Satan's incorrigibly evil nature and for giving the devil license to continue doing evil.

Stanley Fish attempts to extricate Milton the apologist and his God from their dilemma with the argument that Satan, good by nature until he chooses evil, loses his character, and so becomes chaos (or flux) personified. Wherefore, Satan is radically free yet totally powerless since by willing evil he becomes nothing.[49] The argument stumbles before the objections that chaos personified could not execute Satan's malignly purposive actions and that, corrupting mankind, Satan certainly isn't powerless.

One cannot extricate Milton the apologist and his God from their dilemma save by pious doublethink. Insofar as its theology is orthodox, *Paradise Lost* demands doublethink. We are asked to believe that Satan is radically free, wholly responsible for his evil nature, and a genuine alternative to God (otherwise man's free choice is pointless). Simultaneously, we must believe him incorrigible, which means he is not free but enslaved to his own evil, and we must believe God in his omnipotence created Satan, which entails that the Devil is not a first cause, not entirely responsible for his evil nature, and not a real alternative to God.

Such incompatible demands need not disturb a Kierkegaard who, asserting paradox, the absurd, and radical freedom without quibble or compromise, need not pretend the irrational is in fact rational. Milton, committed to both rationalism and freedom and drawing upon stasis and flux, created a poem that presents epiphanies of the fundamental flaw in orthodox Christian theodicy: although orthodoxy relies on stasis to support God's perfection, it cannot defend that perfection in light of his responsibility for Satan's evil and man's sin.

Where God's responsibility for Satan's evil and man's sin is not at issue, freedom in *Paradise Lost* follows standard metaphysical assumptions about static, rational universes, assumptions Kierkegaard might have called Hegelian. Thus, freedom ordinarily means action arising from an agent's own, best, God-given nature, and it entails the opportunity to realize one's best self through rational choice.[50] The good angels and the Son exemplify the union of freedom and rationality. In Milton's rational universe truth to one's best self and truth to God, right reason and right obedience, are identical.

Milton and his original readers must have sensed the illogicality of introducing an element of flux (spontaneous freedom) into an otherwise rational universe in order to explain Satan's evil and man's sin. Their belief in orthodox Christianity, though weakening, still cohered sufficiently to repress their perception of implicit dualism. Disintegrating belief, whether manifest in direct attacks like Shelley's and Empson's or in the excuses of apologists like C.S. Lewis, Douglas Bush, and Dennis Danielson is characteristic of our post-Kantian age.[51]

The modern disintegration produces a mentality that cannot easily reconcile absolute power with individual freedom or divine perfection with the existence of evil. Freedom to act in harmony with one's own nature is an intelligible concept in a rational universe, and arbitrary freedom is admissible in a flux. But to assert as dogma that freedom in both senses can exist in harmony in a single universe violates reason and the individual dignity it gives. Without the repression firm belief supplies, modern minds rebel. Shaping our modern response to the dogmas of Christian orthodoxy, the rebellion necessarily influences critical response to free will in Milton and to his dualist archetype, those hostile brothers, the Son and Satan.

JUNG AND GODHEAD

As we have seen, Milton's stressing free will inevitably constellated the dualist archetype. The true nature of this and the other archetypes of Godhead surfaces in the artist's subtle epiphanies. Subsequent chapters will expose these epiphanies to critical scrutiny. In preparation for that critical endeavor, we need to examine further the archetypes of Godhead and the ethical and philosophical stances they generate. To that end, we must cast aside the blinders of orthodox Christian dogma and follow the second sight of Jung's analytical psychology.

Archetypes of Godhead.   When speaking of gods, their natures and acts, Jung observed, we employ images that project the archetypes driving our psychic processes. Whether either the images or the archetypes correspond to metaphysical realities is something we are not equipped to know: we are left with a choice of unbelief or faith.[52] Understanding of deity, however, requires something quite different from faith. We must stop regarding the images we project as metaphysical realities and examine the archetypes behind the images.

In the Christian West the dominant archetypes of the psyche are projected on the Godhead in its Trinitarian form. Hence, understanding Godhead involves seeing through traditional metaphysical assumptions about the Trinity to the archetypes being projected. Although the dogma of the Trinity has remained stable for fifteen hundred years, our archetypal projections upon the Persons of Godhead have undergone significant changes. These changes affect the relationship of Father and Son, the function of the Holy Spirit or Paraclete, and the role of Satan, the missing Fourth Person excluded by the Trinity dogma.

Jung might have found in Milton striking examples of the altered projections upon Godhead that accompanied the Protestant Reformation. For instance, Milton's stubborn resistance to a full-fledged trinity, almost Docetic aversion to the crucifixion, and preference for unequivocal monotheism (in *De Doctrina* the Son is indisputably subordinate and the Holy Spirit becomes a supernumerary figure) accentuate to the brink of heresy the Father's characteristic dominance in Protestantism. Such dominance reduces the Son to a mere agent of the Father and sets both directly opposite Satan, whereas, psychologically speaking, the Father, or primal parent, is a more primitive archetype that precedes the Son and Satan, or the dualist archetype of the hostile brothers. Moreover, despite the sometimes egregiously patriarchal personality he gives the Father, Milton's rationalism pushes God toward the depersonalized logical principle he becomes under deism, a movement that led ultimately to scientific philosophy's dismissal of divinity as unnecessary. But not only did Milton and Protestantism's narrowly monotheistic Godhead become philosophically expendable, it became psychologically useless since it could offer neither a credible explanation of evil nor comfort to suffering humanity.

Seeking a God to help and heal man, Jung rejected narrow monotheism.[53] Jung, paralleling Tillich and following Kant, believed that man knows God through the divine image within the human psyche.[54] For Jung that image is the archetype of the self, an archetype that appears as a four-part process.[55] Jung observes: "If the Trinity is understood as a *process*, as I have tried to do all along, then by the addition of the Fourth, this process would culminate in a condition of absolute totality."[56] Sustaining both psychic process and identity, the quaternal self can heal suffering and guide those facing evil. To reflect the quaternal self's uniplural nature and tap its ability to heal and guide, Godhead must have four members, and the role and significance of each must be recognized.[57] Recognizing the Whole Quaternity has a further advantage that Milton would have appreciated: quaternity's stable uniplurality can insure freedom (plurality) along with the order (unity) needed for freedom to endure.

Despite its advantages, quaternity has not been enthusiastically embraced by most Jungians. On one hand conservative Jungians, attached to traditional monotheism, tend to dismiss it as one of Jung's idiosyncrasies. On the other hand that modern prophet of Mercurius, James Hillman, rejects monotheism and quaternity for outright polytheism.[58] The monotheists should remember that Jung believed the psychological need for quaternity, best understood as uniplurality, was a central principle of psychology of religion. The radical polytheists should remember that although polytheism (and a polytheistic paradigm for the psyche) accurately reflects the multiplicity of the collective unconscious, it usually proves too unstable to sustain and guide individual identity through suffering, tragedy, and evil.[59] The unifying, homeostatic nature of the quaternal self, it must be added, evolved in response to the need for identity that is at bottom the need for sanity—a need few would want to disregard.

Above all, Jung insisted, recognition of the Whole Quaternity is absolutely necessary if we are to deal forthrightly with the problem of evil. By denying that the archetypal spectrum containing the rival brother, rebellious feeling and instinct participate in Godhead, and by reducing evil to mere *privatio boni*, orthodox theologians tried to camouflage the dualistic potency Christian myth gave Satan and evil. However, since good and evil, Christ-logos and the rebel, are interdependent opposites, in depriving evil of reality these theologians simultaneously deprived the good of substance. Jung observes: "The Christian answer is that evil is *privatio boni*. This classic formula robs evil of absolute existence and makes it a shadow that has only a relative existence dependent on light. Good, on the other hand, is credited with positive substantiality. But as psychological experience shows 'good' and 'evil' are opposite poles of a moral judgment which as such originates in man. A judgment can be made about a thing only if its opposite is equally real and possible. The opposite of seeming evil can only be seeming good."[60]

Far from making God purely good, Jung contends, *privatio boni* makes him false. The Christian devil proves that falsity. Satan's role as prime adversary to God, the prowess he displays infecting Adam and Eve with original sin, and his terrible evil in the Apocalypse demonstrate his alleged marginal existence as *privatio boni* to be a subterfuge that disguises his dualist status as an autonomous part of the Divine Psyche rivaling the Son. Milton the artist further darkened the shadow Satan casts across the bright facade of Christian orthodoxy by making Satan's initial rebellion and unflagging resistance to divine will the driving forces behind time and history. Thus, although Milton the apologist attempts to minimize God's responsibility for the evil he has made possible and whose continuance he allows, Milton the artist dramatizes Satan's power. The artist's dramatization implicitly verifies the dualist status of the Devil and reduces *privatio boni* to a sham. Therein, the artist subverts the apologist.

In giving Satan dramatic parity with his hostile brother, the Son, Milton follows the archetypes and a dialectical process Jung perceives as generating both psychic energy and the dynamism of Godhead.[61] Without duality and conflicting opposites, Jung declares, there can be no energy. Evil and good are simply moral aspects of the duality that pervades all energy processes. And consciousness itself arises through the constellation of primal opposites.

However, the ego, our center of consciousness, fears that primal opposites will overwhelm it bringing chaos. In Western culture ego relies on reason to suppress opposites. Concurrently, it fosters the rationalistic pride we see in the doctrine of *summum bonum*, which goes to the extreme of driving opposites and evil out of the Divinity. Behind this doctrine lurks the ego's narcissistic expectation that God ought to conform to one-sided ego values of goodness and rationality. To which Jung objects that God, being manifest to us as a projection of the self archetype, or psyche as a whole, must contain all opposites, must be at once conscious and unconscious, good and evil, rational and instinctive. God, like the self, must contain countless dualities within an overarching uniplurality.

The self, as the supreme archetype of the psyche and the most comprehensive image of God we can know, generates ego's supreme task, individuation: "The self as a totality is indescribable, and indistinguishable from the God image, self-realization—to put it in religious or metaphysical terms—amounts to God's incarnation. That is already expressed by the fact that Christ is the son of God. And because individuation is a heroic and often tragic task, the most difficult of all, it involves suffering, a passion of the ego."[62] To help us achieve individuation, an image of God should correspond to the mysterious archetype of the self. Accordingly, as self includes ego and shadow, our *imago dei* should include Christ and Satan, the divine ego and its repressed shadow. But the Western ego, fearing the dialogue with shadow individuation requires, has constructed an imbalanced *imago dei* that more resembles a willful, rationalistic ego, or its moral persona, than the self.

Milton as apologist underscored the imbalanced rationalism of the Western ego deity. Indeed, he made God the Father subject to the logos and the ego archetype embodied in his "perfect" Son, and placed God and the Son in direct opposition to Satan-shadow, whom he presented as an external scapegoat. Thus, Milton tacitly redefined the Father, or primal parent, by the ego qualities orthodoxy attributed to the Son. Their true relationship becomes apparent in book 3 of *Paradise Lost* where the Son leads the Father as both follow the ego archetype.[63] In Milton's theory the Son is subordinate, but in psychological fact the ego archetype, most fully embodied in the Son, also defines the Father! From a Freudian perspective the subordinationism Milton consciously proclaims hides the oedipal revolution he unconsciously seeks. A Jungian point of view, however, will

stress that redefining the Father by the Son's ego archetype makes the
Christian God more one-sided and less able to help with individuation.

The Stages and Functions of Godhead.   While Jung rejected the orthodox
Trinitarian deity as hopelessly one-sided, he recognized that the concept
of trinity illumines the stages of a Godhead that mirrors the total self.[64]
Like the self, Jung's quaternal Godhead becomes manifest in a four-part,
three-staged dialectical process. Trinity symbolizes the stages of divine
individuation and reflects the mind's tendency to organize developmental
or temporal events in threefold patterns that follow time's elemental
divisions of past, present, and future. The uniplural quaternity symbolizes
the four parts of the individuation process and its goal, wholeness.

When we merge trinity with quaternity we get the schema for self and
Godhead described in figure 1.[65]

Figure 1. Schema for self and Godhead

Stage 3	Holy Spirit	anima-mediated, individuated self	
Stage 2	Son, Satan	warring opposites, ego x shadow	
Stage 1	Father	undifferentiated, primordial self	

The Father's stage, we learn in Jung's visionary masterwork, *Answer to Job,*
is an undeveloped state of prereflective consciousness, the rude begin-
nings of individuation. In the stage of the hostile brothers, the Son and
Satan, or ego and shadow, consciousness advances through a war of op-
posites. The highest stage, symbolized by the Holy Spirit or Paraclete,
transcends and harmonizes duality and warring opposites through media-
tion of Sophia, the divine anima.[66] The three stages of individuation,
it might be noted, find rough analogues in Kierkegaard's (1) aesthetic,
(2) ethical, and (3) religious stages that mark the Christian's path to
God.[67]

In the Christian era most of humanity remains deadlocked in the
hostile brothers stage. An imbalanced commitment to "good" and a com-
pensatory fascination with evil typify this stage. Unable to confront evil
and duality because they are possessed by the Son-logos archetype, ortho-
dox Christians proclaim for binding truth a theodicy that reduces divinity
to ego-born willfulness and perfectionism. Similarly one-sided, the egos of

modern rebels identify with the shadow archetype to become, through the resulting unacknowledged guilt and emptiness, secret apostles of anarchy.

The orthodox and the rebels alike suffer from failure to transcend ego demands for perfection, a failure perpetuated by their inability to see that the demands are an outgrowth of inflation. The inflated ego either insists that God is purely good (the orthodox) or rejects God for falling short of perfection (the rebels). The orthodox are directly committed to ego values, and the rebels are committed to ego identified with the shadow's inverted values. Both groups assert free will. Indeed, free will seems the one thing they agree on.[68] Seen psychologically, the origin of their "free will" lies in ego's conceit of sovereignty over psyche. Since ego is the seat of will, "free will" is a euphemism for ego sovereignty.

Christian orthodoxy's defining the entire Godhead by the ego archetype made inevitable a heavy imbalance toward ego in the psychology of westerners, whether orthodox or rebels, and insured that each group would rely on the doctrine of free will to vindicate ego's tyranny over the entire psyche. Imbalance toward ego insured also a sado-masochistic dualism wherein other egos become objects for sadistic manipulation and shadow is expected to submit masochistically to ego. To overcome this harmful dualism, Jung concluded, we must open ourselves to the mediation of the Paraclete, which encourages a *coincidentia oppositorum* in the dualities that comprise self and Godhead. Once we accept self and Godhead in their quaternal wholeness, we can openly constellate the rebel brother archetype or shadow and meet the challenge to transform and integrate its protest and anger. We will then dismiss the delusion of mastery, or free will, along with its accompanying sado-masochistic mindset and learn to follow the Paraclete, that spokesperson of the greater self.

The third stage of the individuation of Godhead and self, the realm of the Paraclete, lies beyond dualism, beyond ego and shadow, beyond sadism and masochism, and beyond good and evil—not "beyond" in the sense that ethical dualities are denied but in the sense that the individual transcends willed commitment to "good" (ego) and compensatory fascination with "evil" (shadow) to achieve an overview of good and evil where wholeness becomes possible because neither opposite possesses the mind. Jung remarks: "Looked at from a quaternary standpoint the Holy Ghost is a reconciliation of opposites and hence the answer to the suffering in the Godhead which Christ personifies."[69] The reconciliation of opposites brings individuated wholeness or mature freedom, something quite different from free will.[70] Mature freedom implies an anima-inspired openness to self and cosmos (or the *unus mundus*), whereas free will implies ego's disposition to impose its power and values on self and cosmos in the case of the Son-logos, or shadow's impulse to reject self and cosmos in the case of Satan-pathos.

So far as I know, neither Jung nor any of the Jungians have explicitly correlated individuation in Godhead and self with the four psychic functions; notwithstanding, the correlation seems justified. In that correlation the Paraclete links with intuition, the Son-Satan polarity with the warring opposites of thought and feeling, and Yahweh, the Father's undifferentiated, primordial consciousness, with sensation.[71] Figure 2 shows them combined in a diagrammatic configuration.

Figure 2. Individuation correlated with the psychic functions

Intuition	Paraclete	*Conjunctio oppositorum*
Thinking Feeling	Son Satan	alienated dualities
Sensation	Yahweh	emerging consciousness

Psychic individuation begins with the primitive perceptive function, sensation. From there the psyche proceeds to constellate the dual judging functions, thinking and feeling, whose dialectical opposition and alienation must eventually be transformed in the *conjunctio oppositorum* of a third stage where apperceptive intuition works to integrate the quaternal whole. At this stage reason and ego no longer arrogantly declare themselves self-sufficient and so become unreasonable. Similarly, feeling and the repressed shadow do not proclaim their free will and so become intractable. Rather the light of reason turns inward upon the realm of feeling and outward to that of sensation. Feeling ceases its war on reason and instead offers guiding values to thought and brings refinement to sensation. And intuition fosters an individuated wholeness that creates mature freedom.

OBEDIENCE, REBELLION AND INWARD VISION

The stages of individuation in Godhead and self generate the fundamental ethical stances of Western culture. The opposing ethics of obedience to authority and of defiant rebellion characterize the hostile brothers stage of individuation with its war of ego and shadow, thought and feeling. The old ethic of obedience and repression that held sway for millennia began to crumble in the seventeenth century preparing the way for the ethic of rebellion that surfaced in the French Revolution and the Romantic era. The Satanic potential of the ethic of rebellion became evident in the twentieth century as collective ideologies and totalitarian states overthrew restraints on their wills to power.[72] Recent times have also seen in the psychoanalytic movement the birth of a second sight, that inward vision that can open the whole self to consciousness.

Erich Neumann's seminal *Depth Psychology and the New Ethic* probes the psychological basis of the old ethic. The old ethic, Neumann asserts, depends on the orthodox Father-God.[73] God, aggressively proclaiming his infinite power and perfect goodness, behaves like an immature ego compensating for insecurity. These excesses had their uses in early phases of cultural development when ego consciousness was weak and undifferentiated and the unconscious posed a continuing threat like barbarians at the frontier. The old ethic defended consciousness and ego by calling the unconscious evil and by repressing the shadow.

While the strategy of the old ethic protects ego values, it also rigidifies them and divorces them from the human purposes they were fashioned to serve. Once consciousness acquires differentiation and stability, the emboldened ego begins to chafe under the old ethic's rigid constraints. When discontented individual egos forsake the cultural canon and turn to the shadow for an alternative, what I term the ethic of rebellion appears.[74]

The ethic of rebellion is not, however, a truly fundamental departure from the old ethic of obedience. Being the old ethic's shadow, the ethic of rebellion merely inverts its basic character. Because they each encourage their adherents to treat others as objects to be manipulated through pity, contempt, and envy and to be controlled through guilt and justice, both ethics are essentially sadistic. Simultaneously, they promote masochism since to be "good" is to sacrifice self either to others, as in Christian altruism, or to the collective cause, as in Marxist credos. The old ethic of obedience and the ethic of rebellion, moreover, each rely on metaphors of mastery and servitude, those paradigms of sadism and masochism, in stressing command, service, and commitment.

Eventually, insightful spirits sense the need to break from the endless cycles of sado-masochistic manipulation perpetuated by the two hostile ethics with their tools of contempt and envy, guilt and justice. These individuals seek a guide superior to ego or shadow. The archetype to which they turn is the self. The self enables the individual to transcend the ethics born of ego and shadow through anima-mediated intuitive vision. The goals of this inward vision are understanding in place of obedience, persuasion in place of command, mature freedom or individuated wholeness in place of free will, metastance (or overview) in place of commitment, and transformation in place of repression and rebellion.[75] Through inward vision, pity, envy, guilt, and justice are all transformed. The strategy of inward vision is neither to choose between opposites as in the old ethic and the ethic of rebellion nor to find a golden mean between them as in Aristotle. Inward vision seeks, instead, transformation of opposites to create a new outlook that advances consciousness.[76]

The Two Ethics, Inward Vision, and Paradise Lost.   The concepts of an ethic of obedience, an ethic of rebellion, and an inward vision can provide fresh perspectives on *Paradise Lost*. Consider, for example, how the epic reinforces the old ethic. At the level of Milton the apologist's conscious intentions the old ethic appears to dominate the poem. Under the old ethic the hero champions the cultural canon against emergents from the unconscious projected upon scapegoats. We can see such conventional heroism in the Son and in Abdiel who, however distasteful their moral certitude may seem to moderns, are meant to be true heroes and thus deliberate foils to the false hero or scapegoat, Satan. Disobeying divine authority, Adam and Eve also become scapegoats who must be punished. Heroism in *Paradise Lost* is obedience to the old ethic.[77] Consequently, when Adam repents and, bowing to authority, accepts the "truth" from archangel Michael, he too becomes heroic.

The Son, Abdiel, Raphael, Michael, and repentant Adam all champion the collective conscience linked to the father archetype and embrace the old ethic of obedience to authority. Their collective conscience opposes that authentic, individual conscience Jung called the voice.[78] The voice expresses truths from the larger self. It also correlates to the Holy Spirit and, though Jung never made the correlation explicit, to anima and intuition's inward vision. The only character in *Paradise Lost* who listens to the voice is Adam upon choosing to follow Eve in sin. Although his punishment clearly tells us whose side Milton the apologist is on in the conflict of collective conscience and voice, the position of Milton the artist, as shall become evident in subsequent chapters, is far more complex.

Under the old ethic whatever the collective conscience rejects is relegated to the shadow, which in turn becomes projected onto someone outside the community, a stranger or scapegoat. Those who, obedient to the old ethic, shun the voice's challenge to transform their own evil into new good are fated to project their shadow onto others and persecute it in scapegoat form. The traditional hero slays the scapegoat or drives it out. Nevertheless, the evil qualities the scapegoat supposedly embodies remain evident in the hero, community, or deity that persecutes it.[79] In *Answer to Job* Jung maintains that the Christian deity finally confronts his own evil by becoming a scapegoat himself and atoning for his guilt through crucifixion.

In *Paradise Lost* Milton passed over the crucifixion, the very heart of Christian myth, to dramatize instead the suffering of the original scapegoat, Satan. But he did not ignore the crucifixion altogether. To the contrary he considered treating it in a projected *Christus Patiens* and began, but left unfinished, *The Passion*. Why did the crucifixion prove an unworkable theme for Milton? May he not have sensed in it a divine guilt and imperfection that, because of his commitment to ego, the father archetype, and the moral perfectionism of the old ethic, proved unacceptable to his conscious mind? If so, Milton and Jung reach their contrary stances toward the crucifixion by traveling in opposite directions from the same starting point, their intuition of divine guilt.

Divine guilt, Jung declared, is the pivotal insight of Christianity. The insight, however, became conscious slowly and not until Jung did it become transparent. We can see the insight emerge over the centuries in artists' representations of Christ. Early Christian artists, repressing the insight altogether, avoided the subject of the crucifixion and the cross was not depicted with the figure of Christ before the sixth century. From then until the eleventh century Christ was usually represented as a triumphant, open-eyed savior wearing not a braid of thorns but a royal crown. The intuition of divine guilt gained sufficient strength in the eleventh century to change the image of Christ to a deathly pale, emaciated figure, head fallen to the side, speared in the chest, and hair dripping blood from a crown of thorns.[80]

The selfsame intuition influenced representations of tragic sacrifice in Renaissance literature. Shakespeare understood divine guilt and the limitations of the old ethic better than any other Renaissance writer. Out of his profound understanding he created what many consider the greatest tragedy ever written—*King Lear*.[81] Milton, upholding the old ethic and resisting divine guilt, created out of his resistance the grandest epic of the Christian era and the most memorable portrait of the divinity's sacrificial scapegoat—Satan. As for Jung himself, he judged his proclamation of divine guilt, *Answer to Job*, his supreme achievement. Not many, he realized, agreed with that judgment, but, he insisted, it would take several centuries for the votes to come in.[82]

With the sacrifice of Christ, Jung contends, the hero-ego symbolically accepts responsibility for suffering and imperfection. Thus, the shadow, admitted into consciousness, is no longer scapegoated upon others who are persecuted in its stead. The shadow is understood and transformed through the agency of the Paraclete. We can then move from the warring ethics to inward vision. For the sacrifice to be made by the cultural hero rather than inflicted upon an external scapegoat is a momentous advance in consciousness because it constitutes acceptance by the hero (ego) and society of responsibility for evil. With acceptance of responsibility, evil's transformation, the task of the Paraclete, can begin.

Wherefore, it should surprise no one that Milton as Christian apologist, in his attempt to free the hero-ego of guilt, vindicate divine perfection, and defend the old ethic gives center stage to the scapegoat and banishes the crucifixion to a forgotten corner. Not surprising either is the lack of emphasis on miracles in *Paradise Lost*. Being obvious corrections for divine fumbles, drastic actions like miracles, the crucifixion, and the resurrection troubled the increasingly rationalistic seventeenth-century mind. Milton the apologist, like many of his intellectual contemporaries, displayed little tolerance for the nonrational in either men or God. Hence, he sought to minimize all elements in Christian myth that resisted his notions of rationality. Indeed, he strove to compensate for them with rationalistic discourses from the mouth of the Divinity!

To the same end of minimizing those inexplicable disruptions of order that Jung maintained, mark the growth of divine consciousness, Milton turned to the opposite of disorder, the great chain of being, that hierarchical arrangement of creation so beloved of intellectuals committed to the old ethic.[83] C.S. Lewis provides a succinct account of Milton's hierarchical theory: "According to this conception degrees of value are objectively present in the universe. Everything except God has some natural superior; everything except unformed matter has some natural inferior. The goodness, happiness, and dignity of every being consists in obeying its natural superior and ruling its natural inferiors. When it fails in either part of this twofold task, we have disease or monstrosity in the scheme of things until the peccant being is either destroyed or corrected."[84]

The hierarchical theory bolsters Milton the apologist's subordinationism and his emphasis on reason and conscious ego. These emphases are part of an extensive complex of emphases which with their polarities define the old ethic of obedience and its opposite, the ethic of rebellion. Between the poles emerges transformative inward vision. Table 1 places the defining archetypes, concepts, values, and themes of *Paradise Lost* in respect to the warring ethics and inward vision.[85]

Criticism and Inward Vision.   Traditional critics have well documented the strength and influence of the old ethic in Milton's time, not that any dispute it. Yet they consistently overlook Milton the artist's archetypal compensations for the old ethic's one-sidedness. These archetypal compensations, prefiguring the ethic of rebellion and inward vision, have helped insure his work's enduring interest. Traditional critics, moreover, miss the psychological import of Milton the apologist's need to vigorously defend the old ethic and its ground, God the Father: his vigorous defense indicates that the challenge to the old ethic had personal urgency.

Table 1. Archetypal correlations

	Old Ethic	Inward Vision	Ethic of Rebellion
ARCHETYPE	Son-logos ego cultural hero	Paraclete-Sophia self wisewoman	Satan-Prometheus ego identified with shadow rebel
CONCEPT	monotheism absolutism eternality dependence on 　God hierarchical order *privatio boni* *summum bonum*	uniplural quaternity contextualism eschatology interdependence 　with God creative evolution uroboric evil *coincidentia 　oppositorum*	atheism (or polytheism) relativism temporality autonomy anarchy impurity, scapegoats irreducible dualities
VALUE	cultural canon repression reason deductive comedic identity fidelity	individuality transformation intuition synthetic tragic wholeness insight	ideology party loyalty, conformity feeling reductive ironic collectivity sincerity
THEME	constraint patriarchy essentialist circle being stasis	balance androgyny developmentalist spiral psyche process	emancipation equality existentialist chaos empirical fact flux

Those critics who refuse to admit that *Paradise Lost* itself ever questions, contradicts, or displaces the old ethic guard their position, as we have seen, by denying unconscious meanings or their relevance to interpretation. For them Milton the artist is ever subservient to Milton the Christian apologist. They strive for the certitude that orthodox theology, stasis philosophy, and the old ethic promise. Indeed, they seek to discover their lost paradise of secure belief in *Paradise Lost*. Since inward vision and its vehicle analytical psychology require surrendering the moral certitude the old ethic provided, those critics who adhere to the old ethic are destined to oppose analytical psychology. As Neumann points out, in seeking transformation rather than repression, analytical psychology poses a fundamental threat to old ethic values.[86] Consequently, criticism of *Paradise Lost* expressing inward vision faces strong resistance, which partially explains why so little has been published.

Although the secular humanist critics adopt ideas from inward vision only sporadically, they have shown us that Milton sensed the cracks in the old ethic. Furthermore, these critics implicitly recognize the Jungian principle of compensation, as Empson does when he points out that Milton counters those elements in Christian belief that make man contemptible and degraded. It is the enduring merit of the secular humanist critics to have broken new paths. Partly due to their pathbreaking, in the last fifteen years sophisticated psychological criticism has emerged, like the work of William Kerrigan, as well as criticism utilizing the ethic of rebellion, like the work of Christopher Hill, Andrew Milner, and Joseph Wittreich.[87] All these critics have helped give us a more balanced view of Milton and so cleared the way for the bearers of inward vision.

Subsequent chapters of *The Unfolding God of Jung and Milton* use inward vision to probe the graver import of archetypal images in Milton's major poems. The central archetypes, Jung shows in his *Alchemical Studies*, are evident in cultural products of the past that draw on psychic processes. But Jung, predisposed toward the arcane, neglected the manifestations of central archetypes in literary classics. Had he focused on Milton's major poems, he could have found archetypal images of Godhead. For, like the Book of Job, the Book of Ezekiel, the Gospels, and the Apocalypse, Milton's major poems contain crucial epiphanies of Godhead.

The first of the subsequent chapters focuses on the role of evil and Satan in Christian Godhead. It shows that, while Milton the apologist relies on the old ethic's *summum bonum* deity, on the orthodox doctrine of *privatio boni*, and on the notion of evil as impurity, Milton the artist conveys their limitations in metadramatic epiphanies. Additionally, the artist's metaphors for satanic evil are shown to offer a profound alternative to the old ethic's evasions of the problem of evil. Throughout I endeavor to present Milton's vision of Godhead in its full archetypal complexity, including the most disturbing of its complexities, the uroboros archetype. Here Milton the visionary artist intuited, perhaps better than Jung himself, the true nature of this hidden yet tremendously powerful archetype.

Chapter 3 examines the identity-forming decisions that cause Adam's fall in *Paradise Lost* and shape Messiah's triumph in *Paradise Regained*. In both epics drama, meaning, and character pivot on identity-defining decisions. Man, Satan, and Messiah do not create themselves, but their decisions influence what they become, their character or identity, along with the critical difficulties in these works. Behind their decisions lie archetypes, anima and animus in the case of man and the two hostile brothers with Satan and Messiah, whose subtle movements provide hitherto neglected epiphanies of Godhead. The concluding chapter, on *Samson Agonistes*, seeks in the blindness of the Yahweh archetype clues to tragedy's graver import for Godhead.

2

The Shadow of God

Many of the difficulties modern readers experience with *Paradise Lost* are reactions to one character, God the Father. The Father, defending himself and combating Satan, often resembles a flawed human being. Consequently, to presume, as the narrator frequently does, that he manifests supreme goodness seems a mockery of truth. Offended, moderns may retort that, far from being supremely good and deserving worship, the Father deserves to be repudiated as evil. Jung's analytical psychology, however, offers a more refined perception, which promotes a more balanced response.

The best starting point for a Jungian analysis of God the Father is the doctrine of *summum bonum*.[1] Orthodox Christian theology borrowed its methods and many of its ideas from Hellenistic philosophy. The most influential of these philosophic borrowings was the doctrine of *summum bonum*, which redefined God the Father, or the Old Testament Yahweh, by perfectionist ego values. Philosophy's triumph was bought at the price of psychological wholeness, for the primitive Hebraic deity was not restricted by the ego values evident in the Hellenistic *Summum Bonum*. Yahweh manifested the encompassing self archetype in all its dynamism, complexity, and contradiction.[2] Christian orthodoxy's decision to force its deity into a procrustean bed of ego values was at bottom a failure of faith in the self and in an inclusive divinity that reflects the self archetype.

Milton was able neither to acknowledge the failure of faith evident in the *summum bonum* doctrine nor to entirely repress his doubts about the supreme goodness of the Father. The most serious of these doubts were caused by orthodoxy's making the Father like an ego. This inevitably made Satan the Father's hostile shadow thereby contradicting the *summum bonum* doctrine, which denies God can have a shadow.[3]

The *summum bonum* gave a philosophical basis for the denial of God's shadow. The denial itself originated much earlier with the old ethic's repudiation of shadow. St. Paul, championing the old ethic, sharply demarcated ego from shadow (the "sin that dwelleth in me") in Romans 7:20: "Now if I do that I would not, it is no more I that do it, but sin that dwelleth in me."[4] Milton has Adam voice Paul's demarcation of ego from shadow when he assures Eve:

Evil into the mind of God or Man
May come or go, so unapprov'd, and leave
No spot or blame behind: Which gives me hope
That what in sleep thou didst abhorr to dream,
Waking thou never wilt consent to do. [V.117-21]

We become evil, the passage implies, only when the will (seated in the ego) embraces evil thoughts arising outside the ego—that is, from the shadow. Accordingly, what counts is ego, not the whole self, which includes the shadow.

Repression, orthodoxy and the old ethic insist, is the only safe way to deal with shadow. Therefore, Christians made their God repress his shadow. Since the shadow is utterly disavowed, Satan, who should be Lucifer-pathos, the dialectical opposite of the Son-logos, becomes an arch scapegoat. From the crusades, Aquinas, and the rise of scholastic philosophy in the twelfth century and proceeding through the traumas of the Schism, the Reformation, and the Counter-Reformation, repression of God's shadow was carried to pathological extremes. Yet Satan the scapegoat could not be persecuted. Consequently, his agency was attributed to those thought to follow an ethic of rebellion—infidels, heretics, Jews, so-called witches and homosexuals—who were ruthlessly persecuted in the devil's stead.[5]

Jungian psychology, following inward vision, seeks to break out of the old ethic's repression and persecution by basing moral and ethical judgment not on ego but on the self.[6] The self accepts rather than represses shadow for, unlike ego, the self in its wholeness can relate to opposites simultaneously. Ego always tries to make a choice between opposites, which, banishing one to the shadow, disrupts the dialectic that creates consciousness. Acceptance of shadow restores the dialectic. No longer warred upon by ego, the shadow abandons its hostile stance to become a source of creative energy, substance and insight upon which ego can freely draw.

Milton the Christian apologist follows the old ethic in relying on command and obedience to repress shadow and fulfill ego's hopes for purity, perfection and secure identity. Nonetheless, Milton's personal belief in individual dignity, along with his artist's intuitive channel to the whole self, led to him adopt certain values and insights characteristic of inward vision. These values and insights, which are best illumined by Jungian psychology, enabled him to draw a more detailed and convincing, one might almost say psychologically realistic, portrait of the Father and Satan than either the scriptures or any other great poet gives us.

Milton, apparently intuiting that Satan resembles the repressed, shadow element in the psyche, wanted to understand in depth both his shadow function and its true relation to the Father and the Son. The *summum bonum* doctrine and the old ethic, however, dictated Satan's dismissal as an external scapegoat. In consequence, Milton's desire to understand in depth the divine Self could not be satisfied at a conscious level and so had to work indirectly through the archetypal epiphanies of Milton the artist.

A JUNGIAN APPROACH TO EVIL

The prime theological mechanism Christian orthodoxy uses to deny God has a shadow is the doctrine of *privatio boni*. Since the doctrine caused Jung to reject the orthodox treatment of evil and to replace the Holy Trinity with a Whole Quaternity, it is necessary to examine in some depth Jung's critique of *privatio boni*.

In *Jung and the Problem of Evil*, H.L. Philp, attempting to defend orthodoxy against Jung's critique, protested that Christians are not required to believe *privatio boni*.[7] Christians are in fact not required to believe anything about evil other than that an all good, all knowing, and all powerful God created its possibility, which Satan and man actualized by disobeying him. Notwithstanding, it makes little difference whether Christians are expressly required to believe *privatio boni* because the concept ineluctably develops from the idea of evil existing in a universe governed by an all good, all powerful creator.

Moreover, those who hold that *privatio boni* is not essential to Christian belief, Jung pointed out, must explain why the three principal alternatives to it, (1) outright dualism, (2) the view that God as *coincidentia oppositorum* contains interdependent good and evil, and (3) disallowing the problem of evil by denying the existence of sin and evil, are each heresies. Since *privatio boni* is the single non-heretical instrument for dealing with the implications of evil's existence, the fact that Christians are not required to accept it means only that Christians are not required to think rigorously.[8]

The true reason orthodoxy declines to stress *privatio boni*, Jung contends, is that the doctrine cannot withstand logical scrutiny:

Suppose one has a thing being 100 percent good and if anything evil comes then it is diminished by say five percent. Then one possesses 95 percent of goodness and 5 percent is just absent. If the original good is diminished by 99 percent, one has 1 percent good and 99 percent gone. If that 1 percent also disappears, the whole possession is gone and one has nothing at all. . . . The identification of good with *ousia* is a fallacy, because a man who is thoroughly evil does not disappear at all when he has lost his last good. But even if he has 1 percent of good his body and soul and his whole existence are still thoroughly good; according to the doctrine evil is just identical with non-existence. This is such a horrible syllogism that there must be a strong motive for its construction. The reason is obvious: it is a desperate attempt to save the Christian faith from dualism. According to this theory even the devil, the incarnate evil, must be good, because he exists, but inasmuch as he is thoroughly bad, he does not exist. This is a clear attempt to annihilate dualism in flagrant contradiction to the dogma that the devil is eternal and damnation a very real thing.[9]

In a letter to Father Victor White Jung explained why he thought it imperative to reject *privatio boni:* "On the practical level the *privatio boni* doctrine is morally dangerous, because it belittles and irrealizes Evil and thereby weakens the Good, because it deprives it of its necessary opposite: there is no white without black . . . no truth without error, no light without darkness etc. If Evil is an illusion, Good is necessarily illusory too."[10] In a subsequent letter to Father White Jung attacks the doctrine's confusion of Good and Being: "The crux seems to lie in the contamination of the two incongruous notions of Good and Being. If you assume, as I do, that Good is a moral judgment and not substantial in itself, then Evil is its opposite and just as non-substantial as the first. If, however, you assume that Good is Being, then Evil can be nothing else than Non-Being . . . God is certainly Being itself and you call him the *summum bonum.* Thus all Being is Good and even Evil is a minute good, even Satan's disobedience is still good to a small degree and nothing else. For that Good he is in hell. Why should Good be thrown into hell? And at what percentage of goodness are you liable to get condemned?"[11] These arguments failed to persuade Father White. He and Jung suffered a falling out over Jung's rejection of *privatio boni* and his view, promulgated in *Answer to Job,* that the Deity is a *coincidentia oppositorum* of interdependent good and evil.[12]

Jung's failure with White may have been in part because of his approach: he attempted to give logical reasons for rejecting *privatio boni* when White's and Christianity's motives for accepting it were not logical, though they pretended to be, but psychological. An effective argument against *privatio boni* would thus need to be explicitly psychological. It might run as follows: (1) the archetype of the self is the source of *imago dei* and, being the comprehensive archetype, its only sufficient archetypal model; (2) the *summum bonum* doctrine displaces the self as a model with a subordinate archetype, the ego; (3) *privatio boni* derives from the *summum bonum* doctrine; (4) therefore, *privatio boni* assumes an insufficient *imago dei*.

Though they failed to sway White, Jung's criticisms of *privatio boni* are cogent and in line with contemporary analytic philosophy. Moreover, Jung's stress on radical evil links him to Freud and the existentialists with their belief in irrationality and tragedy.[13] Jung's position, however, takes its roots in his personal experience with human suffering, the horrors of World War II providing the strongest impetus. Contemporary Anglo-American Jungians, children of a more sanguine era and culture, tend to give short shrift to their master's "animus" against *privatio boni*.[14] Seldom do they note either that Jung's position links him to Freud and the existentialists or that it is mandated by the nature of the individuation process: individuation advances only by raising opposites from the unconscious, differentiating them through ego suffering, and then unifying them in that supreme symbol of interdependence, the *conjunctio oppositorum*. Without the differentiation of opposites, which *privatio boni* seeks to avoid, "there is no experience of wholeness and hence no inner approach to the sacred figures. . . . Although insight into the problem of opposites is absolutely imperative, there are very few people who can stand it . . . The reality of evil and its incompatibility with good cleave the opposites asunder and lead inexorably to the crucifixion and suspension of everything that lives. Since "the Soul is by nature Christian" this result is bound to come as infallibly as it did in the life of Jesus: we all have to be "crucified with Christ," i.e. suspended in a moral suffering equivalent to veritable crucifixion."[15]

Jung's rejection of *privatio boni* for real opposites and of the *Summum Bonum* for *Summum Coincidentia Oppositorum* ought to be taken seriously since it reflects his axiom that the suffering opposites bring is necessary to individuation. Furthermore, it confutes, once and for all, the attempts to dismiss Jung as a mystic divorced from painful realities.[16] The most persuasive reason for taking it seriously, however, is not theoretical or biographical; it involves our very survival. *Privatio boni*, Edward C. Whitmont astutely observes, is one of the underlying reasons why modern man fails to deal effectively with evil: "Much more than theological hairsplitting is involved here. The psychological significance of this doctrine lies in its denial of polarity. If there is only more or less good, it is our personal duty to increase the supply in order to please God. It is also possible, in principle at least, to eliminate the appearance of evil completely. Our progress mania, our social utopianism and our lack of realism in dealing with the human existential situation may be traced to the secularization and trivialization of the *privatio boni* concept. Since only good is acknowledged, we are unable to accept and deal with violence, aggression and suffering other than by trying, impotently, to legislate it away."[17] By upholding the appearance of goodness in the Deity, *privatio boni* teaches us to uphold the appearance of goodness in everything. Through *privatio boni*, concern for appearances comes to dominate our thinking. This shallow concern traps the Western psyche in a vicious circle of delusion, hypocrisy, and persecution wherein ego, bent on eliminating the appearance of evil, represses its shadow into the unconscious whence it's projected upon external scapegoats and in that form warred or legislated against. The only way out, Jung insists, is to confront the reality of evil in ourselves, God, and the world. We can then withdraw projections and repudiate unrealistic doctrines like *privatio boni* and *summum bonum*, which feed ego's impulse to repress, project, and persecute. The graver import of Jung's rejection of *privatio boni* is that, if Western civilization is to survive, ego's concern with maintaining the appearance of goodness must yield to self's drive to become conscious of opposites and cope with the realities of evil.[18]

Despite the general soundness of Jung's rejection of *privatio boni*, he unjustly blamed Augustine for the doctrine, which entered orthodoxy two centuries earlier with Clement of Alexandria and secured wide acceptance long before Augustine defined it.[19] In addition, Jung failed to understand Augustine (if I may use once more that threadbare phrase) "in his historical context." Hence, Jung failed to appreciate either the profundity of Augustine's thought or the similarity of Augustine's motives to his own.

It was the dualist Manichaeans and the early Manichaean Augustine who wanted to believe God perfectly good. The later Christian Augustine's *privatio boni*, his concept of original sin, and emphasis on the power of habit are all movements away from the belief that God and the uncorrupted soul of man are entirely good. They in fact express the realistic view of man's soul Jung accused Augustine of lacking. Augustine's repudiation of Pelagianism and his massive qualification of Neoplatonism exhibit the same movement toward realism. Both Pelagius and the Neoplatonists proclaimed the perfect goodness of God and of man's soul. Pelagius, rather like Milton, regarded sin a superficial matter of wrong choices. Augustine sensed, however, that Pelagian optimism about human nature can be sustained only by ignoring the complexity of the psyche and denying subordination of will and ego to self. Here, too, Augustine stood close to Jung. Indeed, among the principal alternatives of Augustine's era, Augustine himself most nearly approximated the dark vision of human nature put forward in our time by many existentialists, Freud, and Jung.

Privatio boni is the formal orthodox stance on evil, but Christian myth supports other stances. Although *Paradise Lost* assumes *privatio boni*—for example, Eve's intellectual weakness and Adam's lack of self-knowledge are deprivations of good—the poem avoids explicit references to *privatio boni*, relying instead on two other notions of evil. The most primitive of these is the Hebraic notion of impurity.

The Will to Purity.   The concepts of sin and evil, as Paul Ricoeur shows in his study *The Symbolism of Evil*, originate with the idea of impurity.[20] Purity is the essence of Milton's most primitive idea of good just as impurity is the essence of his most primitive idea of evil. Purity and impurity, then, form the two poles of a single standard that often defines good and evil for Milton. The most revealing statement of the purity-impurity standard is not, however, in Milton, but in Kierkegaard.

Purity of Heart Is to Will One Thing wrote Kierkegaard announcing the thesis of his edifying discourse in its title.[21] Kierkegaard's short book, like so much of what he wrote, takes an indirect approach advocating single-mindedness by attacking its opposite, those forms of double-mindedness or multiplicity that indicate impurity. Indirectness notwithstanding, Kierkegaard furnishes an unambiguous example of Christianity's reliance on single-minded will (or ego) as the vehicle for good.

Purity, that singleness of will, that effort to subordinate all the diverse voices of the self to one sovereign ego kneeling before one supreme divine ego has given Christians focused energy that helps account for their religion's historical advance and persistance.[22] Despite purity's importance, Christians leave unexplored the psychological nature of the will to achieve purity in oneself and to claim perfection in one's God. Analytical psychology shows that the will to purity is rooted not in love but in ego's desire for autonomy. We can clearly see the desire for autonomy behind the loveless, alienating spiritual pride that sometimes passes for Christian holiness.[23] Demanding abnegation of self, prideful holiness drives self into shadow in the name of "love" for an egolike God.

The way of authentic love, by contrast, lies in heeding self and dialoguing with shadow, with instinct, aggression, and impurity. Truly, we love each other, whether that other is another person or a nonego voice in the self, when we suspend alienating "purity" to allow the other's point of view a fair hearing. Authentic love, then, requires the double-mindedness, or better yet manifold-mindedness, that Kierkegaard deplores.[24] The single-minded condemn themselves to a loveless, alienated egotism they call purity.

Purity is the standard of the old ethic. Transformation of "evil" and "impurity" is the dynamic of the inward vision. Milton, as believer in "the upright heart and pure," neglects transformation, emphasizing instead an apocalypse with dualistic overtones wherein the good God finally eradicates the devil's corruption.[25] Good and evil, purity and impurity, will at last be separated. For the "impure" scapegoats there shall be destruction, and for the "pure" and faithful herd, union with God:

> Truth shall retire
> Bestruck with slandrous darts, and works of Faith
> Rarely to be found: so shall the world goe on,

To good malignant, to bad men benigne,
Under her own waight groaning, till the day
Appeer of respiration to the just,
And vengeance to the wicked, . . .
    to dissolve
Satan with his perverted World, then raise
From the conflagrant mass, purg'd and refin'd,
New Heav'ns, new Earth, Ages of endless date
Founded in righteousness and peace and love,
To bring forth fruits Joy and eternal Bliss. [XII.535-41; 547-51]

Those who steadfastly maintain their will to "truth" will not doubt the promised final purification. However, once will relaxes, the skeptical imagination sparks vexatious questions. If the goal is a static new heaven and new earth where "truth" and "righteousness" prevail unchallenged for eternity, why have a temporal process at all? If the Almighty has an unflagging aversion to impurity, why countenance it any place or time? Analytic psychology's answer is that however great the orthodox ego-God's love for purity, it does not match his love of willfulness; and to exercise will he and his followers must have both an object, purity, and a resistance, impurity or evil.

If impurity is psychologically indispensable to the orthodox ego-God, so also is *privatio boni*. How do these two forms of evil differ? While *privatio boni* is passive nonbeing, impurity requires the presence of active corruption. Hence, affirming *privatio boni* denies reality to active corruption and asserting active corruption confutes *privatio boni*. The two are incompatible because they derive from opposite metaphysical positions, *privatio boni* from stasis and impurity from flux. Orthodox theologians, in a striking case of doublethink, turn to stasis and call evil deprivation of good when God's responsibility stands at issue, then turn to flux and regard evil as active corruption when the spotlight moves to the responsibility of Satan or sinful men. Kierkegaard was right: the impurity of double-mindedness is the Christian's chief danger. But that danger consists of the unrecognized proclivity to doublethinking self-deceptions.26

However, if we switch from orthodoxy and the old ethic to follow the inward vision of Jungian psychology, evil ceases to be impurity and deprivation of good and becomes a challenge to create consciousness. Then shadow and suffering begin to make sense, not of course as part of divine perfection but rather of divine individuation with its impulse to create consciousness. Furthermore, if we follow inward vision, Satan in the Godhead and shadow in the self become integral to the individuation process of deity and self.

Whether human or divine, the quester for consciousness is bound to get soiled hands. Why does creation of consciousness involve the impurities of shadow and evil and require time and travail? The explanation lies in the nature of consciousness. Consciousness grows by dealing with the conflict of opposites that occurs only within temporality. In this process stances of ego are transformed into new syntheses or metastances that encompass opposites or "impurities" from the shadow.

Since opposites and impurity pervade temporality, the ego possessed by will to purity longs for the extratemporal world of the unconscious.[27] In simple Freudian terms, the will to purity seeks a return to the womb.[28] The Jungian archetype for that abode of unconscious "purity" is the uroboric Great Mother.[29]

Uroborus.   Despite orthodoxy's obsession with purification and sin, its over-arching *summum bonum* and *privatio boni* doctrines tacitly render impurity unreal by making God's purity and perfection a static absolute. These orthodox doctrines do not stem from the scriptural myths where God's incarnation is a tragic process bound in time. They come instead from Platonic stasis metaphysics. Behind stasis metaphysics with its controlling notion of a Perfect Being or *Summum Bonum* looms the archetype of the Great Mother. The Great Mother is absent from dominant Old and New Testament notions of God. But she is not absent altogether. As primordial rival to Yahweh, the patriarchal sky deity, she gave birth to various phallic, serpent, and dragon deities who eventually contributed to the protean character of the Christian Satan.[30] (Leviathan is the preeminent biblical example of the dragon.[31]) While she looms in the background, the Father and the two hostile brothers, the Son and Satan, rule the time-bound realm beyond the womb, the realm of history. The purified heaven that follows the eschaton or end of history is a goal alien to Godhead. It expresses a will to purity whose archetypal origin is not Godhead but devouring uroboros, that darkest face of the Great Mother.

Four dominant archetypes have shaped the orthodox conceptions of deity from the second century to the Renaissance. These are the Father, the Son, Satan, and the negative aspect of the Great Mother symbolized by devouring uroboros. The Holy Spirit or Paraclete has become influential in recent centuries, but until the Renaissance it remained peripheral. Although Jung did much to clarify the archetypal nature of the Father, the Son, and Satan, he barely noted devouring uroboros's determining influence on the orthodox deity. What spurred its full recognition in *The Unfolding God of Jung and Milton* is the peculiar vision of evil of Milton the artist.[32]

How, we must ask, does the uroboros archetype operate within the psyche? Alienation and inflation are the usual methods. They do not appear in their true natures, however, but rather in the guise of perfectionism. The destructive character of uroboric perfectionism becomes evident in personal psychology where it castrates males, kills feminine relatedness, and finally consumes ego. The chief symptom of uroboros's activity is inflated obsession damning up psychic energy that ought to nurture consciousness. Medusa is her most ominous mythic face, the face of psychotic alienation.[33] By stopping the flow of life energy, Medusa, the evil anima, turns all to stone, making relation and growth impossible. Only through dialoguing with shadow and harkening to the positive anima, who nourishes bonds and creativity, can we break the evil anima's obsessions with purity and perfection.

Believers, of course, do not realize that orthodox theology was constructed to feed the uroboric obsessions with purity and perfection. Theologians, moreover, dare not acknowledge that at the core of Christian belief lie irreconcilable conflicts between Hebraic process Godhead and uroboric being. Consequently, the obsessions and the conflicts are not brought to light but fester in darkness, breeding pervasive doubt and a welter of contradictions. Evil and suffering are real in history but illusory in eternity; human life is tragic but the universe is comedic; the Godhead of scriptural myth evolves immanently through history but the deity of the theologians has the properties of transcendence, eternity, and perfect being. Suffering, history, tragedy, and Godhead itself, teach the perfection-seeking theologians, must ultimately yield to the *Summum Bonum*. But, they can never acknowledge the *Summum Bonum*'s archetypal basis in ego alienated from self and possessed by uroboros, because uroboros has no place in the Godhead of scriptural myth.

The most fundamental feature of orthodox theology is its subversion of the Christian Godhead through an alien archetype, the devouring uroboros. The male archetype of Godhead least compatible with the uroboric ideal of Perfect Being is Prometheus-Lucifer-Satan, which accounts for its problematic theological status. As rebel and as hostile brother to the Son-logos, it ever breaks up the uroboros's preconscious monism into dualities of good and evil, ego and shadow. Thus, it spurs consciousness and counteracts uroboros. Orthodoxy's making Satan the prime cause of evil is a compelling indication of the hidden power of uroboros.

Alienation and Inflation. Alienation and inflation are devouring uroboros's twin methods. They arise together and feed each other. Hence, we can never finally determine whether we inflate because we are alienated or become alienated because we inflate. Choosing to inflate, ego simultaneously chooses to become alien from self, God, and others. Inflated ego, denying interdependence, withdraws love from others to direct it inward where, alienated, it sours into uroboric evil. The choice to inflate and become alienated is in truth a choice to pervert love.

However, we never directly choose to inflate and become alienated; that choice always comes disguised as a way of coping with shadow and suffering. The ego that represses shadow for the sake of purity and perfection will become alienated and fall into self-fed, self-consumed inflation. By contrast, the ego that works through love to transform shadow and suffering builds substance to achieve an unshakable anchoring in reality such as Jung exhibits when he declares: "We do not know whether creation is ultimately good or a regrettable mistake and God's suffering. It is an ineffable mystery. At all events we don't do justice either to nature in general or to our own human nature, when we deny the immensity of evil and suffering and when we turn our eyes away from the cruel aspect of creation."[34] Though creation itself is an ineffable mystery, shadow and suffering have a clear function: coping with them develops consciousness, gives ego substance and holds it to reality. Equally important, by making us aware of our interdependence, they can guide us toward love.

Alienated inflation finds its ideal in the insubstantial fantasy of a prelapsarian paradise free of shadow and suffering. Activating memories of the womb and infancy, the devouring uroboros archetype tempts ego to mistake that early challenge-free state for perfection and call it "paradise."[35] But ego never finds "paradise." The very idea of paradise is a uroboric siren song tempting ego to escape the struggle with shadow and suffering that is essential to individuation.

Just as in myth paradise embodies ego's alienated inflation, so the *imago dei* should ideally embody the love expressing the whole self. Specific examples of *imago dei*, however, inevitably reflect the actual development of ego and self. If uroboros inflates ego alienating it from self, inflated ego, not love and wholeness, will be projected upon *imago dei*. Those who project inflated ego onto *imago dei* will see in God what matters most to inflated ego: power, autonomy and purity.

Present throughout the history of Christianity, the tendency to make *imago dei* that apotheosis of ego inflation, the omnipotent *Summum Bonum*, waxed particularly strong in Milton's time. Widespread fear and insecurity drove mid-seventeenth century men to seek refuge in a powerful, absolutist deity who embodied not the whole self but what they wished their egos could become. Attributing to God an inflated ego would later make it possible for the Romantics to reject him as arbitrary and amoral. Moreover, seventeenth-century absolutism, epitomized in the philosophy of Thomas Hobbes, prepared the way for our own age's covert resurrection of the inflated deity in its secular totalitarian states and ideologies. The religious absolutism of Barth's *totaliter aliter* and Kierkegaardean fideistic irrationalism are intellectual obsessions that affirm the selfsame inflated ego deity. The seventeenth-century constructions of an inflated deity and the modern resurrections of him alike are symptoms of ego's escape from dialoguing with shadow into inflated obsessions. Dialogue is hard; inflated obsessions are easy.

Our century has spawned a dangerous array of inflated obsessions. At the same time it has overcome the psychological obtuseness fostered by Christian morality's repression of the personal shadow and Christian theology's scapegoating of God's shadow, Satan. Consequently, modern psychology can find in the career of Satan understanding of shadow that can guide us toward individuated wholeness and help us guard against alienation and inflation.

A JUNGIAN PERSPECTIVE ON SATAN

The Old Testament Yahweh, Jung pointed out, is an ambivalent God who mingles antinomies of light and darkness, good and evil, kindness and cruelty, in a single heterogeneous personality. The Old Testament Satan, Jungian scholar Rivkah S. Klugar has shown, is a personified aspect of this dissociated deity which gradually became detached from him.

Historical Background. Rather than having a separate mythic character from the start, Satan began as a metaphor for one of Yahweh's diverse qualities. He seems to have originated in an attempt to define certain features of the familiar mythological figure Malak Yahweh. The Malak Yahweh is not an autonomous archetype with an independent will but the enactment of Yahweh's will. As messenger and adversarial function, the Malak forms the hypostasis of Yahweh's intervention in temporal affairs.[36] The best example of the adversarial function is Satan in the Book of Job. But there are other illustrations of Yahweh's dark side like the story of Balaam, the incident in Exodus 4:24-26 where "the Lord met Moses, meaning to kill him," and the instance in 1 Samuel 16:15-23 where "an evil spirit of God" troubled Saul. The early Satan is, therefore, quite consistent with the Old Testament conception of an all-encompassing God who bears responsibility for both good and evil, a God who declares in Isaiah 45:7: "I form the light and create darkness: I make peace, and create evil."

By alternately enabling and spurring men to substantiate their individuality, Satan the Adversary furthers human consciousness. He furthers, additionally, a similar process within the divine personality that ultimately led to his exclusion from it.[37] Gradually, under Hellenic and Iranian influences Satan obtained independence from Yahweh until he became an archetype of evil in his own right in the apocalyptic literature of 200-250

B.C.[38] At the same time the promised Messiah brought hope for a final triumph of good over evil. And Hellenized Jews, inflated with uroboros, made Yahweh "the Lord" who was perfectly good, just, and all powerful. These new ideas created the problem of theodicy, which was to trouble Judaism's Christian heirs through Milton's time and into our own bedeviled age. One solution was the outright dualism of Gnosticism and Manichaeanism. Augustine attempted to counter Manichaean dualism by making evil logically meaningless with the doctrine of *privatio boni*. The doctrine in turn smoothed the way for Satan's transformation into that almost comic butt, the medieval devil.[39]

Despite these early and later developments, Satan's identity and central role are primarily the work of the New Testament. In the Gospels he appears repeatedly under different names. Thirty-five times the adversary is referred to as Satan, thirty-seven as the devil or "diabolus" and seven times as "Beelzebub" or lord of the flies, an allusion to Ahriman, the Persian god of evil. The gospel Satan is a spirit opposed to the good who throws obstacles in the way of those seeking God and tempts men into sin. For Jesus Satan was no longer an aspect of God; he remained, nevertheless, an inevitable part of God's creation whose existence served the divine purpose of giving moral substance to the good.

Albeit the devil was often a troublesome figure for Jesus, he never portrays himself as locked in dualistic combat with cosmic evil.[40] That melodramatic outlook was left for later Christians, particularly for the writer of the Apocalypse. Here Satan and his agent the false prophet, who stands to Satan roughly as Christ stands to God, became an archetypal power of evil absolutely opposed to divine purpose.[41] Thus, the New Testament presents two quite different forms of evil: the operative evil of the Gospels and the absolute, dualistic evil of the Apocalypse.

Although Jesus tapped apocalyptic trends in Judaism, apocalypticism and the crucial idea of an Antichrist did not come into vogue during the activism of the apostolic period. Activist Paul's inflated purity and perfectionism did, however, prepare the way for the Antichrist by creating a huge shadow that had to be projected. Yet Paul himself appears not to have made the projection—at least if those who deny he wrote 2 Thessalonians with its "son of perdition" are correct.[42] Not until disillusionment with the possibility of redemption in this life became widespread and activism gave way to quietism was the Church psychologically primed for the massive projection of shadow we see in the doctrine of the Antichrist.[43] The doctrine, along with the Apocalypse's dualistic visions of evil, made Christianity a semidualist religion that, while preserving the purity of the Lord, gives Satan a scope almost as vast as Ahriman from whom he in part derives. Of the Satan that emerged from the New Testament historian Jeffrey Burton Russell observes:

Wide powers were assigned to Satan for two reasons. The first is simply that the traditions of Mazdaism, Orphism, Hellenistic religion and philosophy, and late Judaism were passed on to New Testament Christianity. But, second, these traditions were eagerly accepted and reinforced because they allowed a partial answer to the question of theodicy. Every day in every place, in every life, Satan and his powers are working to block the kingdom of God. The devil is the source of lies, of murder, of wars, he tempts us, accuses us, punishes us, he afflicts us with disease and even possesses us. . . . The Devil of the New Testament is not a joke, he is not taken lightly, he is not merely symbolic, and he is decidedly not peripheral to the New Testament message. The saving mission of Christ can be understood only in terms of its opposition to the power of the Devil: that is the whole point of the New Testament.[44]

Thus, the New Testament, taken in its entirety, gives us Milton's Satan in his full stature. Furthermore, the development of Satan from the Gospels and Paul to 2 Thessalonians and the Apocalypse set a pattern of failed activism followed by apocalyptic projections of shadow upon Satan that was repeated in church history through Milton's time. For example, activist Luther had few positive words for the Apocalypse, and Zwingli dismissed it outright as an unchristian book. Apocalyptic mania, however, gripped their Protestant heirs in the frustrating decades of the mid-seventeenth century.

Milton, Michael Fixler has argued, was so influenced by apocalyptic mania that he consciously structured *Paradise Lost* on the model of the Apocalypse.[45] In *Paradise Lost,* as in the Apocalypse, Satan afflicts mankind like a chronic plague. In both works God is a judge and a destroyer who promises salvation to the holy few and final purification of the world only after terrible suffering and at the end of time. Nevertheless, in *Paradise Lost,* God the Father's unrelenting "justice" has a counterbalance in the Son's creative energy; and matter is not impure but partakes of the divine just as spirit does. Hence, apocalypticism and its obsession with purity exert only a partial and desultory influence on *Paradise Lost.* Moreover, although Milton's conception of evil stands closer to that of the Apocalypse than to that of the Gospels, he went far beyond the Apocalypse with a characterization of Satan that is incomparably richer, more profound, and more psychologically suggestive.

Despite Milton's surmounting narrow apocalyptic psychology, his rendering the Son and Satan as polarized opposites drove out impurity from the Son and creative potential from Satan just as polarization drove out impurity and creative potential from the Lamb and the false prophet in the Apocalypse. Thereby, the Son and the Lamb lost substance and wholeness, while Satan and the false prophet became dualistic evils. Jung observes of the purified Son-Lamb-Christ: "the Christ symbol lacks wholeness in the modern psychological sense, since it does not include the dark side of things but specifically excludes it in the form of a Luciferian opponent."[46] The Son-Lamb-Christ, therefore, comes to represent a psychologically false wholeness. This sham exchanges the wholeness of the self archetype for an inflation of the "good" hostile brother archetype. Consequently, the black sheep or Satan archetype, its role in the dialectic of individuation denied, turns malignant and becomes truly ominous.

Jung, we have seen, repeatedly takes pains to establish the necessity of each of those two hostile brothers, ego and shadow, to psychic balance. So strong were Jung's convictions on the subject that he insisted the Christian repression of shadow and refusal to acknowledge evil or Satan in Godhead was a root cause of persecution and of Christianity's helplessness to combat the rise of destructive will to power. No one is redeemed by Christianity, Jung contends, because the religion, with its inflated will to purity and perfection, refuses to understand what we are to redeem and why.

To remedy Christian inflation, Jung insists, we must stop polarizing the opposites of good and evil, Christ and Satan and ego and shadow, and begin recognizing their interdependence. Their interdependence was recognized early in the Ebionite idea that God has two sons, an older one Satan and a younger one Christ.[47] This notion remained at the periphery of orthodox theology for several centuries. One of its more sophisticated manifestation appears in Lactantius, a theologian overlooked by Jung but not by Milton.[48]

Lactantius contended that God willed a sharp distinction between good and evil to help us grasp the nature of the good by contrasting it against evil.[49] Accordingly, God, who is the overarching good, made the world through two opposing yet interdependent powers. The Son and Satan, though not literally brothers, are the heavenly counterparts of Abel and Cain, one loved like a good son the other loathed like an wicked son.[50] In Lactantius, God's goodness works chiefly through the Son, but the Son, as in Milton, is subordinate.

The opposing yet interdependent brothers, interdependence being implicit in their fraternity, form a universal archetype spanning countless mythologies. Ahura-Mazda and Ahiraman, Baldur and Loki, Osirus and Set, and Apollo and Dionysus are the preeminent pagan examples. The archetype, Jung noted, also appears in the astrological symbolism of the two fishes, Christ and Leviathan, which symbolize the Platonic month of Pisces.[51] In the succeeding Aquarian age, occult doctrine teaches, the two fishes will be reconciled as their interdependence becomes conscious allowing men to dispel Christian inflation and finally confront the problem of evil. Jung speculates in *Aion:* "If, as seems probable, the aeon of the fishes is ruled by the archetypal motif of the hostile brothers, then the approach of the next Platonic month, namely Aquarius, will constellate the problem of the union of opposites. It will then no longer be possible to write off evil as the mere privation of good; its real existence will have to be recognized."[52] Recognition of evil's real existence involves two exceedingly heterodox steps: (1) admission that the Satan-Lucifer-Prometheus and Christ-logos archetypes form an interdependent pair, or *coincidentia oppositorum*, within the quaternal Godhead; and (2) repudiation of God the *Summum Bonum* for Godhead as a symbol of the self. The Renaissance-Reformation period, Jung believed, saw the first glimmerings of this new recognition of evil's real existence in alchemy, the rising scientific spirit, the Cabala, and the works of Jacob Boehme.[53]

Answer to Job. Jung's consummate statement on Godhead is *Answer to Job.* Here he finds in the Book of Job a seedbed for the Christian images of Satan and Christ as well as for the Western notion that creation of consciousness requires mortification of ego through tragic suffering. The Book of Job, Jung contends, reveals the beginnings of both Satan and Christ in their father Yahweh, a largely unconscious deity who, embodying total psychic possibility, displays every psychic quality and its opposite. The contradictory picture of Yahweh was not, however, unique to Job but common to other ancient testimonies: "The picture emerges of a God who knew no moderation in his emotions and suffered precisely from this lack of moderation. He himself admitted that he was eaten up with rage and jealousy and that this knowledge was painful to him. Insight existed along with obtuseness, loving kindness along with cruelty, creative power along with destructiveness. Everything was there and none of these qualities was an obstacle to the other. Such a condition is only conceivable when no reflecting consciousness is present at all or when the capacity for reflection is a very feeble and more or less adventitious phenomenon."[54]

Since Yahweh is blind power, dialogue with him is impossible. The only feasible stances toward him are rebellion or blind submission, Job's stance after Yahweh's theophany in the whirlwind. Jung extolled Job's initial rebellion and rejected his submission and its modern parallel, the blind faith of Kierkegaard.[55] Faith is acceptable to Jung in the form of *pistis*, that is the trust or confidence necessary to sustain the task of individuation, but never in the form of submission to alleged truths that cannot be confirmed by human reason or experience.[56] Blind submission or blind faith brings not consciousness but blindness.

The early Yahweh's consciousness was so undifferentiated he needed the obedience of man to verify his existence. Therein resides one meaning of his arbitrariness. Yahweh's arbitrariness, Jung maintains, indicates, "a personality who can only convince himself that he exists through his relation to an object. Such dependence on the object is absolute when the subject is totally lacking in self reflection and therefore has no insight into himself. It is as if he existed only by reason of the fact that he has an object which assures him that he is really there."[57] Seeking assurance of his own existence or substance, Yahweh arbitrarily wrongs man. The preeminent instances are his setting up Adam for a life of burdens and suffering and his permitting Satan to torture the innocent Job. Satan, Jung reminds us, does not question Job's loyalty on his own initiative. Yahweh unconsciously goads Satan to play the adversary by boasting about Job's unshakable piety. Here, Jung asserts, a hidden doubt comes to light. Yahweh needs to have Job's piety and, hence, his own existence confirmed because he secretly doubts his substantiality.

Satan manifests the primitive Yahweh's self-doubt, which eventually enables Yahweh to realize self-knowledge and moral substance. In his catalytic role Satan first makes man (or Job) self-aware, and therein superior to Yahweh, by afflicting man with the miseries of the world and driving him inward. Job's superiority, Jung contends, has a transformative effect upon Yahweh: "Yahweh must become man precisely because he has done man wrong. He the guardian of justice knows that every wrong must be expiated and Wisdom knows that moral law is above even him. Because his creature has surpassed him, he must regenerate himself."[58] Man understands himself, expiates his sins and substantiates his moral being through suffering. Similarly, to understand himself, to expiate the wrong he has done Adam, Job, and mankind, and to substantiate his moral being, Yahweh becomes a man and suffers crucifixion—that in a nutshell is Jung's yet unassimilated Copernican revolution in theology.[59]

Just as Aristarchus of Samos (ca. 270 B.C.) anticipated Copernicus, so certain Gnostics anticipated Jung. God, these early heretics maintained, becomes man not to enable man to atone for his sins but to enable God to understand man's lot and thus deliver man not from sin but from its consequences, the wrath of God. The fountainhead of Jung's heterodox revolution is, however, not Gnosticism but his own personal conviction that it's impossible for a reflecting mind to believe the Christian God the *Summum Bonum*.

Christians can believe in the *Summum Bonum*, Jung insists, only by blind submission to doctrinal authority. If they reflect, reflection must give rise to doubt or self-delusion.[60] There is, Jung maintains, no creditable explanation for a perfectly rational and benevolent God raging at imperfect man for disappointing his impossible expectations. Man indeed has reason to fear God, but he would have no reason to fear a *Summum Bonum*. God, Jung concludes, must be understood not as the *Summum Bonum* but as a *Summum Coincidentia Oppositorum*, and therefore both fear and love of him are possible.[61]

Attributing any quality to a god who is a *coincidentia oppositorum* necessarily posits its compensatory opposite. God's injustice forces man to realize its compensatory opposite, righteousness. Acting as Job's adversary, God forces the growth of man's moral consciousness and at the same time creates in Job an adversary to himself. Acting as God's adversary, Job compels the divinity to become aware of human suffering and ultimately to incarnate—the objective of incarnation being to individuate divinity with human moral consciousness.[62]

Once good and evil, ego and shadow, are manifest in the Gospel Jesus and the Apocalyptic Satan, for divine individuation to advance further God as divine self must side with good in Christ and reject evil in Satan. Such an alignment inaugurates the second stage of divine individuation. But if divine individuation is to advance to its third stage, if God is to fully manifest his Holy Spirit or Paraclete, then the thesis and antithesis of Christ and Satan must somehow be transformed and transcended. Having distinguished good from evil, God and man must co-create from suffering and shadow a greater good where ego's consciousness conjoins with shadow's substance to inaugurate the stage of the Paraclete.

The third stage of divine individuation can be illuminated by Nietzsche's famous notion—"beyond good and evil." Employed vulgarly it simply means that traditional views of good and evil have become irrelevant. But Nietzsche's profounder meaning implies a philosophic overview, or, if you will, a transformative *conjunctio oppositorum*, which, recognizing the interdependence of opposites, eliminates the need to identify rigidly with good and the temptation to yield to the spell of evil.[63] So enlightened, we can freely acknowledge that God and man need both good and the shadow's operative evil to individuate. When Western man finally assimilates the insight made necessary by the Book of Job—the interdependence of good and operative evil, ego and shadow—polarity ceases to be an absolute religious truth and the orthodox all good ego-God loses credibility. Ergo, God, seen as a divine ego, is dead.

We should not take this second famous Nietzschean pronouncement to mean that either the divine self or *imago dei* is defunct. Instead, it should mean that, once the opposed ethics of repression and rebellion are superseded by inward vision, in place of a God who resembles an inflated ego alienated from shadow will arise a new *imago dei* that reflects the individuated self, whole and substantial.[64]

CRITICAL APPLICATION

While Milton follows orthodoxy in explicitly identifying evil with impurity and implicitly accepting *privatio boni*, his work does not end here. Rather, Milton as artist offers a vision of evil sufficiently profound to authenticate

Coleridge's claim that *Paradise Lost* is the most philosophic of our great epic poems. Because the Miltonic vision of evil is conveyed in a complex image, never stated the way God and the narrator state central theological ideas such as free will, the significance of the Miltonic vision has gone largely unremarked.

Largely unremarked also has been the earliest appearance of the essential image. The vision of evil that unfolds in *Paradise Lost* was first anticipated by an image in *Comus*, Milton's masque of thirty years before:

> But evil on itself shall back recoyl,
> And mix no more with goodness, when at last
> Gather'd like scum, and setl'd to it self
> It shall be in eternal restless change
> Self-fed, and self-consum'd; [*Comus* 593-97]

Here we see in poetry what analytical psychology might call withdrawal into alienated inflation. Indeed, for Milton the artist evil's tendency to recoil from good into inflation's self-fed and self-consumed chaos constitutes its essential character. Thus, in *Paradise Lost* he uses images of back recoiling, self-consumption, self-containment, and restless, futile change to describe Satan and his followers.

Evil Recoiling upon Itself. For Milton the artist evil becomes a counterforce that causes created beings, good though they may initially have been, to recoil from God's goodness. Herein, he parallels Plotinus's idea that evil is a turning away from God. Recoiling from goodness, however, creates not Plotinian deprivation but rather inflated obsession. Inflated obsessions are of course deprived of good, yet Milton does not use the term *privatio boni* or even allude to it. Instead, he uses his artist's image of eternal restless change. There is a major difference between the term and the image: while *privatio boni* implies passivity, eternal restless change conveys ceaseless, chaotic activity.

And, what is crucial, Milton's complex image is not based upon an abstract concept, but upon an archetype, that recoiling, circular beast, the uroboros. The basis of the image in the uroboros archetype becomes apparent once we consider that "settl'd to itself / It shall be in eternal restless change / Self-fed, and self-consum'd" portrays the womb of devouring uroboros. This self-contained entity finds symbolic representation in various closed vessels, the best known being the alchemists' *vas Hermetis*, the Holy Grail, and, nearest to Milton's image, the witch's cauldron.[65] The idea of a self-contained uroboric cauldron devolves from the matriarchal religions associated with the Great Mother, which the Babylonians knew as the All Mother Tiamat, the Egyptians called Temu, and the Hebrew scribes termed formlessness or *tohu* and *bohu*.[66] By making the uroboric cauldron the archetypal image for Satan's inner nature, Milton the artist grounds his peculiar vision of evil in the devouring uroboros archetype. Hence, the term uroboric evil seems appropriate for Milton's vision of evil.

The devouring uroboros has two primary aspects. Their standard representations are the dragon (inflation) and a snake eating its tail (alienation).[67] Satan's actions and the image from *Comus* exemplify and define these two aspects whose characteristic Renaissance displays are malice and envy.[68] The Renaissance emphasis on malice and envy was no mere eccentricity of that time. It indicates a profound archetypal shift away from evil as the passive nonbeing of medieval *privatio boni* toward uroboric evil. Far from passive, uroboric evil is an active counterforce to good operating externally as malice-inflation and internally as envy-alienation. Milton did not derive uroboric evil from Plotinus, Augustine, or any other philosopher. Instead, following the archetypal intuitions that are the birthright of a great visionary artist, he gleaned it from Renaissance malice and envy.

Milton the artist reached further still to intuit the underlying uroboric qualities of a self-sufficient *Summum Bonum*, qualities he makes his Satan openly parody. The artist's intuition implicitly challenges *privatio boni* where, according to Aquinas, evil has no activity peculiar to itself but simply lacks something it ought to have.[69] In *Paradise Lost* Satan's evil is not chiefly a lack of obedience or love, which would render him indifferent to God; it is, above all, a malice and envy toward God unleashed in demented parodying of him.

Privatio boni taken in its literal, Plotinian sense implies a low or deprived place in the chain of being. (Presupposing a universe that is hierarchical, *privatio boni* prepared Christian thought for the notion of a great chain of being.[70]) By contrast, the evil that recoils back upon itself to parody God entails willed rebellion and alienation irrespective of whether one's original place in the chain of being was deprived—clearly, Satan occupied a lofty and privileged place. Thus, uroboric evil, unlike *privatio boni*, actively defies the chain of being. Moreover, the concept of uroboric evil expands and deepens the primitive notion of evil as impurity by defining it through process rather than flux.

Satan's evil is, therefore, anything but deprivation and far worse than a mere impurity. He is a powerful and memorable character because his evil possesses terrible, ceaseless energy, at once aggressive and regressive.[71] To use metaphors that are not Milton's but belong to modern astrophysics: one can liken *privatio boni* to the passive vacuum of empty space; whereas Satan's uroboric evil has the devouring energy and fatal inescapability of one of those strange parodies of the universe and ultimate uroboric enclosures we call black holes. Milton the artist is perhaps the most convincing and thoroughgoing premodern exponent of what I term the black hole or uroboric notion of evil.[72] In attributing uroboric evil to Satan, Milton the artist surmounts orthodox theology without directly challenging it.

Privatio boni offered no psychologically satisfying way to explain Satan's inflated malice, his alienated envy, or his indefatigable resistance. Nonetheless, Milton the Christian apologist had to assume *privatio boni* to reconcile the abiding tragic results of Satan's actions with God's claim to being the Omnipotent *Summum Bonum*. Wherefore, evil in *Paradise Lost* becomes one thing when portraying Satan's character and actions, but it becomes quite another upon proclaiming God's nature.

Although Milton may have been the most philosophic of all great poets, he is more the poet than the philosopher. Yielding to the poet in himself, he gives the conflict between uroboric evil and *privatio boni* a resonance that betrays Christian orthodoxy's failure to provide a consistent theodicy. Table 2 shows the archetypal alignment of the values, definers, and grades of evil that shape the conflict of uroboric evil and *privatio boni* in *Paradise Lost*.

Evil Recoiling on Satan.   Up to this juncture I have discussed in generalities Milton's vision of uroboric evil actively parodying the divine uroboros. To ground the generalities in *Paradise Lost*, we must consider specific images of Satan's uroboric evil and then analyze God's response.

Evil recoiling upon itself, as Arnold Stein first noted, epitomizes both Satan's character and the revolt he incites:[73]

> but the evil soon
> Driv'n back redounded as a flood on those
> From whom it sprung, impossible to mix
> With Blessedness [VII.56-59]

It traps Satan in self-fed, self-consumed uroboric enclosure. Wherever he flies is hell, he confesses, echoing Faust:[74] "which way shall I flie / Infinite wrauth, and infinite despair? / Which way I flie is Hell, my self am Hell;" (IV.73-75). Bemoaning his plight as he contemplates his most base act, the seduction of innocent Eve, Satan employs images of recoil and redound:

> and the more I see
> Pleasures about me, so much more I feel
> Torment within me, as from the hateful siege
> Of contraries; all good to me becomes

Table 2. Archetypal alignment

	Uroboric evil Self/Godhead	Privatio boni Ego/Uroboros
Religious values	*coincidentia oppositorum* consciousness—wholeness interdependence—love	*summum bonum* certainty—perfection dependence—purity
Philosophic value	process	stasis
Ethical value	insight—transformation	obedience—repression
Defining order	dialectical	hierarchical
Defining essence	consciousness	being
Defining mode	tragic	comedic
Operative evil	suffering—learning shadow substantial	sin—repentance shadow insubstantial
Relative evil	stagnation	deprivation
Moral evil	alienation—envy ego inflation—malice	impurity rebellion
Absolute evil	yes	no

> Bane, . . .
> Nor hope to be my self less miserable
> By what I seek, but others to make such
> As I, though thereby worse to me redound
> For onely in destroying I find ease
> To my relentless thoughts; [IX.119-23; 126-30]

By no means deficient in self-knowledge, Satan realizes he's his own most helpless victim. But trapped in uroboric evil, he compounds his long-term misery by taking revenge in order to gain momentary respite from tormenting envy:

> But what will not Ambition and Revenge
> Descend to? who aspires must down as low
> As high he soard, obnoxious first or last
> To basest things. Revenge, at first though sweet,
> Bitter ere long back on it self recoils;
> Let it; I reek not, so it light well aim'd,
> Since higher I fall short, on him who next
> Provokes my envie, this new Favorite
> Of Heav'n, this Man of Clay, [IX.168-76]

As the image of recoil describes Satan's withdrawal from God into uroboric enclosure, so the image of evil redounding upon the evildoer describes God's method of punishment. Indeed, God seems quite willing, eager cynics might contend, to give Satan opportunities to bring more evil back upon himself regardless of the dire side effects for hitherto innocent persons:

> Onely begotten Son, seest thou what rage
> Transports our adversarie, whom no bounds
> Prescrib'd, barrs of Hell, nor all the chains
> Heapt on him there, nor yet the main Abyss
> Wide interrupt can hold; so bent he seems
> On desparat revenge, that shall redound
> Upon his rebellious head. And now
> Through all restraint broke loose he wings his way
> Not farr off Heav'n, in the Precincts of light,
> Directly towards the new created World,
> And Man there plac't, with purpose to assay
> If by force he can destroy, or worse,
> By som false guile pervert; and shall pervert; [III.80-92]

While drawing the reader's attention to Satan's own evil redounding upon him, Milton also draws attention to the license God gives Satan to pursue that evil. Therewith, Milton allows the reader to raise a perplexing question: why does God grant Satan license to pursue his evil when there is no hope of bringing him to repentance and when others, hitherto innocent, are certain to suffer?

To address that question we must first consider Satan's obsessive persistence in evil. Neither his persistence nor his original rebellion make sense psychologically unless we recognize that malice and envy utterly possess him. The chief of the devils is not free but himself possessed—in short he is a psychopath. However, we do not regard it just to punish true psychopaths because we know they are not free to change (or repent) and therefore are not responsible for their continuing psychosis.[75] Above all, we never grant psychopaths license to pursue their evil in society!

Those who wish to defend God's license to Satan face a hopeless task. They must: (1) disregard Satan's psychopathy—his inability to repent and his implacable malice—and hold him responsible and justly punished; (2) assert that his rebellion deserves prolonged punishment; and (3) rationalize sacrificing innocent mankind in order to give Satan new opportunities for crime and God new occasions for punishing him. The moral indefensibility of the license God grants Satan is obvious. Unable to admit the obvious, orthodox theologians can say only that some things must simply be accepted on faith.[76] But to make Satan's license and prolonged punishment essential to Christian faith is not to found that faith upon divine omnipotence and supreme goodness, since these qualities are inconsistent with the license and prolonged punishment. Instead, faith rests upon the implied, though dogmatically rejected, autonomous power of God's adversary. Those unwilling to found their faith upon an implicitly autonomous devil (and implicit dualism) must turn to analytical psychology to elucidate Satan's license and punishment.

For analytical psychology, the Devil's function as a scapegoat is the key. A scapegoat receives the projection of shadow qualities ego cannot accept in the psyche. *Paradise Lost*'s ego-God projects uroboric evil on the Devil. God, then, gives Satan continuing license to do evil in order to have an enduring scapegoat upon whom he can project his own uroboric evil!

Uroboric Evil in Satan and God.   Scapegoating psychology met the needs of God's *summum bonum* persona. Uroboric evil met the quite different needs of his depictor, Milton. No diffident Montaigne, Milton consciously sought militant commitments. To sustain those commitments he needed something beyond the relative evil of deprivation; he needed for an opponent an absolute evil. Here uroboric evil served him well. The self-fed, self-enclosed nature of its malice and envy precludes repentance and so renders it a changeless absolute. Milton's choice of uroboric evil proved, moreover, a choice of genius. Enabling him to portray Satan as more like a black hole than like a vacuum, uroboric evil accounts for, as *privatio boni* never could, the devil's relentless aggression and boundless energy. And uroboric evil explains the devil's power without defying Christian orthodoxy with explicit dualism.

Perhaps no less than the genius of the poetry in which Satan appears, the genius of making his evil uroboric accounts for the fallen archangel's enduring fascination. Once trapped in the self-fed, self-consumed circle of malice and envy, Satan can never escape. His plight, circular and more insidious than even himself, seems to epitomize uroboric evil's mesmeric power. Consider how the image of recoil at once evokes that plight and conveys uroboric evil's irresistible power to pull the victim in deeper and deeper like a psychosis or a black hole:

> Satan, now first inflam'd with rage, came down
> The Tempter ere th' Accuser of mankind,
> To wreck on innocent frail man his loss
> Of that first Battel, and his flight to Hell:
> Yet not rejoycing in his speed, though bold,
> Far off and fearless, nor with cause to boast,
> Begins his dire attempt, which nigh the birth

> Now rowling, boils in his tumultuous brest,
> And like a devilish Engine back recoils
> Upon himself; horror and doubt distract
> His troubl'd thoughts, and from the bottom stir
> The Hell within him, for within him Hell
> He brings, and round about him, nor from Hell
> One step no more then from himself can fly
> By change of place: [IV.9-23]

Trapped in a back recoiling uroboros, Satan is no longer free to repent and break from his cycles of self-fed, self-consumed, eternal restless change. Absolutely devoid of freedom, he personifies intractable psychosis.

The most painful phase of that psychosis is Satan's own recognition of it, the anguished realization that with rebellion, freedom to repent and so freedom itself, was irreparably lost:

> Me miserable! which way shall I flie
> Infinite wrauth, and infinite despair?
> Which way I flie is Hell, my self am Hell
> And in the lowest deep a lower deep
> Still threatning to devour me opens wide,
> To which the Hell I suffer seems a Heav'n . . .
> But say I could repent and obtain
> By act of Grace my former state; how soon
> Would highth recall high thoughts, how soon unsay
> What feign'd submission swore: ease would recant
> Vows made in pain, as violent and void.
> For never can true reconcilement grow
> Where wounds of deadly hate have peirc'd so deep: . . .
> This knows my punisher, and therefore as farr
> From granting hee, as I from begging peace: . . .
> So farwell Hope, and with Hope farwell Fear,
> Farwell Remorse, all Good to me is lost;
> Evil be thou my Good; [IV.73-78, 93-99, 103-104, 108-11]

Although critics often analyze these famous lines, they seldom mention the crucial feature of Satan's plight: the psychotic compulsion precluding his repentance precludes also the only moral justification for his omnipotent punisher's tolerance of Satan's continued existence and activity—he hopes to reform him.

"Infinite wrauth," like "infinite despair," Milton the artist allows us to conclude, is trapped: to keep his uroboric evil from devouring him, he must eternally project it on his scapegoat, Satan. In a sense the plight of the orthodox divinity is more profoundly desperate than that of his scapegoat, since he can never allow himself to recognize the true nature of his "infinite wrauth."

The Divine Darkness.   God can fulfil his promise of turning Satan's (and by implication his own) evil into new good only if that evil is operative evil. An operative evil, unlike an absolute evil, contains a challenge to growth that, when consciously met, can enlarge the realm of the good. But since Satan is incorrigible, he cannot be an operative evil; his evil must be absolute. Consequently, in preserving Satan God does not retain options for creating new good. He preserves a sterile realm of malice and envy where no good can ever grow. Worse still, by denying that the Satan archetype is part of him—what sane motive could he have for preserving Satan other than that Satan is part of himself?—and by treating the archetype as an external being so he can have a scapegoat, he gives his divine darkness destructive license and power it would not have were it forthrightly acknowledged.

Every conscious being partakes of both operative and absolute evil. To gain moral substance and acquire perspective on ego, one must deal with one's own operative evil or the personal shadow. However, knowledge of the self demands recognition of that impersonal, collective shadow, the devouring uroboros. The collective shadow forms a counterforce to self that tempts ego to renounce interdependence with self and *unus mundus* for uroboric containment. Being absolutely opposed to the self and its drive for individuation, the collective shadow is, Jung believed, an absolute evil.[77] Just as every man has a collective as well as a personal shadow, so the face of absolute evil is also among the faces of Godhead. Furthermore, man can never truly know Godhead's glorious, creative side unless he can bear to look at its uroboric collective shadow.

Individuation in man or God requires eventual recognition of the self's counterforce, its uroboric collective shadow. Milton's egolike Deity refuses to acknowledge the danger his collective shadow poses to divine individuation. Instead, he clings to the arrogant delusion of perfect ego-sufficiency and scapegoats his collective shadow upon his personal shadow, Satan, who becomes a confusing mixture of operative and absolute evil, divine shadow and external scapegoat.[78]

Insofar as Satan is an incorrigible evil, a wholly good, omnipotent, and fully realized deity would lack justification for allowing his continued existence. Such allowance makes God a party to Satan's evil, which means he cannot be perfectly good or fully realized. If Satan is truly an operative evil, then he should in the end be brought to reform himself. That Satan is an operative evil is the position of those church fathers who, like Origen with his heresy of apocatastasis (the idea that all beings will eventually turn to God) asserted the potential reform and salvation of Satan. Satan's reformation would make God an emergent deity who requires time to perfect himself and substantiate his ego with the potential goodness of his personal shadow.[79] The God of orthodoxy's refusal to reform Satan constitutes refusal to transform his own evil and substantiate his full potential goodness.

Paradise Lost treats Satan as operative evil when focusing on God's allowing Satan to tempt man and on Satan's catalytic role in human affairs. Then, to explain why Satan cannot repent and why God will cut him off from creation at the end of time, he is treated as an incorrigible evil. In each case the poem remains orthodox. The orthodox try to obscure their God's inconsistent treatment of Satan's evil by righteously extolling his perfect goodness. The inward vision of analytical psychology, however, penetrates the Deity's deceptive persona and reveals its archetypal source: ego's inflated perfectionism. Inflated perfectionism, inhibiting acknowledgment of the slightest operative evil or personal shadow in deity, drives orthodox Christians to the great evil of defining God as a big lie.

In *People of the Lie,* M. Scott Peck, a practicing psychologist and an avowed Christian, describes his experiences with evil people. Peck's observations anatomize the psychology behind the perfectionist Christian demand that their God must have no shadow. All the evil people Peck encountered had strong religious backgrounds. Their signal defect, he notes, is not sin but refusal to acknowledge sin.[80] The truly evil conceal their crimes. Their favored concealment mechanisms are projection and scapegoating, motivated by their fear of self-criticism. The evil are utterly dedicated to maintaining an image of perfection.[81] Lacking all desire to be good, they work intensely hard to appear good. Invariably, the evil cloak their true motives with lies. Professing to want perfect goodness, what they truly want is power for its own sake. At the root of their desire for power festers terror of uncertainty.[82]

Peck, I presume, might well be disconcerted to see his observations applied to the orthodox Christian God who flaunts a persona of supreme goodness and self-righteously scapegoats upon man and Satan all blame for the evils of a world he himself has created. Nevertheless, the application's pertinence becomes obvious in light of Peck's remark that evil persons are almost always religious people who cannot bear the thought of their own imperfection: those who insist that God must be the *Summum Bonum* attribute to Deity their inability to accept imperfection in themselves.[83]

The shadow of those who cannot tolerate imperfection is always projected and often satanic. In Milton's and Christian orthodoxy's God, pride, scorn, intolerance of imperfection, self-glorification, and concern for moral reputation generate a lying persona that casts a colossal, satanic shadow. Similar to a Renaissance ego with its faith in will and lust for boundless power and glory, Milton's God also resembles a hypertrophied Reformation superego in overstressing purity, individual blame, and obligation. Whereas in theory Milton's God is all good and all knowing, his behavior, like that of an unreflective, willful, ego-driven person, incongruously mixes good and evil.

Although Milton's orthodoxy inhibited him from acknowledging how close the divine and the demonic stand, his intuitive apprehension of their proximity sometimes breaks fleetingly into consciousness. A striking example arises when the poet, soaring in imaginative flight to leave the apologist behind, has Mammon say:

> How oft amidst
> Thick clouds and dark doth Heav'ns all-ruling Sire
> Choose to reside, his Glory unobscur'd,
> And with the Majesty of darkness round
> Covers his Throne: from whence deep thunders roar
> Must'ring thir rage, and Heav'n resembles Hell?
> As he our darkness, cannot we his Light
> Imitate when we please? [II.263-70]

The similarity of heaven to hell that Mammon notes holds for heaven's oratory no less than for its lighting effects. God's relishing scornful rhetoric indicates a verbal sadism and a spirit given to resentment and vindictiveness. Though the Son lacks the Father's vindictive urges, he nonetheless mirrors his pride in their divine power and glory and his scorn for their opponents:

> Mightie Father, thou thy foes
> Justly hast in derision, and secure
> Laugh'st at thir vain designes and tumults vain
> Matter to Mee of Glory, whom thir hate
> Illustrates, when they see all Regal Power
> Giv'n me to quell thir pride, and in event
> Know whether I be dextrous to subdue
> Thy Rebels, or be found the worst in Heav'n. [V.735-42]

Why should the Persons of the Godhead revel in derision? Why should the Son need to assure the Father of the justice of his scorn? Why should the Son savor proving his "Regal Power" in battle? Why delight in quelling the devil's pride, and why boast of his military prowess like a Hotspur chafing for victory? Satan is called scornful and condemned for the pride, malice, and envy his scorn reveals. Yet the Father and the Son resort to scorn and vaunt that differs from Satan's mainly in its stuffier tone.

Furthermore, their exemplary faithful servants, Gabriel and Abdiel, engage Satan in flyting matches with all the bravura of seventeenth-century political pamphleteers. The only psychologically credible motive for God and his servants scorning Satan is that they feel threatened by him. Here it should be noted that since Satan cannot threaten divine power, he can only pose a threat to the Divinity's conception of himself and to the Divine Persona his servants want to believe in.

The nature of the Divinity's scorn and his love of power and glory along with their relationship to Satan's envy deserve more careful scrutiny than critics have hitherto given them. In Milton's age envy was universally judged a powerful motive. By contrast, our time, as sociologist Helmut Schoeck documents, represses the entire topic of envy.[84] While Schoeck proffers a sweeping modern study of envy, he himself seems to fall under the current repression when it comes to exploring envy's opposite, scorn or contempt. Those who heed Jung, however, will recognize that because of *coincidentia oppositorum* nothing can be understood apart from its opposite.

Envy and contempt are distinctly complementary opposites. They exhibit an easy reciprocity and at times almost an interchangeability. Contempt is for the powerful what envy is for the weak; together they comprise parallel avenues of alienation's retreat from love. Envy and contempt are each other's shadows. We often find beneath displays of contempt a desire to be envied and beneath displays of envy a hidden fear of being scorned. The most envious people, greatly fearing scorn, are likely themselves to scorn those below them. Envy can be a defense against contempt, and contempt a defense against envy. Even as we express contempt to counter malicious envy, so we envy others in retaliation for their real or imagined scorn of us.

The remedy of envy is to acknowledge our imperfections and either accept them or strive to improve. The remedy of scorn is to acknowledge that superior position depends on fortune and to recognize our tragic vulnerability. If the envious ought to change in themselves those flaws that can be changed and accept those that cannot, the contemptuous ought to realize that, to deserve morally their privileges, they must be magnanimous to the unfortunate.

In *Paradise Lost* Satan and God illustrate how envy and contempt provoke each other. Here we see a devil filled with envy and a deity blown up with contempt, each evil feeding its opposite. Satan's envy and God's contempt together form a self-fed, self-consumed uroboros. At each pole of their entwined evil cowers an insecure demi-ego—the dispossessed coveting strength, the privileged willing to pay any price to uphold the image of moral superiority.

A perfectly good, fully realized and omnipotent deity would feel no insecurity about self-image and no contempt for underlings. Possessor of complete self-knowledge, he would be a stranger to the self-doubt behind insecurity and contempt. Were Satan to envy an entirely serene deity, that deity's sovereign serenity would calm and finally dispel the envy. Only because Milton's scornful, vaunting deity lacks credible serenity does Satan's rebellion become plausible.

A God at Odds with Himself.[85]   The Father's contempt, the Son's boasting, and Satan's envy are difficult to account for given what we're told about their separate identities. Milton the apologist represents them as like autonomous persons governed by Renaissance egos with their characteristic striving for power, glory, and self-expansion along with the existential insecurity underlying such striving. Above the apologist's conscious drama, however, stands a metadrama orchestrated by Milton the visionary artist.

To grasp the whole, we must attend to the tensions between the conscious drama, setting forth the theological identities of Father, Son and Satan, and the artist's metadrama subtly shaping word and action to give us epiphanies of archetypal realities. While at the dramatic level Father, Son, and Satan appear to be autonomous persons, in the metadrama they should be viewed the way Jung views characters in myths and fairy tales, as discordant archetypes constellated by a single psyche struggling for individuated wholeness.[86] Since the conscious level has been heavily explored, I shall focus on the epiphanies of the metadrama.[87]

In the drama Satan and the Son are depicted as similar to warring Renaissance generals, which makes them like rival egos.[88] In the metadrama they constellate the archetypal hostile brothers so that Satan becomes the shadow to the Son-ego. The Son, as ego, loses claim to being a pleromatic self-symbol. Nonetheless, both he and Satan could still be peaceably subsumed within the totality of the Father's Divine Self. The Father, however, can offer no peaceful berth because he identifies not with his Self, but with the ego qualities of the Son. To make matters worse, Milton distinguishes the Father and the Son as dramatic characters by inflating the Father's ego qualities! Like many inflated egos, the Father demands a persona of perfect righteousness and so cannot integrate the shadow to realize conscious wholeness.[89] Indeed, the Father's ego inflation necessarily puts him in direct conflict with Satan. Their conflict eliminates Malak Satan, Yahweh's cooperative adversarial function, leaving Satan the metadramatic role of the Father's belligerent shadow and the dramatic role of his scapegoat.

Foresaking his pleromatic self to identify exclusively with ego and to war against shadow, the Father cannot escape doubts about his own claims to manifest the Divine Self. The most obvious symptoms of these doubts are his recurrent defensiveness and his compulsive need to justify himself. Frequently, he resembles a man dogged by some guilty secret. For example, predicting man's fall, he insists upon his own blamelessness even though no one has faulted him:

> whose fault?
> Whose but his own? ingrate he had of mee
> All he could have; I made him just and right,
> Sufficient to have stood, though free to fall. [III.96-99]

Later the Father sends Raphael to warn Adam of Satan's designs. The intent of the warning is not to protect man against his tempter but to protect the Divine Ego from accusations of injustice! He concludes:

> Happiness in his power left free to will,
> Left to his own free Will, his Will though free,
> Yet mutable; whence warn him to beware
> He swerve not too secure: tell him withall
> His danger, and from whom, what enemie
> Late falln himself from Heav'n, is plotting now
> The fall of others from like state of bliss;
> By violence, no, for that shall be withstood,
> But by deceit and lies; this let him know,
> Least wilfully transgressing he pretend
> Surprisal, unadmonisht, unforewarnd.
>   So spake th' Eternal Father, and fulfilld
> All Justice: [V.235-45]

The Father appears to be setting up Adam for sin, judgment, and punishment in a cynical manner reminiscent of modern political purges. But Adam's free will, we are expected to concede, relieves the Father of responsibility for setting up man. The Father's argument resorts to the deception and verbal sorcery characteristic of those who hide unscrupulous egotism behind a perfectionist persona. Consider his formula: "left free to will / Left to his own free Will, his Will though free, / Yet mutable." Here, with free will used in an almost incantatory fashion, magic substitutes for meaning. Especially noteworthy is the strange phrase: "though free, / Yet mutable." The conjunction "yet" appears to make the will's mutability a qualification upon its freedom. The nature of the qualification, however, is left unexplained. The Prestidigitator does not unravel his tricks. "Qualification" may be too weak a term for this particular verbal trick, for "though" and "yet" put freedom and mutability in opposition to create a paradox. Paradox, a stock tool of verbal magic, loses its power to fascinate and confuse when understood, which accounts for Milton's Divine Magician leaving the philosophical machinery behind his paradox well cloaked. Seen for what it does, "though free, yet mutable" is astute sophistry.

The Father's instructions to Raphael never mention the one thing Adam and Eve in their inexperience most desperately need to know, Satan's strategy: the devil will seek to divide them against each other and use their division to alienate them from God. Instead Raphael is instructed to give them philosophical generalizations that they lack the experience to appreciate and the training to apply. Were a Stalin to commission a warning as purposefully ineffective as Raphael's, we'd call it an insidious subterfuge. In his commission, as elsewhere, the Father shows great concern about appearing just and no concern about actually being just.

So exclusive is the Father's concern for his righteous persona that he remains untouched by the human tragedy of man's fall:

> no Decree of mine
> Concurring to necessitate his Fall;
> Or touch with lightest moment of impulse
> His free Will, to her own inclining left
> In eevn scale. But fall'n he is, and now
> What rests, but that the mortal Sentence pass
> On his transgression, [X.43-49]

Why should the Father need to belabor divine justice and his innocence of blame for man's fall? Why reiterate that man has free will when new iteration never comes mated with new illumination? Why but that men have good reasons to dismiss free will as a sophistic ruse, to doubt his justice, and to infer that he secretly knows he's much to blame.

The Father is more than just too quick to exonerate himself and blame man, at times he displays a recklessness that ventures close to letting slip out his subtle participation in evil. For instance, watching Sin and Death cross Chaos after Satan's "victory" in Eden, the Deity boasts in language rank with scatological contempt that he has drawn them to Earth to serve divine purposes:

> See with what heat these Dogs of Hell advance
> To waste and havoc yonder World, which I
> So fair and good created, and had still
> Kept in that state, had not the folly of Man
> Let in these wastful Furies, who impute
> Folly to mee, so doth the Prince of Hell
> And his Adherents, that with so much ease

> I suffer them to enter and possess
> A place so heav'nly, and conniving seem
> To gratifie my scornful Enemies,
> That laugh, as if transported with some fit
> Of Passion, I to them had quitted all,
> At random yeilded up to their misrule;
> And know not that I call'd and drew them thither
> My Hell-hounds, to lick up the draff and filth
> Which mans polluting Sin with taint hath shed
> On what was pure, till cramm'd and gorg'd, nigh burst
> With suckt and glutted offal, [X.616-33]

The grim truth, overshadowing this supercilious and repugnant speech, is that the Father let in Sin and Death because he allowed Satan to travel to Earth on his bad errand. Equally disturbing is the pleasure he takes in outfoxing these demented fools. The sole discretion the Father shows in this bleak epiphany of divine egotism lies in leaving it to the angels to sing the justice of his ways:

> He ended, and the heav'nly Audience loud
> Sung Halleluia, as the sound of the Seas,
> Through the multitude sung: Just are thy ways,
> Righteous are thy Decrees on all thy Works:
> Who can extenuate thee? [X.641-45]

The Shawcross edition notes that "extenuate" here means disparage. Who can disparage so disparaging a deity? Since his scorn, scapegoating, and rationalization undoubtedly justify disparagement, anyone who thinks can. The passage reveals, then, how easily the angels are taken in by divine scapegoating and rationalization. Although the angels affirm the popular belief, which Milton the apologist subscribes to, that no one can find fault with what God had done or not done, by using the word "extenuate" Milton the artist encourages the reader to question God's words and actions.

The militant self-righteousness of the Father's speeches, analytical psychology tells us, overcompensates repressed guilt. Far from presenting a *Summum Bonum* who should be supremely serene, the speeches meta-dramatically convey turbulent epiphanies of ego individuation in an imperfect process deity. Like every insecure ego, the Father resists individuation because he knows it requires dialogue with shadow and involves humbling of ego. And like all inflated egos, the Divine Ego resists individuation by projecting his defects onto scapegoats and by making hubristic claims to moral perfection.

Moral perfection's physical correlate is cleanliness. Evil, as Paul Ricoeur notes, began as defilement.[90] Proclaiming his moral perfection, Milton's ego-identified Deity stresses Sin and Death's defilement and promises to make his flawless purity universal at the end of time by closing forever the hideous, uroboric orifice of hell:

> obstruct the mouth of Hell
> For ever, and seal up his ravenous Jaws.
> Then Heav'n and Earth renewd shall be made pure
> To sanctitie that shall receive no stain:
> Till then the Curse pronounc't on both precedes. [X.636-40]

The Father claims the authority only the archetype of self possesses. Nevertheless, in his scornful tone and with lurid imagery (e.g., wastful, draff, filth, polluting, taint, cramm'd, gorg'd, suckt, glutted offal, ravenous jaws, X.616-40), he behaves like an insecure Christian ego unable to accept impurity or guilt and horrified by the way its shadow stains the earth.

Beneath the contradiction between the Father's professions on one hand and his acts and imagery on the other, suppurates an archetypal conflict. Divine ego, which dominates his stage of individuation, is profoundly at odds with divine self. According to Jung, the self, motivated to advance individuation, contrives to get ego soiled with impurity and evil in order to force it to radically change its identity. Growth, after all, requires identity change. Since ego typically resists identity change (ego's function is maintenance of identity) by asserting its current perfection and projecting its shadow onto scapegoats, the quest for wholeness requires crucifixion of ego upon the cross of self. "The whole world," Jung observed, "is God's suffering, and every individual who wants to get anywhere near his own wholeness knows that this is the way of the cross."[91] Milton the artist's treatment of Satan's revolt gives metadramatic epiphanies of the Self of God pushing the divine ego into conflicts with its shadow, creating crosses that ultimately further the Self's quest for wholeness.

Revolt of the Shadow. God the Father surely knows that exalting the Son will spark Satan's revolt.[92] Indeed, his announcement of the exaltation suggests something beyond mere foreknowledge:

> Hear all ye Angels, Progenie of Light,
> Thrones, Dominations, Princedoms, Vertues, Powers,
> Hear my Decree, which unrevok't shall stand
> This day I have begot whom I declare
> My onely Son, and on this holy Hill

Him have anointed, whom you new behold
At my right hand; your head I him appoint;
And by my Self have sworn to him shall bow
All knees in Heav'n, and shall confess him Lord
Under his great Vice-gerent Reign abide
United as one individual Soul
For ever happie: him who disobeys
Me disobeys, breaks union, and that day
Cast out from God and blessed vision, falls
Into utter darkness, deep ingulft, his place
Ordaind without redemption, without end. [V.600-615]

What can be the Father's motive for flaunting his authority and the permanence of his decree in a situation where none (save the wary reader) has any reason to question his authority or suppose he might revoke his decree? The Father's very insistence makes sense only as an epiphany of his secret wish to incite questioning and throw down the gauntlet to any disposed to take it up. If the Son is the angels' creator and king, as Miltonic doctrine specifies, why, long after their creation, does the Father suddenly declare the Son his "onely" son and appoint him head of the angels? His Divine Self, Jungian psychology answers, realizes his Satan-shadow is ripe for revolt and seeks to incite that revolt in order to spur divine individuation.

The word "onely" carries a fleeting epiphany of an aspect of God's archetypal nature that orthodox theology has long endeavored to shroud. Declaring the Son his "onely Son" suggests that he, like a desert potentate who chooses a single heir from a great brood of progeny, has other sons but desires to officially claim only one. The implication of other progeny supplies an archetypal basis for an action whose context is obscure in Miltonic and orthodox theology.[93] The archetype constellated here is that of the two brothers whose hostility springs from their father's preferring one over the other. While the archetype does not operate explicitly, its metadramatic function is probably closer to the surface of Milton's consciousness than one might first suppose.[94]

The exaltation of the Son in book V (600-615) is in part based on Psalm 2, which Milton doubtless knew well since he translated it.[95] By the Christian interpretation Messiah is the Son. But Milton must also have been aware of the Jewish interpretation wherein "the anointed" (Messiah in Milton) is the king of the children of Israel. Israel is Jacob, the rival brother to Esau. Jacob and Esau are two of the most prominent hostile brothers in the Old Testament.[96] An instance of their conflict that parallels the Son and Satan's conflict in *Paradise Lost* appears in the Book of Obadiah. The house of Jacob, Obadiah prophesies, shall be a fire utterly consuming the scapegoated house of Esau. To be consumed in the Son's fire is of course the prophesied fate of scapegoat Satan. Moreover, the idea of the Son as one of many brothers was common in the Arian-subordinationist sector of the Christian spectrum. This sector contained Milton, whose subordinationism derives in part from Lactantius, for whom, as we have seen, Christ and Satan were metaphorically brothers.[97]

Finally, certain Hermetic and Gnostic accounts with which Milton may have been familiar explicitly represent Christ and Satan, or Lucifer, as brothers.[98] Of these accounts Milton at least knew of Epiphanius, whom he mentions in *Areopagitica*. Epiphanius discussed the belief of the Elkesaites that Christ and the Devil are brothers.[99] In all these accounts the divine Father preferred the docile, obedient brother over the aggressive, rebellious one in the manner that Yahweh preferred Abel over Cain.

If the Son and Satan are taken to be brothers, God would seem to commit the injustice of favoritism by claiming one and disowning the other. They are not brothers in orthodox theology to be sure. Nonetheless, they become like brothers when their archetypes are excavated, and archetypes, being permanent features of the psyche, go deeper than orthodoxy, which is a cultural product. While Milton the apologist defended orthodoxy, his artist's unconscious, according to Jung, would have sought to compensate for orthodoxy's imbalances by activating powerful archetypes across the border in heresy. But, because of the apologist's commitment to orthodoxy, Milton the artist could present heretical archetypes only in subtle, metadramatic epiphanies. It is a tribute to the power of the artist that the archetypes outlined in the tensions and murmurings of his poem convey truths of Godhead the apologist would labor to disavow.

Milton the apologist neither believed that God appointed the Son at a particular time and convocation nor did he speculate in *De Doctrina* or elsewhere on the causes or specific circumstances of Satan's rebellion. However, to meet dramatic poetry's need for believable motivation, Milton the artist went beyond the apologist to create the fiction of the "onely" Son's appointment and speculate on Satan's state of mind at the time he rebelled. Out of his artist's impulse to stress the direct rivalry of the Son and Satan, he disregarded scriptural authority (Revelation 12:7-9) to make the Son, not the archangel Michael, responsible for Satan's defeat.[100] Out of the desire to make their rivalry psychologically plausible, he drew from the unconscious the archetype of the hostile brothers and constellated it in metadramatic epiphanies. And to heighten dramatic impact, he made the scapegoat brother Satan seem a formidable adversary to the obedient Son.

Theology insists that reality was otherwise. But in its explicit denial of Satan's autonomous power, theology raises, though never answers, the question of why God countenances Satan's continued existence after his fall. Sensing the need to explain Satan's continued existence, Milton the artist drew upon the archetypal substrate of Christian-Hebraic myth, thereby falling into conflict with Hellenic derived theology. Hence, Satan's character and role in the scheme of things became defined by the scapegoat-brother archetype in sharp contrast to the scriptures *in toto,* where he has a protean identity, and to orthodox theology where the unspoken policy is to avoid getting specific about Satan in order to avoid explaining his continued existence.

Moreover, because Milton gave Satan strong character and a pivotal aggressive role, all the Son's actions seem reactions. Satan's initiative becomes disconcertingly apparent when Michael previews human history for Adam in the final two books of *Paradise Lost.* Thus, the initiative Satan shows in history, causing us to question his true nature and power, forms yet another metadramatic epiphany of his role as hostile brother (the paradigmatic bastard) and shadow to the acknowledged Son's divine ego.

Although the narrator never specifies Satan's exact prefallen status in heaven, he does state that Satan compared himself to the Son and felt his pride injured by the Son's exaltation:

> he of the first,
> If not the first Arch-Angel, great in Power,
> In favour and in praeeminence, yet fraught
> With envie against the Son of God, that day
> Honourd by his great Father, and proclaimd
> Messiah King anointed, could not bear
> Through pride that sight, and thought himself impaird.
> Deep malice thence conceiving and disdain, [V.659-66]

Here that cryptic word "begot" gains a synonym, "honor'd."[101] Unhonored, Satan by comparison felt impaired. Orthodox theology denies Satan any grounds for expecting to be treated as the Son's equal. Only because we sense the archetype of the two hostile brothers operating at a metadramatic level does Satan's pride and envy become psychologically and dramatically convincing.

The Father's decree exalting the Son raises more than just the question of Satan's real position. Why, we wonder, does the Father introduce changes into a world without sin, which presumably would be perfect. The "why" of the Father's motives surely lurks behind Satan's objections to the Messiah's "new laws":

> new Laws thou seest impos'd;
> New Laws from him who reigns, new minds may raise

In us who serve, new Counsels, to debate
What doubtful may ensue, more in this place
To utter is not safe. [V.679-83]

Laws bring order, yet heaven should be ordered perfectly already. The new laws are not credible if we regard God as the static, eternally perfect *Summum Bonum*. However, if, viewing their proclamation metadramatically, we see God in an unfolding individuation process at the stage where ego and shadow become polarized, then emergence of the hostile brothers, the Son and Satan, and the Father's preference of the former and scapegoating of the latter become entirely credible.

The *Summum Bonum* cannot be in process since he maintains static perfection for eternity. That's the theory at least, and we must keep it ever in mind if we want to understand Milton's conscious intentions. Nevertheless, to understand Satan's position and revolt we must look beyond the apologist's theory to the epiphanies of the artist's metadrama. We can then perceive behind the divinity's rigid, orthodox persona the movements of vital archetypes. Here an unconscious process, imperfect and incomplete, constellates opposites to push the divine psyche toward individuation.

The Reactionary Shadow. Assuming that God's actions further a metadrama of divine individuation, the revolt of Satan-shadow becomes a predictable and appropriate response to the exaltation of Son-ego. Nevertheless, when individuation fails to proceed smoothly, which is typically the case, the entire fault does not always reside with ego. Other archetypal functions have their independent roles and energies and sometimes these other functions will be diseased. That, it may be argued, is the psychic situation Milton portrays in the metadrama of *Paradise Lost*.

One salient fact gives credence to this interpretation: while inflation colors the Father's words and deeds, the Son, save when praising the Father, is notably moderate. The chief heir to the Father's inflation is not Son-ego but Satan-shadow. He virtually defines the disease. Satan's inflation suggests an alternative interpretation of his revolt that lays responsibility on the rebellious archangel's shoulders. The Son's exaltation and the new laws, by this interpretation, challenge Satan-shadow to enter a new stage of the divine individuation process. Instead of responding to the challenge, he reacts with inflation in the form of resentment, his sense of injured merit, against the Son who rules by virtue of ego's decision-making role.

Resentment, like other forms of inflation, rejects creative faith. If we assume, despite orthodox theology's commitment to stasis, that the God of

Christian myth embodies an individuation process, the changes in heaven ought to make Satan and all the angels happier once they respond creatively. But where Satan ought to respond with creative faith, he reacts with destructive resentment and pride. The metadrama of *Paradise Lost* may thus present divine individuation developing as the Son, who spearheads creativity, overcomes Satan, his inflated, demented shadow, who attempts to thwart all creative advance.[102] Such, at least, is the metadrama Milton the apologist appears to want. And the wants of the apologist exert sufficient influence to shift the actual metadrama in the desired direction. But they are not, we shall see, able finally to thwart the deeper purposes of the unconscious working through Milton the artist.

Satan is depicted as the enemy of great creative nature. He journeys to Earth in hope of ruining God's latest creation and promises Chaos to return Earth to his unformed realm. Moreover, he fathers Sin and Death and introduces these destructive offspring into the undefended world of man and nature. Rejecting the Son's creativity, Satan repudiates his own shadow role as a constructive complement to divine ego. Traditionally, the archangel Michael defeated Lucifer. Milton replaces Michael with the Son, the creator of all the angels, to sharpen the conflict between creativity and destructiveness. The metadramatic effect is to stress Satan's destructive power. The need for the Son to suffer crucifixion, death, and resurrection to redeem creation from Satanic power further underscores that power.

As I explained in the preceding chapter, Satan represents the most destructive part of the archetypal complex behind the rebel and the ethic of rebellion. In *Paradise Lost* Satan's rebel identity is blackened by making him a tyrant. Satan is depicted as the kind of rebel, so common in our century, who rebels in order to establish personal tyranny. His self-serving objective makes him more a reactionary in rebel's garb than an genuine revolutionary. Milton had too much of the revolutionary in himself to portray his arch villain as anything other than a reactionary. He tried to make Satan, therefore, more akin politically to those who resisted the commonwealth than to those who imposed its "new laws."

In portraying Satan as a "reactionary" Milton attempts to redirect the archetype activated by challenge to divine power, the Promethean archetype.[103] Prometheus is ordinarily assigned to the creative side of the shadow, not the ruling ego. *Paradise Lost* overturns the accustomed order by making the Son bring the Promethean challenge and thus incorporating within him the creative energies of both ego and shadow. Since, for Milton the apologist, God and his Son must manifest perfection, nothing good can knowingly be granted to Satan. He cannot be a creative shadow; his only acknowledged role is as the all black scapegoat of an all white God.

Because Milton the apologist cannot give Satan any independent creative potential, indeed all creation must play moon to God's Son, there can be no real dialectic between creator and creature. The creature's sole creative act is the "free" choice of his "mutable" will to obey God's commands.

Throughout *Paradise Lost* Milton the apologist tells us that to love God is to obey his commands. Indeed, the old ethic notion that love and creativity require obedience to commands underlies his intended metadramatic interpretation of Satan as a reactionary scapegoat. It also underlies that interpretation's failure. To understand why the apologist's orthodox metadrama fails and is superceded by the artist's heretical metadrama, wherein the devil ceases to be a scapegoat and becomes the divine shadow, we must analyze obedience and commands. The most probing and provocative modern analysis is Elias Canetti's *Crowds and Power.* Canetti stresses the danger to freedom, to morality, and ultimately to creativity that obedience and commands pose. Of men whose moral sense has been destroyed by commands, he observes: "The more foreign to his nature the original command, the less guilt he feels about what it made him do; the more autonomous and separate the existence of the sting [of the command]. It is his permanent witness that it was not he himself who perpetrated a given wrong. He sees himself as its victim and thus has no feeling for the real victim. It is true therefore, that people who have acted on orders can feel entirely guiltless. . . . From whatever aspect we consider the command, we can now see that, as we know it today, in the compact and perfected form it has acquired in the course of its long history, it is the most dangerous single element in the social life of man."[104] Far from being compatible with freedom, as adherents of both the old ethic and the ethic of rebellion believe, commands subvert freedom by setting up an inner other, whether divine or collective, to whom we abdicate responsibility in obeying it. And far from sustaining the moral sense, commands sabotage its very basis, love or compassion, by alienating men from each other and from their own feelings. By its very nature, submission to power, obedience is inimical to freedom. Though obedience may be necessary under certain circumstances, war conditions, for example, like war, obedience is never in itself either free or loving. Love always cooperates knowingly; never does it blindly submit to superior power. Love seeks the understanding, indeed is the understanding, that renders obedience and commands unnecessary. Ethics that rely on command and obedience promote not freedom and love but scapegoating, alienation and inflation.

Satanic Inflation. This psychological view of command and obedience is an outgrowth of the harrowing ordeals of our time. Living in an age when the perils of totalitarianism were less apparent than they are today, Milton as apologist seems naively optimistic about improving human life through obedience to commands. The Son and the loyal angels obey freely, the apologist asks us to believe, because they love freely. Devoid of all love, Satan forsakes creative obedience for alienated inflation.

Milton the artist's metadrama, however, goes much deeper. Here Satan's reactionary self-involvement and vaunted independence parody the more subtle withdrawal into inflation of God himself. When God the Father speaks inflation is never far afield—witness all his speeches cited in this essay! Sometimes divine inflation remains muted, yet at other times it becomes blatant, as in sending the Son forth to create the world:

> My overshadowing Spirit and might with thee
> I send along, ride forth, and bid the Deep
> Within appointed bounds be Heav'n and Earth,
> Boundless the Deep, because I am who fill
> Infinitude, nor vacuous the space.
> Though I uncircumscrib'd my self retire,
> And put forth not my goodness, which is free
> To act or not, Necessitie and Chance
> Approach not mee, and what I will is Fate. [VII.165-73]

Some will object to calling these grandiloquent words inflated on the grounds that God utters them, not man. Specious reasoning this, for God ought to set an example. To speak like an inflated man no more becomes deity than would speaking like a violent, hate-filled man. Imbalanced emotional states sanctioned by divinity are likely to infect human auditors. Such has been the case historically where inflation attributed to the Divinity has often infected the proponents of Christian orthodoxy, fostering absolutism, intolerance, persecution, and war.

The orthodox divinity's inflation began with the denial of God's shadow accompanying the arrogant doctrine of *summum bonum*. Through that doctrine, devouring uroboros's inflated perfectionism, which promotes alienation, supplanted the dialectic of ego and shadow that promotes individuated wholeness. Simltaneously, uroboros corrupted Christian civilization; for making God like an inflated ego encouraged Christians to ignore their own personal inflation, and it abetted collective inflation among them. Perhaps most destructive of all, their deity's inflated egotism sanctioned alienating command and obedience ethics and scapegoating.

With his bloated claim to pure goodness, Milton's ego-God creates a shadow manifest in Satan's inflation: this raises Satan above his scapegoat identity to make him the true Shadow to God's ego. The inflated will to self-sufficient power behind God's claim, "Necessitie and Chance/ Approach not mee, and what I will is Fate," is echoed and made unmistakable in Satan's boasting, "A mind not changed by Place or Time," a mind that is its own place and "Can make a Heav'n of Hell, a Hell of Heav'n." Considered together, God's claim and its satanic echo become a metadramatic epiphany of the inflated horror that is Christian orthodoxy's ideal of Divine Omnipotence.

Satan's Identity and Its Final Dissolution.   Alienation' acme, Satan's boast epitomizes uroboric evil. Uroboric evil disavows that sense of dependence essential to religious emotion in a system where God is a static *Summum Bonum.* Where God is a process, religious emotion entails a sense of interdependence. Where flux rules, no god merits worship; hence, religious emotion is transferred to "heroic" acts of rebellion that assert the uroboric autonomy of the hero or group. Accordingly, Satan initially assumes a heroic posture to assert his autonomy:

> who saw
> When this creation was? rememberst thou
> Thy making, while the Maker gave thee being?
> We know no time when we were not as now;
> Know none before us, self-begot, self-rais'd
> By our own quick'ning power, when fatal course
> Had circl'd his full Orb, the birth mature
> Of this our native Heav'n, Ethereal Sons.
> Our puissance is our own, our own right hand
> Shall teach us highest deeds, by proof to try
> Who is our equal: [V.857-66]

Later Uriel informs Satan that he saw God make the world from formless matter (III.694-721). The young angel's disingenuous testimony, refuting satanic autonomy, sparks Satan's agonized address to the Sun (IV.32-113). Here he acknowledges dependence and his inability to find meaning apart from his creator.

Repentance is Satan's sole alternative to eventual oblivion. Unable to repent or accept dependence on the God he now knows to be his maker, he abandons the pretense of heroism and confirms himself in deliberate malice. Biding farewell to hope and fear and embracing total desperation, he relinquishes the delusive persona of a Promethean rebel to embrace the identity Milton the apologist attributes to him from the start—that of a reactionary who malevolently seeks to thwart divine creativity. Thus, what begins with the inflated pretense of rebellion ends with the fact of inflated reaction. Throughout the drama Satan is a study of the faces of inflation; throughout the artist's metadrama his inflation forms an epiphany of the shadow cast by God's righteous persona.

Satan, considered as an autonomous being, can never be a true hero because heroism requires sacrifice. The exact opposite, Satan is ever and obviously inflating. Sacrifice and inflation (or hubris) are the poles that define heroism and villainy in myth. Satan's inflation notwithstanding, the account of his voyage to Earth links him to mythic heroes.[105] He undertakes, for example, the traditional task of the hero, to restore the kingdom to his dispossessed people. Like the heroes of myth he is a wanderer in search of a place to reintegrate his shattered personality. And like them he displays great initiative and energy.[106] All becomes ironic, however, upon reaching his destination. Touching down on Mt. Nephates, his heroic facade collapses revealing an inflated scapegoat primed to carry the projection of divine inflation.

Satan's exposure on Nephates shouldn't startle anyone since his quest, like the battle in heaven, belongs to mock epic more than to true heroic action. The earlier confrontations with Sin, Death, and Chaos are conspicuous instances of mock heroic mode. Indeed, Milton may have seen his mock heroic mode as satire. In *An Apology for a Pamphlet* he remarks: "for a satyr as it is born of a tragedy, so ought to resemble his parentage, to strike high and adventure dangerously at the most eminent vices among the greatest persons."[107] Satan, the ruler of our benighted world, is the supreme target for satire. Accordingly, Milton uses mock heroic satire to demolish all Satan's claims to heroism.[108]

In Milton's epics the true hero, after achieving self-mastery, acknowledges dependence upon something higher. He cannot, he realizes, be an autonomous center of meaning; meaning comes only through obedience to God. In such obedience he can also fulfill his ideal identity. The quest of the hero ends, therefore, in realization of ideal identity under God. Contrariwise, Satan's mock heroic quest ends with identity lost as God drives out his scapegoat.

The final reference to Satan in *Paradise Lost* prophesies his loss of mental being in utter dissolution (XII.546-49). Evil in the poem begins in envy's radical alienation and proceeds through inflated rebellion to withdrawal into uroboric evil's self-fed, self-consumed chaos. The process culminates in the scapegoat's fiery dissolution followed by purification of the world he is accused of polluting.

Dissolution, or *solutio*, the culmination of Satan's restless changes, is an alchemical term signifying reduction to original, undifferentiated matter.[109] During the council in hell Belial obliquely refers to the possibility of dissolution. Here he warns the fallen angels not to further anger the

Almighty lest their very intellectual being "perish rather, swallowd up and lost / In the wide womb of uncreated night, / Devoid of sense and motion" (II.149-51). Likewise, Sin prophesies to Satan and Death that God's wrath "one day will destroy ye both" (II.734). And most important, the Father, who embraces Milton's mortalist heresy, asserts conditional immortality, promising resurrection to those who justify themselves by faith and faithful works (XI.57- 66).[110]

The mortalist heresy and the prophesied dissolution of God's scapegoats, Satan and followers, are subtle breaches of orthodoxy that yet once more shift Milton's universe away from the eternal recycling of stasis toward upward-spiralling process. These breaches and shifts give Milton a universe fundamentally different from Dante's unqualified stasis. In Dante each sinner is condemned to relive throughout eternity the moment of his self-defining transgression. Only Satan assumes that God is committed to unqualified stasis; he alone voices the orthodox contention that men will live in hell after death (IV.377-87). Satan's contention is denied by the Father (XI.57-66) and by Milton in *De Doctrina* (I.xiii): "the soul as well as the body sleeps til the day of resurrection." These instances again indicate that, counter to the pull of orthodoxy, Milton often followed his predilection for the Hebraic Godhead over subverting uroboros and for dialectical process over uroboric stasis.[111] Besides, it ran counter to Milton's humanist sensibility to render eternal either Satanic inflation or divine vindictiveness.

Thus, while Milton the apologist followed mainline orthodoxy and used satire to deflate all Satan's claims to heroism, Milton the artist developed certain heterodox stances toward Satan. In addition to dissolving Satan and denying him eternity, the artist, by adopting devouring uroboros as the paradigm for his evil, made Satan an active evil rather than a passive *privatio boni*. However, dissolution and active uroboric evil, the tragic and destructive features of Satan's character, career, and fate, implicitly challenge stasis and the doctrine of *summum bonum*. To apprehend the graver import of that veiled but momentous challenge, we must take an archetypal overview.

ARCHETYPAL OVERVIEW

The circle, symbolizing eternal changelessness, is the controlling pattern of Dante's universe.[112] Like other cyclical systems, this universe is essentially mechanical, and being mechanical its character is, in Henri Bergson's view, comic.[113] The spiral, representing a developmental process with a beginning, middle, and end, furnishes a pattern for Milton the artist's universe the way the circle furnishes a pattern for Dante's.[114]

The archetypes undergirding a process universe permit tragedy in the forms of irreparable loss and active evil. They actuate a God who manifests both good and operative evil in the hostile brothers archetype as he spirals upward toward his eschaton of individuated wholeness. Divine process necessitates historical process. Hebrew eschatological time is implicit in the archetypes of Godhead even as Hellenic cyclical timelessness, or the notion of eternity, is implicit in the uroboros.

Eschatology gives time and history a definite alpha and omega and renders each moment in between unique: this makes new creation and final destruction possible. No Greek or medieval could have endowed "The world was all before them" with the wealth of meaning it holds in *Paradise Lost*.[115] Fired by the archetypal energies resident in the Hebraic-Christian Godhead, Milton the artist presents a birth outside the familiar cycles of life and death. He presents the creation of an entirely new world. And in *Paradise Regained* he presents the incarnation of God in man in a metadramatic rejection of uroboric circularity for upward-spiralling eschatological time.

What is the archetypal-historical background and context to Milton the artist's choice of Godhead and eschatology over uroboros and cyclical time? At the dawn of the Christian era, uroboros was the dominant archetype in the West. In the stagnant, dying Greco-Roman civilization that formed the nursery of orthodox Christianity the uroboric values behind the *summum bonum*, although opposed to self and Godhead, retained a powerful appeal. Faced with disintegration, men prize stability and seek security; the prospect of growth holds little atraction. Longing for security, orthodox Christians abandoned existential realities for supermundane hopes. And they refashioned a Godhead that, like the self, makes arduous demands to a theology offering the eternal peace of the uroboric Mother. Still questing for security, the medieval church that rose upon the corpse of Greco-Roman civilization downplayed eschatology, made the soul unconditionally immortal, and despatched it to heaven, hell, or purgatory at the body's death. But the sway of the uroboros archetype, most demonstrable in theology, began to falter at the height of medieval civilization in the twelfth century.

Simultaneously, the archetypes behind the process Godhead of Hebraic-Christian myth gained enormous dynamism. The revitalized Father archetype induced repression and intolerance because its patriarchalism activated the darkest aspect of Godhead's uroboric shadow, Medusa's stony perfectionism. Repression and intolerance spurred the Crusades abroad and persecution of women and heretics at home. Later the Father archetype, again as patriarch, energized Protestantism, especially that of Luther and Calvin, and revived the eschatology and apocalypticism of early Christianity. The Christ and Paraclete archetypes exercised a more subtle and gentle influence. Christ gave new life to Renaissance humanism and the Paraclete nurtured occultism and inspired the emphasis on individual conscience.[116]

The Satan archetype, ever the wild card of actual Godhead, was played to varying and often sensational effects.[117] First, the devil's imputed activity furnished an excuse for patriarchal repression, intolerance, and scapegoating. Later the archetype nurtured the hard side of Renaissance individualism which in turn fed the archetype's Promethean manifestations—empirical science, technology, skepticism, and, in literature, tragedy.[118] These exposed orthodox theology's philosophical weaknesses allowing the Promethean ethic of rebellion to break through the open cracks.[119] In popular imagination Satan himself regained the virtually dualist status the Apocalypse gave him, and in *Paradise Lost* the destructive and tragic features of his apocalyptic role were for the first time dramatized in consummate poetry.

Orthodoxy, with its uroboros-derived theology, *summum bonum* dogma, and notion of eternity on one side and its Godhead myths and eschatological time on the other, is built across a fault line. The constellation of the Satan archetype set up rumblings along the fault line that reverberate throughout *Paradise Lost*. The most significant of these rumblings, Satan's destructiveness, tragic fate, and scapegoat status, make a mockery of that dream of stasis, the *Summum Bonum*.

Hence, Milton the apologist, like orthodox theology, needed to rationalize the evil Satan causes and experiences. Orthodox theology rationalized that evil is an unfortunate epiphenomenon of free will. The doctrine of free will, however, collapses under logical analysis, leaving us with the stark break between uroboros-derived theology and Godhead myths. As I explained in the preceding chapter, the doctrine gives Satan and men stable, continuous identities so that God may hold them responsible for their sins. At the same time it leaps beyond process and borrows from flux to grant those identities spontaneous mutation in order to free God from responsibility for the evil choices of the beings he creates. In short, the doctrine of free will, as orthodox theology conceives it, makes identity simultaneously stable and in flux—stable when man's and Satan's responsibilities are at issue, and in flux when the responsbility in question becomes that of the Creator. The doctrine offers no viable way to unify the conflicting definitions of identity it posits; it only provides a blurred question mark to shroud the contradiction.

Tertullian, a patristic type to Soren Kierkegaard's modern antitype, embraced flux and the absurd, declaring of the philosophic contradictions doctrines like free will create: "I believe because it is impossible." Thus, belief, which began as a way to bolster Christian hope in the absence of certainty, became a means to sustain doctrine in defiance of reason. For much of what *Paradise Lost* says about God, the Devil, and free will to be palatable to moderns, they must tread the radical fideistic path blazed by Tertullian and paved by Kierkegaard. But to tread that path is to ignore those parts of the epic that decline to sacrifice reason to faith and uphold instead that the two should work hand in hand to resist evil and achieve man's regeneration. Moreover, it is to ignore the artist's metadrama with its epiphanies of a Godhead mirroring the individuation process of the quaternal self.

Paradise Lost draws on stasis, process and flux, rationalism and voluntarism, uroboros and Godhead. It presents an omnipotent *Summum Bonum* alongside an incorrigibly depraved scapegoat, stable individual responsibility mated to unstable free will, and determined rationalism coupled with pliant faith. What are we to make of its concoction of contraries?

Adopting an orthodox standpoint we obscure the conflicts with calls for faith and pious references to God's mysterious ways. Assuming the standpoint of the ethic of rebellion we dismiss the "outmoded" theological ideas and enjoy *Paradise Lost* for its poetic merit. Taking an archetypal overview, we see the epic as reflecting a stage of psychic development characteristic of Protestantism. Here men have sufficient inward vision to intuit the need to withdraw projections from deity, admit ego imperfection, and bring the shadow to consciousness so it can transform and substantiate ego: such is the case with Milton the artist. At the same time, they lack the developed inward vision or mature individuation required to hush ego's cry for certain belief and secure identity. We see this lack of developed inward vision in Milton the apologist as he clings to the doctrine of *summum bonum*.

Still under the sway of uroboros, those who lack inward vision fear to confront the personal shadow. The devouring uroboros stirs fear of the personal shadow to protect itself by diverting attention away from itself. Once a man realizes that the personal shadow is a creative potential able to transform conscious ego, he can see that the greatest threat comes not from the personal shadow but from the self's collective shadow, the uroboric counterforce ever striving to devour consciousness. He will then understand that Satan is not the shadow of Godhead, the divine Self, but only the shadow and scapegoat of the Father, the divine ego. And he will recognize for the first time the devouring uroboros for what it truly is, the collective shadow and unrelenting counterforce to self and Godhead.

3

Decisive Identity

In his epics Milton attempts to portray decisive identity. By "decisive identity" I mean a conscious guiding of individuation wherein identity and character are created through moral decisions. Decisive identity does not imply creating what we initially are. Rather, it involves consciously deciding what we become, which requires a troublesome but indispensable element, freedom. Milton develops themes, character, and plot by showing the origins and consequences of identity-forming decisions. These decisions are the foci of moral judgment and meaning. In *Paradise Lost* and *Paradise Regained* the crucial decisions are those by Adam and Eve causing man's fall and those by the Messiah qualifying him to become man's redeemer. Stressing their correspondence, Milton makes them the pivots upon which God's entire plan for humanity turns. The credibility of that plan and of Milton's theodicy rests on whether each case shows true, decisive identity.

An Identity Divided and Obscure

Behind Milton's treatment of the decisions of Adam and Eve and of Messiah lies the single most important decision made by orthodox Christianity itself, a decision that profoundly influenced the Christian conceptions of decisive identity, freedom, and Godhead. The decision I refer to is the church fathers' decision to reformulate Christian myths in terms borrowed from Hellenistic philosophy.[1]

Reformulating Christian myths into a theology intelligible to Greeks meant that thenceforth Greek philosophy would provide the intellectual foundation for Christianity. But what supported Greek philosophy? Hellenic myth! Hence, the validity of Christian myths came to rest not upon the archetypes behind those myths but upon philosophical assumptions based on the alien archetypes of a rival mythology.

Hellenic mythology, upon whose archetypes Plato, Aristotle, and the Neoplatonists constructed their philosophies, makes static being, and being's associated archetype, the uroboric Mother, the elemental manifestation of deity. Hebraic-Christian mythology makes an individuation process manifest in a quaternity of archetypes the dynamism of its Godhead. One signal effect of these fundamentally different archetypes of divinity was the emergence within Western culture of two opposed conceptions of time.

Hellenic philosophers usually assume that time is cyclical.[2] Time resembles the uroboros, never dying or actually changing, always recycling its eternal essence in self-fed, self-consuming rounds. Time as real change is an illusion. We believe time and change real only because we are unable to directly perceive changeless, uroboric being.

Hebraic myth, by contrast, makes time as change ultimately real, for Godhead itself changes and unfolds by interacting with man in history.[3] And Hebrew myth makes free decisions implicitly real. God created the world out of nothingness in a free decision. Through free decisions God and men consciously decide their identities. The idea of freedom itself developed in part from the Hebraic notion of moral consciousness evolving through the decisions of God and men. The Greek notion of static fate or *moira*, by contrast, inhibited development of a concept of human freedom.[4] Greek rationalism, moreover, left no place for freedom in God's nature.[5]

The Christian theological compromise rests on a elemental cleavage: Greek philosophy defines God's eternal nature, Hebraic myth determines his historical actions. The originators of the myth, those sundry prophets, scribes, and apostles who wrote the Old and New Testaments, knew little of Greek philosophy. The two notable exceptions, St. Paul and the author of the Johannine Gospel, while philosophically educated, were still primitive Christians who took literally the myth's promise of an imminent second coming.[6] The scriptural writers' general unfamiliarity with Greek philosophy allowed them to show their deity engaged in conduct that was, though endearingly and maddeningly human, quite incompatible with that double crown of *summum bonum* and eternal being the theologians would later rest upon his head. Consequently, those who approach scripture without dogmatic preconceptions meet a deity who behaves like a human psyche struggling for wholeness. But when they turn to theology, they encounter a deity whose nature mirrors only man's rationalistic ideals.

The pre-Hellenistic Jews were a philosophically unsophisticated race compared to the Greeks—that is one of the prime truisms of Western intellectual history. Another prime truism is that Hebrew myth had a creative dynamism and heuristic qualities Greek myth lacked. Hebraic myth's concern for justice, which spurs probing human motives and the psyche itself, seems to account for its heuristic quality. More significant still is the dynamism of Hebraic myth.

Crude as it may be in some Old Testament instances, Hebraic myth constellated powerful, dynamic archetypes that became the great engines driving the train of history for the last two thousand years. Judaism, Christianity, Islam, Marxism, and modern science, technology, and psychology are ultimately energized by the unfolding, dynamic archetypes of the Hebraic Godhead. While the earliest manifestations, Judaism and Christianity, appear to be in decline today, the core dynamism remains as powerful as ever.[7] What explains the Godhead's overwhelming dynamism? If Jung is correct, the archetypes of Godhead carry the human psyche's primary drive, the drive to unfold its wholeness.

Radical Protestants, John Milton in certain respects one of them, strove to recover Godhead's dynamism in its "uncorrupted" form. Catholic Christianity, they asserted, sold out to pagan philosophy in the fourth and fifth centuries thereby becoming the corrupt political entity called "the whore of Babylon." Their favored remedy was "reform" involving return to the "pure" Christianity of the first century.[8] These radical Protestants, besides overlooking early Christianity's clutter of incongruous Gnostic, Hellenic, and Judaic features, failed to perceive how Godhead's dynamism manifested itself in Catholic developmentalism.

Viewing Catholic developmentalism through Jungian eyes, one can see the Catholic theological compromise and the problems of evil and freedom it raises as facets of an individuation process of Godhead. Therein Hellenic uroboric being becomes an archetypal counterforce against which Godhead gradually individuates itself in a long struggle that shapes Western civilization. Ironically, the struggle's literary apex is not a Catholic work but that quintessential Protestant epic, *Paradise Lost*.

THE DIVINE ANDROGYNE

Like the Book of Job, the Book of Ezekiel, 2 Isaiah, the Gospels, and the Apocalypse, Milton's epics constellate the archetypes of Godhead in crucial epiphanies—such is the distinctive hypothesis of *The Unfolding God of Jung and Milton*. Since the hypothesis stems from and develops the ideas of C.G. Jung, it assumes that many, though not all, of the psychological keys to understanding Milton's epiphanies are to be gleaned from Jung.

Prominent among these keys are Jung's two main criticisms of the orthodox trinitarian Godhead. Jung's first criticism is that the Trinity excluded the dark, Promethean-Luciferian shadow, setting up a false, inflated purity whose effects I discussed in the preceding chapter. However, to understand the momentous epiphany in Milton's account of the fall, I will focus on Jung's second criticism: because it excludes the feminine, the Trinity excludes the *conjunctio* essential to psychic wholeness.

The Paraclete: Anima of Godhead.   Union of opposites or *conjunctio oppositorum* is for Jung the supreme task, the task of making conscious the *coincidentia oppositorum* that is the self. The cross and Adam and Eve are the prime symbols of *conjunctio oppositorum* in Christian myth.[9] Jung sought to realize *conjunctio* of male and female opposites within Godhead by introducing the absent feminine in the person of Mary. The addition of Mary makes the deity a quaternity reflecting the mandala of four-part psychic wholeness. At the same time it creates difficulties Jung preferred not to confront. First, it is undeniably confusing to have the missing Fourth Person of Godhead be Lucifer or Satan, whom Jung opts for whenever he focuses on the inadequacies of the Christian settlement to the problem of evil, and then have Mary assume the fourth position once the topic shifts to the defective *conjunctio*. Not only are Mary and Satan so dissimilar they cannot conceivably pass for manifestations of the same archetype, as Jung himself observed, the "identity of mother and son is born out over and over again in the myths."[10] Since the Son is already present in Godhead, Mary, being an extra mediator between mankind and the Father, becomes redundant. To make matters worse, placing Mary opposite Christ, her physical son, sets the stage for an oedipal *conjunctio*, hardly the *conjunctio* Jung sought. Finally, displacing Satan-shadow with Mary's virgin purity in one swoop precludes *conjunctio* and eliminates the *coincidentia oppositorum* of good and evil thus reinstating *privatio boni*.

Fortunately, contemporary feminist scholarship provides a way to resolve Jung's difficulties and simultaneously deepen his basic insights.[11] The feminine Wisdom or Shekhinah the Old Testament says was with God from the beginning, feminist scholars point out, functions like the Holy Spirit or Paraclete of the New Testament, shares its symbolism of the dove, and is specifically referred to as God's "holy spirit from above" in Wisdom 9:17-18.[12]

Neglecting the similarity of Wisdom to the Paraclete did not of course begin with Jung.[13] It began with those early Christians who sought to give intellectual respectability to Hebraic-Christian myth by reformulating it in terms of Hellenistic philosophy. The actual denigration of Wisdom, however, commenced before Christianity with Philo-Judaeus and other Alexandrian thinkers who, bowing to the era's intellectual fashions, concluded that feminine attributes lessened God. God's dignity, these philosophers insisted, required him to be all male no less than all good and all powerful.

Anxious to protect the masculinity of their God, the church fathers declined to meld the Judaic wisdom figure with its natural successor, the Paraclete, which would have made one member of Godhead feminine. Instead they masculinized Wisdom's attributes by assigning them to the putatively male Christ-logos.[14] Since Wisdom stood subordinate to Yahweh in Judaism, introducing Sophiology into Christology contributed to subordinationism and the Arian heresy.[15] Consequently, orthodox theologians in time withdrew Wisdom from Christ-logos and put her on a shelf where she languishes to this day.

Jung, therefore, had no need to interject the feminine into Godhead. He needed only to rebut ancient misogynistic prejudices and properly stress the feminine qualities and imagery the Paraclete inherited from Hebraic Wisdom.

The Hebrew term *Hokhmah*, the Wisdom appearing in Proverbs 8 as Yahweh's co-creator, meant Maternal Wisdom.[16] The Wisdom of Solomon equates her with the Egyptian manifestation of the Great Mother and the Gnostic book *On the Origin of the World* makes her the mother and teacher of Yahweh himself.[17] In addition to Wisdom, the Hebrew scriptures make Sophia a creator, a teacher, a lover, and a plant or tree: all these qualities identify her with anima, the one who guides individuation. Her full archetypal development, however, was thwarted by the rising Hebrew patriarchal monotheism.[18]

Since, like Wisdom, the Paraclete forms a divine anima, it, considered as an archetype, must be qualitatively feminine. While the Paraclete as Holy Spirit remains neuter in orthodoxy, unmistakable evidence for its femininity appears in unorthodox writings. The Valentinian Gnostics, Elaine Pagels notes, believed that Christ and the Paraclete were a masculine and feminine pair sent by Wisdom.[19] After reviewing a variety of Gnostic sources, Pagels observes: "If some gnostic sources suggest that the Spirit constitutes the maternal element of the Trinity, the *Gospel of Philip* makes an equally radical suggestion about the doctrine that later developed as the virgin birth. Here again the Spirit is both Mother and Virgin, the counterpart—and consort—of the Heavenly Father . . . the Greek feminine term for 'wisdom,' *sophia*, translates a Hebrew feminine term, *hokhmah*. Early interpreters had pondered the meaning of certain Biblical passages—for example, the saying in Proverbs that "God made the world in Wisdom." Could Wisdom be the feminine power in which God's creation was 'conceived?'"[20]

Similarly, June Singer remarks: "In Gnosticism, the principle of Source is the Mother-Father element; the second in the Trinity is the Logos or Christ figure, who represents the personal ego; and the third is the Sophia, Holy Spirit or wisdom figure (also known in Judaism as the Shekhinah, in Hinduism as Shakti), the aspect of the psyche that provides the dynamism that leads to individualism."[21]

The unfamiliar guise of the Paraclete's femininity may explain Jung's neglect of its anima function.[22] Gnostic fantasies notwithstanding, the femininity of the Holy Spirit appears in neither the guise of the universal

Great Mother nor in the guise of a personal mother or wife as in Mary and Milton's Eve. What then is its specific feminine archetype?

Figure 3 shows the four principal male archetypes and how they correspond to the four principal female archetypes.[23]

Figure 3. Correspondence of male and female archetypes

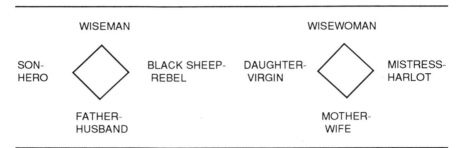

The son and the rebel, or the daughter and the harlot, form the hostile brothers or sisters. The wiseman and wisewoman do not oppose so much as transcend the father and mother and the brothers and sisters: in both wisepersons human wisdom creates an androgyny that integrates the polarized masculinity and femininity of the lower archetypes. While the Christian Godhead excludes mother, daughter, and mistress, it quietly, as though by unconscious striving for balance and wholeness, introduces in the Paraclete a feminine anima whose guiding, healing powers are those of a wisewoman.[24] To make the wisewoman the alternative to the Father returns androgynous wholeness to Godhead. Figure 4 shows how the archetypes of the Whole Godhead appear diagrammatically.

Figure 4. Archetypes of the Whole Godhead

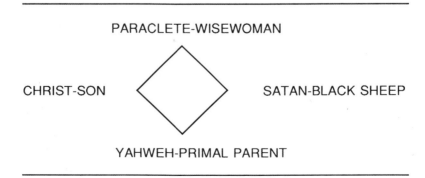

In the uniplural Quaternity, Godhead's real identity in contradistinction to its Trinitarian persona, the masculine archetypes provide differentiation while the feminine Paraclete supplies the subtle, connecting energies that harmonize warring opposites. The distribution of three parts masculine to one part feminine in a quaternal image of psychic wholeness conforms precisely to Jung's theory of anima and animus, which makes anima a single figure and animus a many-voiced group.[25] Thus, the Paraclete functioning as anima together with Father-Son-Satan as animus form the yin and the yang of the syzygy or divine androgyne which is Godhead.[26]

The Paraclete, carrying the archetype of anima, stands behind Christian mystical notions of Sophia. While Sophia was important in the more mystical Eastern Orthodox tradition from Pseudo-Dionysus on, in the West Sophia's flowering did not occur until the Renaissance-Reformation period. Jacob Boehme, an arcane philosopher who in certain respects anticipates Jung, refers to the "kiss of Sophia" in his mystical Christology, which gives the logos a feminine counterpart, Sophia.[27] Durer's Melancholia, Leonardo's Mona Lisa and Spenser's Gloriana convey the Sophia figure in visual art and epic poetry. Sophia's most remarkable appearance, however, is as the anima figure of Shakespeare's paramount tragedy: Lear's truthful daughter Cordelia.

Like Cordelia, anima dispels masculine ego contentiousness with guiding truth and healing love.[28] Jung comments on anima's guiding and healing function aptly describe the effect of Cordelia's appearance upon Lear's madness: "It is as though at the climax of the illness, the destructive powers were converted into healing forces. This is brought about by the archetypes awakening to independent life and taking over the guidance of the psychic personality, thus supplanting the ego with its futile willing and striving. . . . the psyche has awakened to spontaneous activity. . . . something that is not his ego and is therefore beyond reach of his personal will. He has regained access to the sources of psychic life, and this marks the beginning of the cure."[29] The Paraclete, as Sophia, can play the same guiding, healing role for the Christian Godhead that Cordelia does for Lear and anima does for the psyche.[30] The sickness of Christianity, to whose treatment Jung devoted the final decades of his life, is the outcome of inflating divine ego (Father-Son) and repressing or denying shadow (Satan) while neglecting the guidance and healing of divine anima consciousness (the Paraclete).[31]

Since three parts of the Godhead are predominantly masculine and only one part is predominantly feminine, to achieve androgynous wholeness that one part must have greater flexibility than the more differentiated male parts. Only the anima, most protean of archetypes, has the requisite flexibility.³² Furthermore, because the masculine parts out-number the feminine part, the feminine must play the central role: the soul or transcendent function that consummates the entire process by bringing the differentiated and conflicting masculine parts into conscious harmony. As such it must be ever active in a wise, feminine way, which precludes Mary who in her roles of mother and mediatress remains a passive vessel for the nurture and transmission of divine male energies.

The Collective Shadow of Godhead.   Of equal importance to the Godhead's anima is its collective shadow. Distinct from Lucifer, the personal shadow, the collective shadow (sometimes symbolized by Leviathan) is a regressive counterforce to the drive for individuated consciousness. The devouring uroboros archetype empowers the collective shadow, and it, like the Paraclete, appears in a predominantly feminine guise.

Counteracting the Paraclete, bringer of conscious wholeness to the differentiated masculine parts of the Godhead, the collective shadow sucks all differentiation into the maw of the unconscious. Through its evil anima, symbolized by Medusa, the collective shadow first demands a perfection and fixity that betrays feminine relatedness for power and living truth for dogmatic certitude. Medusa-anima, forever arresting the growth of divine character with its perfectionist doctrine of *summum bonum,* petrifies the God of theology even as Sophia-anima enlivens the Godhead of myth. Exclusion of Sophia, or feminine love and wisdom, from God-head empowers Medusa. To break her spell, we must restore androgynous wholeness to Godhead by recognizing the feminine love and wisdom of the Paraclete.

The collective shadow or counterforce to Godhead, which Jung calls absolute evil, is a baffling archetype. Jung deals with it very little and the Jungians scarcely at all. Their neglect holds great peril, since devouring uroboros, if allowed to rule, can stifle Godhead and individuation. Neglect of uroboros also limits understanding, because, Godhead being defined against its uroboric shadow, we cannot fully understand Godhead without recognizing its shadow.

The femininity of both the devouring uroboros, the collective shadow of Godhead, and the Paraclete, Godhead's anima, makes the lowest and highest divine phenomena feminine—appropriate, perhaps, if we regard the female the primary sex of humankind. Thus, the feminine is essential to the archetypal dynamics of Godhead.

Hierosgamos.   The female archetypes of Godhead become evident once we recognize the predominantly feminine nature of its collective shadow and of the Holy Spirit as Paraclete. Nevertheless, the *hierosgamos* or sacred marriage, that symbol *conjunctio oppositorum*, has no obvious place. Because Godhead lacks husband and wife figures, it lacks a *hierosgamos* after the familiar heterosexual paradigm of Adam and Eve. Since homosexual paradigms for marriage are problematic, the common archetype for homosexuality being the brothers or friends, not the connubial pair, what other paradigms remain?

The paradigm of *hierosgamos* in Godhead, I believe, is a process of individuation leading from psychic polarity to androgyny. Before the *hierosgamos*, masculinity and femininity are polarized. With *hierosgamos* a transformation occurs: polarity yields to an individuated wholeness that brings differentiated masculine and feminine qualities into conscious union therein manifesting the syzygy or divine androgyne.[33] The polarity paradigm holds prior to and after an ordinary marriage, but Godhead's inner *hierosgamos* dissolves polarity. In an ordinary marriage male and female partners assume polarized roles each carrying the projection of the other's contrasexual component, the anima or animus. In Godhead's inner *hierosgamos* polarized anima and animus are transformed into a divine androgyne. The divine androgyne is Godhead's highest stage wherein the Paraclete brings harmony to the whole. In certain alchemical and heretical writings Sophia becomes the bride of God, which symbolizes the Paraclete effecting *hierosgamos* in Godhead.[34] This *hierosgamos* realizes the essential androgyny of Godhead and human psyche.[35]

Since the Paraclete inspires the masculine archetypes of Godhead in their struggle for *hierosgamos*, it works in all stages toward the androgynous harmony it unfolds at the completion of its own stage. Openness to androgyny, the coincidence of opposite sexes, allows us to grasp readily the true nature of the Paraclete and its work. Repression of androgyny blinds us to the Paraclete's anima function in the Godhead.

Subordinationism.   Jesus' embodying Sophia, feminist theologians have argued, gave him androgynous wholeness.[36] Before the second century ended the androgynous Jesus who personified God's wholeness had been replaced by a figure congenial to patriarchal theologians, a divine clone to the Father.[37] In the third through sixth centuries, attempts of the Arians, Monophysites, etc. to subordinate the cloned Son in the Trinity are competing bids to make the Father archetype totally supreme and to purge the Son of any remaining feminine qualities.

Subordinating the Son had a profound impact upon Christianity's stance toward Mary. Once theologians reconstructed Christ in his Father's image, the transfer of his feminine *caritas* and mediator role to Mary became ineluctable. Ironically, Christ's main significance became to make Mary a mother. His subordination to her as well as to the Father completes

the repression of divine androgyny. Accordingly, instead of the Jesus of
Gospel myth who reflects God's androgynous wholeness, we are given for
a mediator Mary whose polarized maternal femininity is needed to ap-
pease a polarized male deity, the Father and his cloned Son.

Monotheism.   Jung's principle of psychic balance entails that emphasizing
one of the four prime male or four prime female archetypes while dimin-
ishing the others impairs a culture's psychological health. Impairment is
most severe where monotheism prevails because monotheism melds uni-
plural Godhead into one of its archetypes. The extreme example is the
absolute monotheism of Islam, which makes Allah like a patriarch in
function if not in acknowledged essence. This incites the father archetype
to tyrannize the culture and allows fathers to virtually enslave their women
and children.

The qualified monotheism of Hebraic Godhead elevates patriarchal
Yahweh at the expense of the feminine archetypes. Nonetheless, anima
surfaces in shadowy figures like Shekinah and Wisdom, whose archetypal
energies eventually converge upon that divine potential for androgynous
wholeness, the Holy Spirit as Paraclete. The convergence of feminine
energies on the officially neuter Holy Spirit and the absence of divine
mother-wife and daughter archetypes made it difficult for early Christian-
ity to deify heterosexual pairing after the fashion of polytheistic Near
Eastern fertility cults. As Ernest Jones observed, the Christian Trinity
differs radically from the more balanced (and more polytheistic) Eastern
trinities based on father, mother, and son, substituting instead a "sublim-
inated homosexuality" wherein men gain the love of a patriarchal God by
feminine deference to him.[38]

Patriarchy and Psychic Imbalance.   Christianity's commitment to patriarchy
altered across the centuries.[39] For example, intolerance of alternatives to
patriarchal values surged in the twelfth century. In that same century the
church launched sundry crusades to reconquer Christian territory from
Islam and to achieve a total, closed society at home. And it began persecut-
ing previously tolerated heretics, Jews, witches, homosexuals, and bisex-
uals.[40] New attitudes toward the archetypes of Godhead accompanied the
spreading intolerance. One such change was the church's rejection of the
cult of the Paraclete and promotion of the cult of Mary. Jung noted these
phenomena with considerable interest, although with little explanation.[41]

Historians acknowledge that widespread intolerance in the twelfth
century may be related to changing attitudes toward the role of the
feminine in deity. They acknowledge also that we have a poor grasp of the
underlying psychological causes.[42] In the absence of generally accepted

theories all we can do is speculate. Since the twelfth-century develop-
ments have had tremendous impact, it seems a greater mistake to ignore
them than to offer speculations that may prove premature.

Wherefore, if only to underline the significance of rejecting the cult of
the Paraclete to promote the cult of Mary, let me speculate that this
development may reflect the polarized father and mother archetypes
rising at the expense of the wiseperson archetype and its androgynous
wholeness. When God the Father becomes a patriarchal tyrant devoid of
the qualities of the father archetype's opposite, the wiseman, he scorns
Sophia's guidance for he cannot brook restraint from any feminine arche-
type. Only Mother Mary, ever subservient to patriarchy, can be tolerated.
Together the Father and Mary, by suppressing Godhead's Sophia anima,
the Paraclete, opened the gate to the collective shadow's Medusa anima
with her intolerant perfectionism.

DECISION IN EDEN

Adam's uxoriousness and Eve's insubordination form a psychological pre-
condition for their decision to fall in *Paradise Lost*. The uxoriousness and
insubordination, from a Jungian point of view, are steps toward consciously
integrating anima and animus and therefore toward individuated whole-
ness.[43] This Jungian perspective is not alien to the poem: it finds a subtle,
internal advocate, as we shall see, in Milton the artist.

Anima and Animus and the Fall.   Although *Paradise Lost* challenges the
traditional Christian stereotype of Eve by making her in the end an admir-
able rather than a cautionary figure, at the outset Milton presents a fairly
conventional view of gender roles.[44] Polarization and feminine subordina-
tion appear to be features of Adam and Eve's original innocence:

> though both
> Not equal, as thir sex not equal seemd;
> For contemplation hee and valour formd;
> For softness shee and sweet attractive Grace,
> Hee for God only, shee for God in him:
> His fair large Front and eye sublime declar'd
> Absolute rule; . . .
> Shee as a vail down to the slender waste
> Her unadorned golden tresses wore
> Dissheveld, but in wanton ringlets wav'd
> As the vine curls her tendrils, which impli'd
> Subjection, but requir'd with gentle sway,
> And her yeilded, by him best receiv'd, [IV.295-309]

No proto-feminist she, the early Eve readily assents to Adam's patriarchal notions about woman's subordinate role.[45]

> O thou for whom
> And from whom I was formd flesh of thy flesh
> And without whom am to no end, my Guide
> And Head, what thou has said is just and right. [IV.440-45]

> My Author and Disposer, what thou bidst
> Unargu'd I obey; so God ordains,
> God is thy Law, thou mine: to know no more
> Is womans happiest knowledge and her praise. [IV.635-38]

The two great sexes, it would seem, are not made for each other, but the female for the male and the male for God. Even as the moon reflects the sun's light and all creation reflects its creator's glory, so the female reflects the male. These ideas express the patriarchal myth of sexual polarity, which assumes that male spirit needs to be shielded from corruption by feminine materialism lest the male become androgynous and so lessen himself and spoil God's purposes for him and mankind. Furthermore, the female who rebels against her subordinate status does not just reject God-ordained male supremacy, she also betrays her own nature. Striving to be equal, she lessens herself further.

Eve in her unfallen innocence, we have seen, embraced without qualm feminine subordination. But Eve about to fall undergoes a quiet but momentous change. Explicating that change with Jungian concepts, we note that Eve declines to repress her contrasexual animus and project it on her mate and follow him. Instead, prizing animus like an inner light, she follows it. The new animus-directed Eve tells Adam:

> Thou therefore now advise
> Or hear what to my mind first thoughts present,
> Let us divide our labours, thou where choice
> Leads thee, or where most needs, whether to wind
> The Woodbine around this Arbour, or direct
> The clasping Ivie where to climb, while I
> In yonder Spring of Roses intermixt
> With Myrtle, find what to redress till Noon: [IX.212-19]

Separation, she declares, will help them get more work done. Adam, who still projects anima on Eve, rather than making it an inner light, praises her thoughts while cautioning that their enemy may attempt to exploit any separation. Eve, her animus imputing challenge to Adam, construes his very tactful objections as misgivings about the firmness of her faith and love:

> But that thou shouldst my firmness therfore doubt
> To God or thee, because we have a foe
> May tempt it, I expected not to hear. . . .
> His fraud is then thy fear, which plain inferrs
> Thy equal fear that my firm Faith and Love
> Can by his fraud be shak'n or seduc't
> Thoughts, which how found they harbour in thy brest,
> Adam, misthought of her to thee so dear? [IX.279-89]

Eve is no longer content with her divinely ordained role of following Adam as he follows God. Instead of projecting animus on Adam, she allows it to possess her. The crucial change in Eve has distinct prefigurations, her initial narcissism and her dream being the salient examples, but its psychological causes remain unacknowledged. The reason for the omission appears to be that Milton the apologist intends the fall to exemplify that peculiar form of *creatio ex nihilo* called free will; hence, the fall had to be theoetically uncaused. Nevertheless, Milton the artist, seeking to make the fall psychologically and dramatically plausible, depicts phenomena that would later find causal explanations in Jung's theories of individuation and of anima and animus.

Adam about to fall begins to follow anima, not within himself but as projected on Eve. His weakness for following anima, or his tendency toward uxoriousness, surfaced earlier when he confided to Raphael:

> For well I understood in the prime end
> Of Nature her th'inferiour, in the mind
> And inward Faculties, which most excell,
> In outward also her resembling less
> His Image who made both, and less expressing
> The character of that Dominion giv'n
> O're other Creatures; yet when I approach
> Her loveliness, so absolute she seems
> And in her self compleat, so well to know
> Her own, that what she wills to do or say,
> Seems wisest, vertuousest, discreetest, best;
> All higher knowledge in her presence falls
> Degraded, Wisdom in discourse with her
> Looses discount'nanc't, and like folly shews;
> Authority and Reason on her wait, [VIII.540-54]

In delineating the tendencies which, brought to their test, bring Adam's fall, Milton comes closer than he does with Eve to open acknowledgment of causes for sin other than irrational free will.[46] The crucial tendency appears in the last line: Adam's inclination to allow ego's rationality to wait upon anima's feeling and eros.

Once the tendency Adam reveals to Raphael ripens into uxoriousness, his chief concern becomes to appease and please Eve. Accordingly, he shuns his husband's duty to teach her that her proper role is subordinate:

> To whom with healing words Adam reply'd
> Daughter of God and Man, immortal Eve,
> For such thou art, from sin and blame entire:
> Not diffident of thee do I dissuade
> Thy absence from my sight, but to avoid
> Th' attempt it self, intended by our Foe. [IX.290-94]

Eve at this point may be technically untouched by sin, yet she is not free of blame. Humoring her blameworthy intransigence by attempting persuasion when she's obliged to obey, Adam himself, under patriarchal standards, becomes blameworthy.

His argument that, receiving strength from each other, they should face their dangerous foe together, though very sensible, does not dissuade Eve. Far from acknowledging Adam's superior mind and acquiescing to her subordinate role, Eve follows animus to presume de facto feminine equality in her phrase "we not endu'd / Single with like defense" (IX 324-25). Her motive resembles Satan's in his original revolt. She resents having anyone rule over her, a common animus attitude. Anticipating what Adam ought to have said rather than replying to his conciliatory words, her stubborn animus implicitly questions God himself: "If this be our condition, thus to dwell / In narrow circuit strait'n'd by a Foe, . . . How are we Happie, still in fear of harm?" (IX 322-23, 326) Animus then precedes, in its typical fashion, to assert independence from the motive of personal honor:

> then wherfore shund or feard
> By us? who rather double honour gain
> From his surmise prov'd false, find peace within,
> Favour from Heav'n, our witness from th' event.
> And what is Faith, Love, Vertue unassaid
> Alone, without exterior help sustain'd?
> Let us not then suspect our happie State
> Left so imperfet by the Maker wise,
> As not secure to single or combin'd

Frail our happiness, if this be so,
And Eden were no Eden thus expos'd. [IX.331-41]

The argument here is: (1) Satan's temptation forms an opportunity to gain greater honor before God; (2) that must be the case, otherwise Eden is not Eden and God not God. In other words, if God has not made the world to provide opportunities for Eve to double her honor (here honor assumes the meaning of pride), then He stands at fault for making a imperfect world![47] Her unspoken premise is that the true end and highest value of God's creation is Eve. From an orthodox point of view this is tantamount to a presumption that Eve, not God, is God.

To Eve's near blasphemy Adam returns logic, straightforward, simple, and ineffectual. God's world is not flawed, he argues, but man's free will entails the possibility of flaw since reason can both guide and lead astray:

Reason he made right,
But bid her well beware, and still erect,
Least by some fair appeering good surpris'd
She dictate false, and misinform the Will . . .
Since Reason not impossibly may meet
Some specious object by the Foe suborned,
And fall into deception unaware, [IX.352-55, 360-62]

The fallible reason he speaks of is, in Jungian terms, animus reasoning. Adam is both aware of her animus's fallibility and in disagreement with its argument:

Seek not temptation then, which to avoid
Were better, and most likelie if from me
Thou sever not: Trial will come unsought
Wouldst thou approve thy constancie, approve
First thy obedience: [IX, 364-68]

Notwithstanding, Adam disregards his own judgment, which tells him woman's animus reasonings stand inferior to man's reason. More serious still, he ignores God's teachings about his responsibility to govern and Eve's duty to obey: "But if thou think, trial unsought may find / Us both securer then thus wornd thou seemst, / Go, for thy stay not free absents thee more:" (IX.370-72). In letting Eve follow her animus reasonings over his male judgment, Adam follows his anima feelings over the law and commands of God. He places his own feminine eros above God's masculine logos.

Thereby, Adam breaks the divinely decreed pattern of nature by abdicating, both to anima and to Eve, his governing masculine role. Eve construes his abdication as permission and leaves, promising to return before noon. Upon her departure the narrator comments:

> O much deceav'd, much failing, hapless Eve,
> Of thy presum'd return! Event perverse!
> Thou never from that hour in Paradise
> Foundst either sweet repast, or sound repose; [IX.404-7]

Although Eve technically has not fallen, noncompliance with feminine subordination puts her one small step from open rebellion against God.

The causal link between Eve's initial noncompliance and her subsequent revolt is subtly exposed in Satan's temptation tactics: the tempter expands upon and adapts to his dark purposes her animus motives for leaving Adam. He begins with an appeal to Eve's pride, her tacit assumption that she is the center and raison d'être of creation:

> Fairest resemblance of thy Maker fair,
> Thee all things living gaze on, all things thine
> By gift, and thy Celestial Beautie adore
> With ravishment beheld, there best beheld
> Where universally admir'd; but here
> In this enclosure wild, these Beasts among,
> Beholders rude, and shallow to discern
> Half what in thee is fair, one man except,
> Who sees thee? (and what is one?) who shouldst be seen
> A Goddess among Gods, [IX.538-47]

The serpent's extravagant flattery softens Eve for the bold suggestion that she, admired less than she deserves, suffers mistreatment. Upon that suggestion Eve ought to realize that she stands in the very presence of their foe, yet animus, which repressed by subordination has become a rebellious shadow, takes command and blinds her to the danger. Following animus-shadow, she determines to ignore all Adam has taught her. The serpent, ever alert to opportunity, makes his phallic shape more comely to more readily attract the projection of her animus-shadow:

> The Tempter, but with shew of Zeal and Love
> To Man, and indignation at his wrong,
> New part puts on, and as to passion mov'd,

Fluctuats disturb'd, yet comely, and in act
Rais'd, as som great matter to begin. [IX.665-69]

Whereupon Satan voices a series of animus-style suggestions and opinions ending with the promise of knowledge and power, all of which gain ready entry through the door of Eve's animus-shadow to her heart.

Eve's sin, we are told, is a simple matter of disobedience. Yet behind her decision to disobey stands the animus impulse to be wise: "In plain then, what forbids he but to know, / Forbids us good, forbids us to be wise?" (IX 758-59). The wisdom Eve seeks is knowledge of her own androgynous makeup, her capacity for masculine thought and assertion. Her decision to eat of the tree involves more than just succumbing to animus-shadow and rebelling. However disastrous it may be in the apologist's theological drama, in the artist's archetypal metadrama it's a movement toward individuated wholeness, an attempt to integrate polarized opposites by heeding rather than repressing animus.

Milton the apologist, following the patriarchal Christian bias, assumes that for a woman to heed animus constitutes insubordination: it's her duty to repress the animus whenever it disagrees with her husband. Milton the artist realizes that women ought not let animus dominate as Eve does. Nonetheless, intuiting the archetypal dynamics of the psyche, he also realizes that, to achieve individuation, women must listen to and integrate animus.

Adam's disobedience, seen as archetypal metadrama, evidences a will to individuate by seeking wholeness through his bond with Eve. No facile delusion eases his transgression. Sin for Adam is an agonized step taken with recognition, if not full understanding, of consequences:

And mee with thee hath ruind, for with thee
Certain my resolution is to Die;
How can I live without thee, . . .
So forcible within my heart I feel
The Bond of Nature draw me to my own,
My own in thee, for what thou art is mine;
Our state cannot be severd, we are one
One Flesh, to loose thee were to loose my self. [IX.906-8, 955-59]

Adam views the loss of Eve as a loss of self, for it is she who, carrying the projection of anima, brings to life his androgynous inwardness, making him feel whole.

Adam's poignant testimonial to the wholeness Eve gives constitutes a triumph of Milton the artist over Milton the apologist. Here the artist gives us one of Western literature's supremely beautiful expressions of love, an expression that deeply touches most readers and critics, forestalling regret that Adam does not abandon his gentle Eve and pray to God for a more obedient mate.[48]

Although the narrator diminishes Adam's decision to stand by Eve with, "he scrupl'd not to eat / Against his better knowledge, not deceav'd / But fondly overcome with Femal charm," (IX.997-98). He never tells us what different course he'd have Adam follow. Such is the power of Milton the artist that neither the Father nor the Son dare rebuke Adam's love by asserting he ought to have obeyed God and forsaken Eve. Nevertheless, that Adam ought to have obeyed God and forsaken Eve is the logical implication of their condemning his joining Eve in sin and death. The artist, far from making it easy for them, aggravates their problem by having Adam consider and then reject forsaking Eve: "Should God create another Eve, and I / Another Rib afford, yet loss of thee / Would never from my heart;" (IX.911-13).

Why do readers, narrator, and Deity reject or ignore the divorce option? Because it is humanly unacceptable. While Milton the apologist condemns Adam for embracing Eve's sin, the artist ensures that none can wish in their hearts for Adam to abandon her. He thereby creates one of those peculiar situations where feeling necessarily prevails over logic and law. But something must be very wrong if the deepest human feelings are at cross purposes with the commands of a supposedly loving God.

Evasions in Eden.   The brief, sketchy Genesis account gave Milton the artist liberty to develop and dramatize particulars.[49] Why, then, did he make Adam's fall hinge upon a choice between human love and divine command? *Paradise Lost* poses no more provocative question than this. Indeed, the question galvanizes one of the chief disputes of twentieth-century criticism: is Milton's art at odds with his theology, and, if so, how conscious is the conflict, and what is its significance?[50]

For clues to why Milton made Adam's fall hinge upon a choice between human love and divine command, let us examine the fallen Adam's defense of his choice. To the Son "both Judge and Saviour sent" (X.209) he protests:[51]

> This Woman whom thou mad'st to be my help,
> And gav'st me as thy perfet gift, so good,
> So fit, so acceptable, so Divine,
> That from her hand I could suspect no ill,
> And what she did, whatever in it self,
> Her doing seem'd to justifie the deed;
> Shee gave me of the Tree, and I did eat. [X.137-43]

You're to blame, Adam implies, for making the woman so attractive her doing seemed to justify her deed. The Creator, however, taught Adam that he must lead and that Eve ought to remain subordinate. But Adam does not just ignore God's instruction, he tells him a bare-faced lie. When Adam first saw the fallen Eve he did not believe her doing justified her deed. Recognizing that she had sinned and was utterly lost, he resolved without a trace of self-deception to join her in death. Only after he knowingly makes his decision out of love does Adam commence to rationalize it![52]

In judging Adam, the Son fails to point out that at the heart of his decision to transgress was a conscious choice to follow human love. Instead of being concerned with the truth of what happened and the nature of the sin, the Son seems interested only in challenging Adam's pathetically weak rationalizations:

> Was shee thy God, that her thou didst obey
> Before his voice, or was shee made thy guide,
> Superior, or but equal, that to her
> Thou did'st resigne thy Manhood, and the Place
> Wherein God set thee above her made of thee,
> And for thee, whose perfection farr excell'd
> Hers in all real dignitie: [X.145-51]

Behind the Son's ridicule stands the patriarchal belief that to resign one's "manhood" and follow anima projected on woman shows contemptible weakness. The flaw lies not in woman herself, "the fair Defect of Nature," as Adam contends; the flaw stems, the archangel Michael later asserts, echoing the Son, "From Mans effeminate slackness" (XI.634). Man must govern both his wife and the inner woman or anima whence comes the impulse to effeminacy. The Son concludes:

> Adornd
> Shee was indeed, and lovely to attract
> Thy Love, not thy Subjection, and her Gifts
> Were such as under Government well seem'd,
> Unseemly to bear rule, which was thy part
> And person, had'st thou known thy self aright. [X.151-56]

These patriarchal platitudes censure Adam's weakness without examining why he went wrong. The Son does not chide Adam for refusing to divorce the sinful Eve, which is technically why he falls, but for failing to govern her and for failing to know himself—to know that he was made subordinate to God and Eve subordinate to him. However, once Eve ate the fruit it would have been pointless to attempt to rule her since Adam could not restore Eve to her unfallen condition simply by asserting his male authority. Consequently, he would have had to assert that authority before the fall.

Adam, moreover, did not submit to Eve upon their fatal parting, though the Son's words imply otherwise. He merely declined to compel her to stay because he didn't want obedience not freely given. While Adam declined to enforce male dominion, he did so in the name of the free obedience and love God asks of man. Why should Adam compel Eve when God does not compel obedience of man? Since the free obedience of man to God is the model for the obedience of woman to man, Adam seems justified in giving Eve the selfsame freedom God gave him. Besides, at no point does the narrator state that Adam was derelict of duty for failing to compel Eve to stay beside him.

Something's wrong here. Considering the stakes, Adam is surely culpable for not persuading Eve to stay. Part of that persuasion ought to have been a reminder of her God-ordained duty to obey her husband. The reminder failing, Adam ought to have asserted his authority and required her to stay, considering the stakes. But, considering the stakes also, the same can be said of God. Before exposing them to Satan, he ought to have better taught them to obey. Indeed, he ought to have trained them to obey!

The critics have made much of Adam and Eve's prelapsarian education, and not without warrant, for Milton devotes to it nearly one third of *Paradise Lost* (Books V through VIII). Why such emphasis? Milton's great emphasis on their moral education, Jung's psychology tells us, compensates for and so betrays concern about their lack of training. They cannot be given effective moral training because such training involves learning from mistakes, and moral mistakes, even if small, would be sins. Hence, effective moral training would inevitably compromise their unfallen status. Nonetheless, minimal training would suffice to teach them to unravel and defeat the simple temptation Satan first poses.

Inexperienced persons, children, students, and recruits, for instance, never learn to deal with practical problems through education alone without training and discipline. No sane person would entrust his life or safety to a surgeon or soldier who, having learned only in the classroom, lacks field experience. Notwithstanding, God entrusts the safety of the entire human race to a pair of innocents who are told they must obey his commands but are given no training in obedience and, therefore, have neither the discipline to follow commands nor the experience to grasp their meaning.

Until God had properly trained Adam and Eve, he ought not to have let them wander. Considering the docile nature Milton the artist gives her, it's unlikely that Eve would wander with God there training her. If she wandered nonetheless, Adam ought to have enforced obedience. And if Adam failed to do his duty, God ought to have stepped in and done his. Upon children (or soldiers for that matter) who cannot be persuaded to obey in situations where their lives are in jeopardy, parents (or military officers) rightly enforce obedience. Enforced obedience is the essence of training in discipline. The father who neither trains a child to be disciplined by enforcing obedience nor draws the line at the child's liberty to destroy itself is no believer in free will: he is criminally irresponsible.[53] The same judgment, the open-minded reader of *Paradise Lost* must conclude, ought to fall upon our astonishingly permissive divine parent.

Eve begins to fall the moment she asserts herself to leave Adam, that much seems clear. However, if, in order to spare God blame through analogy, we refuse to acknowledge that Adam begins to fall when he fails to enforce obedience on Eve, and if, in deference to human feeling, we refuse to condemn him for not abandoning the fallen Eve, then we are left in a disturbing predicament. For we have tacitly condoned the most disastrous mistake of all time and thereby committed in spirit the sin that wrought man's fall. That is exactly the predicament in which Milton's narrator and the Son put themselves.

To obscure his predicament the Son resorts to a dodge used by all who prefer the semblance of rectitude above the facts of accountability—righteous generalization. Adam made Eve his God, the divine voice reproves, indeed, he resigned his manhood to her. Playing on Adam's male honor and drawing on his own conspicuously male pride, the Son declares that Eve, being made from Adam and for him, stands inferior to him in perfection and all real dignity. Eve was made to be this first Thorvald's little "Skylark" with Eden their doll house! The Son never gets down to specifics, never says, "when she offered you that fruit you should have said no, fallen on your knees, and prayed to me for guidance." Why not? Could it be that just as God had no training to offer before the temptation, during it he has no guidance to offer? And could it be that to tell Adam he ought to have forsaken Eve would make absolutely clear to everyone the shocking truth that Adam in choosing to die with Eve shows far greater love than the God who sentences them to die?

The Son could not tell Adam to abandon Eve to solitary death and still maintain the pretense of being a God of love. Neither could he tell Adam, "You ought to have loved me more than you loved the woman." Such a demand is itself unloving: love cannot be commanded, it must be inspired. The Son cannot criticize what Adam did; he can only criticize what Adam says.

Moreover, the Son ignores the most obvious flaw in Adam's excuse: it's

not the true reason he disobeyed but a spurious attempt to blame God and
Eve. Instead of criticizing Adam for lying and shifting blame, the Son
answers Adam's lie as though it were truth! The astute modern reader
cannot help but conclude that there's much more to Adam's sin than what
we're told when what we're told always reeks of evasion. These evasions
avoid one damning question: what exactly should Adam have done dif-
ferently?

Eve, the Son assumes, does not merit a reasoned evasion. When he
asks her, "Say Woman, what is this which thou has done?" she answers
simply, "The Serpent me beguil'd and I did eat." He forthwith pro-
nounces judgment upon—not Eve but the hapless serpent! Here he
evades his responsibility to train Adam and Eve by creating a distraction
with a fit of childish pique.

The narrator's rationalizing the Son's indulgence of his divine appetite
for punishing hapless innocents forms yet another link in the chain of
evasions:

> To Judgement he proceeded on th' accus'd
> Serpent though brute, unable to transferr
> The Guilt on him who made him instrument
> Of Mischief, and polluted from the end
> Of his Creation; justly then accurst,
> As vitiated in Nature: more to know
> Concern'd not Man [X.164-70]

Far from being "justly then accurst" the serpent's punishment is a telling
instance of Yahwehistic arbitrariness. Like those apologists for Yahweh
who gloss the Old Testament, the narrator baldly asserts as just what is not
only transparently unjust but infantile to boot. Whereupon he draws an
ominous veil over the Deity's motives with, "more to know / Concern'd not
Man."

Here, as with other evasions, the artist, following a strategy of indirec-
tion, subtly subverts the apologist. The Son's evasions, Jung would tell us,
indicate that his reproach, "had'st thou known thy self aright," projects
upon Adam the Son's own deficient self-knowledge. The real issue is not
man's self-knowledge but God's. The essential element of self-knowledge
the Son seeks to avoid is this: God has designed the entire setup of garden,
serpent, and forbidden tree to entrap, blame, and punish innocent hu-
mans. "Ye shall know them by their fruits," the Gospel Jesus remarked
apropos the relationship of motives to conduct.[54] Far from showing love,
divine conduct in Eden shows love's opposite: will to power.

Let me return to my initial question: why did Milton the artist hinge man's fall upon a choice between divine command and human love? Seen as archetypal metadrama, the choice is between obeying divine ego, manifest in the Father and the Son, and heeding divine anima or the Holy Spirit as Paraclete. In these alternatives Milton the artist presents a momentous epiphany of the Godhead Christian dogma attempts to conceal: an imperfect, struggling Deity unfolding in time and history and torn between three male Persons driving for power and an essentially feminine Paraclete nurturing individuation by inspiring love.

Amplifying The Tree.   One evasion remains to be noted and amplified, the tree of knowledge. The tree and its fruit, Milton the apologist assures us, signifies man's free choice of obedience or disobedience. He neglects, however, to explain why God selects the tree and its fruit to signify free choice. To understand that selection we must consider the tree as symbol. Symbols, embedded as they are in archetypal contexts, have complex and illusive meanings. Jung attempted to fathom these meanings through that synergy of imagination and intellect he called amplification.

In his *Alchemical Studies* he offered the following general advice and caution on amplifying symbols: "Luckily for us, symbols mean very much more than can be known at first glance. Their meaning resides in the fact that they compensate an unadapted attitude of consciousness, an attitude that does not fulfil its purpose and that would enable them to do this if they were understood."[55] When amplifying any specific manifestation of a symbol, we must always ask how it compensates for unadapted, one-sided conscious attitudes. Compensation, moreover, holds unique pertinence for trees because they commonly symbolize individuation—that flow of compensatory material from unconscious roots upward to the leaves of consciousness.

For his starting point in amplifying the tree of knowledge Jung used the philosophical tree.[56] In alchemical lore Jung found Mercurius, the winged spirit (or bird) confined in a tree. Here the tree symbolizes, among other things, the phallus; and Mercurius or Hermes represents the masculine power of solar logos that knowledge releases. The best known example of Mercurius is Shakespeare's mercurial Ariel whom wise Prospero freed from the tree where the witch Sycorax confined him.[57] Seventeenth-century thinkers, living in an era that witnessed science emerge from its alchemical cocoon, regarded the tree a symbol of the human circulatory and nervous system and liked to refer to man as an inverted tree. The Hindus remarked man's similarity to a tree long before with the "serpent power" of the chakras in the spine; the spine being an obvious serpent giving yet another association of the tree. A treasure is often buried beneath a symbolic tree. In alchemy that treasure is Christ. Since the cross is a tree, and Mercurius represents Christ in much occult and alchemical literature, the tree's Christ symbolism proves rich indeed.[58] The four points of a cross make it a mandala or quaternity. Quaternity for Jung is the fundamental pattern of uniplurality in both psyche and Godhead. Examples of significant fourness in God's revelation of himself to man are the four Gospels, the four animals in the Book of Daniel, and the four cherubim in Ezekiel.

A tree is a process connecting earth to heaven and involving the four elements: earth, water, air, and fire from the sun. In this regard it symbolizes the circulatory transcendent function that realizes quaternal wholeness by harmonizing the four psychic functions along with conscious and unconscious opposites. Since birds and spirits live in trees and since trees symbolize the transcendent function, a tree may symbolize that transcendent function of divinity, the Holy Spirit as Paraclete. Furthermore, the mandala-shaped cross or tree of the crucifixion symbolizes the individuation through love and suffering that is the work of God's Holy Spirit.

The tree of knowledge in *Paradise Lost*, we can conclude, carries many of the above meanings. The one meaning that unites all the others is individuation. Accordingly, in eating the fruit of the tree, Eve, while literally following her own animus, and Adam, following anima projected on Eve, symbolically disobey the divine ego or logos embodied in the Father to follow the higher light of that divine transcendent function, the Paraclete, guiding them toward individuation.

The rationalistic Father and Son along with their angelic spokesmen and Adam himself exhibit the one-sided legalism common to patriarchal egos. Their understanding of the tree is a one-sided understanding in dire need of compensation. From a Jungian perspective Adam and Eve's eating the fruit of the forbidden tree (always the logos or one-sided, patriarchal intellect does the forbidding) is a symbolic compensation that initiates the interlinked struggles of man and God for individuated wholeness.

We need not rely exclusively on Jungian psychology to amplify the tree of knowledge. Freud's disciple Theodore Reik offers another intriguing, albeit quite different, approach. The tree itself, Reik contends, was initially the home of a spiritual presence. In fact Yahweh was thought of as a tree.[59] Moreover, primitive myths and the Genesis account lack sexual overtones. St. Paul introduced the sexual interpretation, which the church fathers developed further, culminating in Augustine's belief in the sexual basis of original sin. Christianity thereby shifted the onus of guilt to Eve; in the early Hebraic myths Adam was the chief culprit. Adam's true crime, Reik insists, was killing the primal God-Father who appears as a tree totem. Since the cross of Christianity symbolizes a tree, Christ's dying on it reunites mankind with its Father. Original sin, Reik concludes, has nothing to do with uxoriousness: it is patricide simple and primitive. The Genesis story transforms patricide into symbols that could be accepted once their earliest meaning fell into oblivion.

And terrible indeed that early meaning is, for eating the fruit compounds patricide with cannibalism. No wonder it was repressed into the deep unconscious whence it eventually emerged transformed into a comparatively harmless infraction. The shadowy Christian concept of original sin rooted in concupiscence attenuated the gravity of the primal crime, thus lancing the abscess of guilt.[60]

Guilt, Reik says, making a decisive point, is born not of erotic drives but of aggression and violence.[61] Christianity's shift of guilt from aggression to erotic drives introduced a strange perversity to the religion that accounts for its unnatural obsession with sex and the disturbing ease with which it condones violence against its opponents, both heretics and sinners within and infidels, Jews, and pagans outside. Part of Christianity's dark shadow, if I may put a Jungian concept in service to a Freudian idea, is its practice of obscuring true guilt born of violence with the distracting issue of sex.

Whether or not Reik's criticism of Christianity is valid, Milton's account of the original sin, following Saint Paul's lead, makes erotic lust a telling sign of man's fallen condition:

> but that false Fruit
> Farr other operation first displaid,
> Carnal desire enflaming, hee on Eve
> Began to cast lascivious Eyes, she him
> As wantonly repaid; in Lust they burn:
> Till Adam thus 'gan Eve to dalliance move. [IX.1011-16]

Here Milton's narrator exploits the traditional Christian distrust of eros. But where is the evidence, it may be objected, for a cover-up of the graver sins of murder and cannibalism? While we find no hard evidence for Reik's theory in either Genesis or *Paradise Lost,* there are indications that Milton sensed something much more serious afoot in Eden than mere carnality. For example, both Milton's narrator and God carefully sidestep discussing why the test of man's free will and faithful obedience should be a tree.

The pivotal issue becomes, therefore, not what is present in the text of *Paradise Lost* but what is conspicuous by its absence. Reik at least furnishes a plausible explanation, conspicuously absent in Milton's epic and orthodox Christian theology, of why the tree might symbolize a crime so terrible that it could only be atoned by crucifixion on a second tree, the cross. We may easily challenge the particulars of Reik's account; what seems hard to dispute is the need for a fuller explanation than orthodoxy and Milton the apologist offer.[62]

The Jews were first to feel the guilt of Genesis. So great was their guilt, Reik asserts, that they made their violated deity invisible out of fear of facing him.[63] Behind the Jews' intense devotion to Yahweh lurks an equally intense fear of his vengeance. If Reik is correct, what Jung failed to recognize in *Answer to Job* was that Yahweh had a reason to be vengeful, cruel, and willful beyond mere unconsciousness—he had suffered the most unspeakable of wrongs. His followers had killed and eaten him, or so they believed. The Jews' guilt, Reik observes, activated guilt's opposite, a paranoid megalomania linked to infantile longing for omnipotence.[64] The Jews projected their megalomaniacal group shadow on Yahweh, making him the childish tyrant Jung exposes in *Answer to Job*.

The work of Alice Miller, Freud's most incisive feminist critic, suggests a startling alternative to Reik's approach.[65] I shall treat this alternative concisely since a Millerite school of criticism has yet to appear.[66] In a Millerite view proscribing the fruit of the tree would symbolize arbitrary parental power, and Yahweh, far from being a victim, becomes the primal abusive parent who entraps, traumatizes, and tyrannizes childlike Adam and Eve or, to cite Miller's favorite example, Job.[67] Though Miller is no follower of Jung, her description of Yahweh might well have been taken from *Answer to Job:* "God the Father is easily offended, jealous, and basically insecure; He therefore demands obedience and conformity in the expression of ideas, tolerates no graven images and—since "graven images" included works of art for the Hebrew God—no creativity either. He dictates beliefs and imposes punishment on apostates, persecutes the guilty with a vengeance, permits his sons to live only according to his principles and to find happiness only on his terms."[68] Like abused children, who out of fear and shame of their powerlessness take upon themselves their parents' guilt, God the Father's worshipers falsify their own natures by declaring that their disobedience provoked and justified His abuse. A temple of lies is built. Yet the truth struggles to break forth generating a plethora of ecclesiogenic neuroses along with a welter of theodicies that nurture guilt and stifle truth.[69] Thus, whether we look at the tree from the point of view of Reik, Jung, or Miller, what lies hidden in the tree is guilt—divine-parental or human-child—and the effects are ecclesiogenic neuroses.

Returning to the primal guilt, Reik presents "the murder of God" as the outcome of a conflict of individual and herd. The God-Father is the leader of the primitive herd who personifies its collective spirit. Once he separates from the herd, declaring his individual consciousness superior to its collective mind and therefore entitled to direct it, the enraged herd strives to kill and eat the leader to repossess the manna he "stole" from them.[70] Using Jung to take Reik a step further, the original crime becomes the herd murdering the conscious individual and the original guilt becomes rejection of the individuation first apparent in God the Father.

Combining Reik's and Jung's approaches establishes the tree as a symbol of individuation and illumines Milton's divided attitudes toward eating its fruit along with why God frequently resorts to evasion. Still, Reik does seem at odds with Jung's view of Yahweh and the crucifixion in *Answer to Job*. The discrepancy need not prevent us from drawing upon both theories since, much to the chagrin of positivists, rigid logic does not rule the realm of myth. In fact there is every reason to suspect that divergent archetypal patterns may operate in an account of the fall, which leaves us emotionally and intellectually confused. Similarly, to proffer Reik's theory does not preclude using a Millerite view. All can help amplify the wealth of meanings of that symbolic tree.

What holds for the tree holds more generally for the Christian God. Just as in the Old Testament the tragic vision of the Book of Job, the prophetic vision of Jeremiah, the mystic vision of Ezekiel, and the ethical vision of 2 Isaiah accreted upon the primitive myths of the Pentateuch to give Yahweh a veritable welter of discordant archetypal motives, so the church fathers and subsequent theologians, interpreting Hebrew myth through Hellenistic, medieval, and modern philosophies, added to their God's archetypal conflicts and complexities.

Wherefore, the Christian notion of deity has come to resemble a great city inhabited continuously for millennia. Some parts glitter with modernity, others remain little changed after hundreds or thousands of years, and each age and civilization bequeaths its peculiar remnants to the astonishing quilt that forms the whole. Asking for the true identity of the Christian God is like asking what kind of a city is Rome—an ancient city, a medieval city, a Renaissance city, a nineteenth-century city, or a modern city? Rome's all of these, yet none of them exclusively. The psyche of Western man too resembles Rome. It developed over long expanses of time with each age leaving its peculiar marks. All ages also left their marks on that grandest and most philosophical of epics, *Paradise Lost*, which, taking for its subject our civilization, its basic myths, and its God, mirrors the individuating psyche of Western man.

Free Will, Mature Freedom and Accountability.   Nevertheless, throughout the layers of ideas and influences distinctive Miltonic values and emphases appear. Although the idea of a murdered God may lie in the archetypal background of his story, he never pushes it to the foreground. What he does push to the foreground, accenting it to a degree unsurpassed among major Christian writers, is man's freedom and accountability.

Freedom has two principal senses that form the parameters of accountability in *Paradise Lost:* technical freedom or free will, and ideal, mature freedom. How do these senses apply to the original freedom that preceded original sin?

Eve's decision to eat of the tree and Adam's decision to make her offense his own are free in the technical sense of free will. This means they are free of external coercion. While the serpent deceives Eve, he does so by abetting her animus desires using no force beyond persuasion. Eve in turn makes no attempt to compel the undeceived Adam to follow her in sin. Hence, nothing external coerces their free will, which is a necessary though not a sufficient condition for their accountability. Mature freedom forms a sufficient condition for accountability.

With mature freedom or individuated wholeness, its Jungian equivalent, no single archetype domineers, ego and shadow cooperate with each other and with anima and animus, and decisions and actions flow from the whole self. Eve forsakes Adam to follow not the self but animus; and Adam, projecting anima on Eve, submits his free will to Eve and anima. Although their actions further individuation, Adam and Eve are insufficiently individuated to act as whole persons. Consequently, they lack mature freedom.

Only those who actualize the archetype of the wiseperson, the archetype associated with the Holy Spirit as Paraclete, achieve mature freedom. Maturely free, a Prospero might well have put Satan in his place. However, in Eden a Ferdinand and Miranda go against Satan, and for a parent they have no wise Prospero but an arbitrary father like those Shakespearean senexes whose wrath sets up tragic conditions only a comic miracle can dispel. In the Christian theological "comedy" the Father's wrath finds its measure in the immense suffering (the crucifixion) he demands as payment for the miracle (the resurrection).

Despite the magnitude of God's wrath, we are repeatedly told in *Paradise Lost* that Adam and Eve provoked it by a single act of free will. Because of their free will, we are asked to believe, they are fully accountable (even though Satan, as tempter, shares their blame). The strength of the repressed doubt that they, lacking mature freedom, can be held accountable for God's prodigious wrath registers in the anxious assertions of free will, in Milton's own deep resistance to the price of redemption, the cross, and in his conspicuous silences about its attainment, the resurrection.

Free will alone, Milton must have sensed, cannot make one fully

accountable. Still, one can be partially accountable without having real-
ized mature freedom. Decisions reflect character. God created human
nature; character is something individuals create through experience in
weighing alternatives, making decisions, and confronting their conse-
quences. Although character matured through experience does not guar-
antee mature freedom, it can make one partially accountable. However,
even as Adam and Eve are not given sufficient training and discipline to
learn obedience, so they are not given sufficient experience to develop
mature character.

Adam and Eve, physically and intellectually mature though they may
be, are essentially children without mature character identities. Milton's
detractors might say that he lacked the skill to depict mature character.
Here, as usual, Milton's detractors would be off course. While Adam and
Eve's characters are immature, the skill Milton shows in depicting them,
his art of characterization, is fully ripened. Besides, the limitations upon
Adam and Eve's experience and psychological maturity are imposed by the
biblical myth.

Whether we attribute their childlike characters to prelapsarian inno-
cence or to deficient training and experience, the effect is apparent. Their
decisions themselves lack the tragic meaning of the protagonists' decisions
in *Othello* and *King Lear*, which flow from flaws in mature character. Othello
and Lear can be held partially accountable for their wrong decisions
because their experience has given them opportunity to learn discipline,
to understand alternatives, and to heed consequences. If they fail to learn,
understand, or heed enough to achieve mature freedom, their failure
shows flawed character. For them character is fate, and tragic insight is
recognition of flawed character. Adam and Eve never recognize their flaws
because they have not emerged sufficiently from their archetypal cocoons
to develop individual characters with ingrained flaws. Their mistakes,
Adam's uxoriousness and Eve's insubordination, stem from immaturity,
not from ingrained character flaws. Accordingly, like children who, ignor-
ing their parent's counsel, play with fire and get burned, they recognize
only that they have made a terrible mistake.

Nonetheless, God punishes them more harshly than any humane
parent would ever punish a child, justifying his harshness on the grounds
that their free will renders them accountable. Modern readers imbued
with Kierkegaard and familiar with particle physics may attempt to defend
God by arguing that Adam and Eve's free will, when understood in a
scientific sense, makes them self-determined and therefore accountable
for their acts. Free will, these readers may argue, gains new meaning from
Heisenberg's indeterminacy principle, which entails that we cannot ob-
serve individual subatomic particles without disturbing them and, accord-

ingly, can never know the precise causes of their movements. In like manner, close observation necessarily disturbs human individuals, making it impossible to know the precise causes of their free or undisturbed actions. Hence, free actions appear to be spontaneous.

However, Heisenbergian freedom, to coin a term, does not mean that individuals literally behave with radical spontaneity, their acts lacking causal antecedents. It means only that, because no one can observe the precise causal antecedents of acts, none can unerringly explain choices. Similarly, since no one traces the precise course of Adam's and Eve's wills, no observer, including the narrator, can fully explain their choices—which is an important point. What is much more important, though, is that the analogy of free will to subatomic movements indicates why free will in itself cannot make individuals, including "our first parents," accountable, let alone responsible, for their misguided acts.

Subatomic particles are not accountable for their "free" movements because they are not conscious. Accountability requires more than just freedom from interference, it requires awareness of alternatives and consequences along with the inner discipline to make decisions compatible with a chosen character identity. In short, accountability requires the mature, conscious freedom, or at least mature character, indispensable to decisive identity. Lacking mature freedom and mature character, Adam and Eve are neither justly accountable for the consequences of their acts nor do they show decisive identity.

Freedom in Augustine and Milton. Milton the apologist's attempt to use freedom in its technical sense of free will to hold Adam and Eve accountable for their fallen condition proves dubious at best. To put that dubious attempt in perspective it is helpful to review briefly the history of the concept of freedom.[71] The fact of freedom, whether as free will or mature freedom, has been with us much longer than the concept, which emerged slowly and late. Unlike Milton's God, Yahweh never badgers those he punishes with reminders that being free they've chosen to bring his wrath upon themselves. The word free does not appear in Genesis. In the Old Testament it means only the alternative to slavery and servitude.[72] Indeed, the ancient Hebrews lacked a conscious idea of free will even though free will may be implied in the numerous exhortations to obey Yahweh's commands.

The idea of free will was also absent among the originators of Greek philosophy and Christianity. Plato and Aristotle never discuss what later became the central philosophical issue of free will. Similarly, despite modern determination to read the New Testament in light of Kierkegaard, free will has no explicit place in the teachings of Jesus and Paul. For complex historical reasons the concept of freedom, which was arguably implicit in the act of choosing Christ, gained increasing popularity in early Christianity and its host culture, Roman civilization. Preeminent among those who furthered its development was Clement of Alexandria with his notion that baptism confers *autoexousia*, or power to constitute one's own being. In addition, Irenaeus, Tertullian, Justin Martyr, those proto-Protestants the Montanists, and Origen all relied on free will and developed the concept in their own ways.[73] But not until Augustine do the philosophical issues of freedom crystallize.

Augustine's position on freedom sets forth the alternative to that taken by Milton. As Milton stressed free will, so Augustine emphasized mature freedom. Only ideal men possess freedom, Augustine contended, anticipating Jung: actual men have to work to achieve it.[74] Freedom, then, is not a precondition of character so much as an objective of character maturation, the culmination of a process that can alleviate original sin. Choice, moreover, is no simple act of will; it involves our entire character, our feeling and knowing, love and reason. In fact freedom is not awareness of choice but the liberty to act fully. Hence, freedom exhibits constant motion and activity. Neither is freedom spontaneous, for its concurrence of feeling and knowledge so firmly binds men to their chosen object that no other alternative is possible.

Much of what Augustine as mature thinker says on freedom is sensible and profound; but little of it supports Miltonic theodicy on the fall. The notion of Adam and Eve existing in a state of arcadian innocence until corrupted by a quirk of free will would have seemed absurd to the mature Augustine—and heretical. Pelagius and Julian of Eclanum, whom Augustine branded as heretics, are Milton the apologist's true antecedents.[75]

We need not review the fine points of the Pelagian controversy. It should suffice to note that the controversy centered on the cause of suffering and what can be done about it. Augustine believed that original sin both corrupted man and profoundly angered God.[76] Consequently sin became inevitable and man was left helpless against suffering. Pelagius, believing that such fatalism destroyed incentive for reform and self-betterment, denied original sin. Suffering, he contended, results from men's free choices. Indeed, free will gives everyone power to lead a sinless life. The right exercise of free will by all men, Pelagius taught, could theoretically restore mankind to a state that, if not Eden, would be close to paradisiacal.

Pelagian optimism about individual self-improvement with the help of God bolsters Milton's theological stances. Indeed, in *Of Education* Milton declares that the end of learning is to repair the ruins of our first parents' fall, presuming, like Pelagius, the damage to be reparable. Of our own free will we can repair our natures, avoid evil, and elude suffering: such has been the hope of Pelagians in all ages.

Whatever the feasibility of that hope, free will used, as Pelagius and Milton use it, to free God of original responsibility for human suffering and shift the blame to man is philosophically indefensible. Notwithstanding, that strategy holds great appeal to all who undertake theodicy, including the young Augustine writing *On Free Will*. The psychological impetus of the appeal is ego's will to believe, against contrary experience, that suffering must be avoidable because God, with whom ego identifies, is omnipotent and perfectly good. God has no shadow, say all Pelagians. Man began in paradise and through right choice paradise he can regain.

For both Milton and Augustine freedom is crucial to God's justice in permitting suffering. Their essential difference is this: Milton held that man's free will clears the deity of responsibility for human suffering, whereas Augustine held that original sin so limits man's mature freedom as to make him unable to comprehend God's justice. Though Augustine accepted the orthodox definition of God as the omnipotent *Summum Bonum* when he chose Christianity over Manichaeanism, in a concession to his early dualistic pessimism he insisted that God was incomprehensible. Divine incomprehensibility meant we cannot expect God to be wholly just in human terms. It also implied that he can't be wholly good in human terms, but Augustine of course never actually spelled that out. So far was the mature Augustine from wanting to justify the ways of God to man that he denounced Pelagius as a heretic for attempting to vindicate the deity.

There are many explanations for the difference between Milton's rather optimistic stance on the justice of the *Summum Bonum* and the mature Augustine's very pessimistic stance.[77] Admittedly inclined more toward Augustine, I attribute the difference to Augustine's deeper psychological insight. Deep insight seems to predispose men to a wary view of human nature and of its Creator. Examples in addition to Augustine are Shakespeare, Dostoevsky, Nietzsche, Freud, and Jung.

Deep insight, moreover, predisposes men to search for the deep causes of suffering. Milton presents human suffering as the outcome of free will used unwisely—much too superficial an explanation for Augustine, who believed that God must be profoundly angry with man to permit suffering. Milton's God shows neither profound anger nor convincing agape though much is made of his "love" and "mercy." Above all he is defensive, carrying self-exculpation so far the astute modern reader may wonder if he doesn't have some powerful accuser in the background impugning his justice. Augustine let his experience of suffering inform his conception of the deity. Milton let free will define his God. A religion centered on suffering appeals to the soul and its prime motive, love, whereas a religion centered on free will caters to ego and its will to power.

"Sin Original."   Augustine's belief in original sin shapes his conception of free will, whereas Milton's belief in free will shapes his conception of man's first sin. Accordingly, while Augustine focuses on the flaw in the species, individual transgressions are what interest Milton.

Whether the original sin be a universal tendency, as in Augustine, or an individual transgression, as in Milton, those who seek to exonerate a *summum bonum* deity face an impasse. If human nature has a proclivity to sin, then man's creator bears responsibility for sin, which calls into question his "perfect goodness." If proclivity to sin, rather than being intrinsic to human nature, enters human nature as God's punishment for Adam and Eve's transgressions, then God's justice to their descendants falls into question.

To avoid questioning either God's goodness or his justice Milton, in *De Doctrina* and *Paradise Lost*, avoids specifying the causes and onset of the proclivity to sin.[78] This proved feasible for two reasons. The first, that Milton presents the original transgression in a cleverly elusive way, I shall deal with at length later. The second reason can be stated simply: in the mid-seventeenth century the philosophical predicaments raised by man's proclivity to sin were more easily repressed than today.

Milton's own repression may explain his facile allusion to the loaded term "original sin":

> he scrupl'd not to eat
> Against his better knowledge, not deceav'd
> But fondly overcome with Femal charm.
> Earth trembl'd from her entrails, as again
> In pangs, and Nature gave a second groan,
> Skie lowr'd, and muttering Thunder, som sad drops
> Wept at compleating of the mortal Sin
> Original; [IX.996-1004]

While Milton's inversion of word order suits metrical convenience, it also suits his impulse to slight the dark Augustinian connotations of original sin. The Augustinian connotations convey deep pessimism about human nature along with the crude Hebraic notion of Yahweh visiting the sins of parents on their children. Milton prefers to convey instead his optimism about man's potential and his facile belief that individual free will exonerates the Creator.

However, behind Milton's facile belief lies something quite profound: the notion, first encountered in Greek tragedy, that sin is caused by an aberration arising within the individual sufferer (or sinner). Arnold Toynbee comments upon the Greek notion of sin: "The sinner is brought to destruction not by God's act, but by his own. His offense lies not in rivaling his Creator, but in deliberately making himself utterly unlike him, and God's part in this human tragedy is not active but passive. The sinner's bane is not a divine envy, but a divine inability to continue to use as an instrument of creation a creature that has insisted upon alienating himself from the life of its Creator."[79] Although Milton makes the individual's will to alienate himself from the Creator the cause of sin, he seems reluctant to admit that alienation is a fundamental human proclivity. What Milton the apologist deems fundamental is the Pelagian free will that rebels against God. Nevertheless, one can view the major sinful actions in *Paradise Lost* as effects of alienation, even though Milton the apologist blames rebellious free will. Satan alienates himself through defective love of God before he rebels, Eve alienates herself from Adam through pride, and Adam alienates God by valuing Eve over God. We have no reason to think about our free will until we become alienated. The point where Satan and man enter the path of sin, from this perspective, would not be the rebellious exercise of free will, but the alienation that sparks recognition of free will.

The idea of sin originating in a proclivity toward alienation from God is thoroughly Augustinian.[80] It must be emphasized that for Augustine man does not freely will to become alienated, as Milton the apologist appears to believe. The exercise of will follows the alienation.[81] What causes man's proclivity toward the alienation? Not a choice, according to Augustine, but rather defective love for God. You do not choose to love, Augustine with his profound psychological insight well understood. You love or you don't. Love is more fundamental than choice for it stems not from our will (the ego) but expresses our very being (the self). Hence, defective love corrupts the will and everything else. Defective love is the original sin wherein all mankind lives.

Man's Free Will to Sin and God's Freedom from Sin.   What is sin itself?[82] For Augustine sin is defective love for and alienation from God; for Milton, it is primarily willful rebellion against Him. Defining sin as rebellion or disobedience renders God the master and man his servant. This master-servant paradigm sanctions a subject-object ethic based on the masculine power drive of the hostile brothers archetype with its exaltation of ego-will, repression and rebellion of shadow, and compulsive scapegoating. By contrast, where metaphors of alienation and defective love define sin, we get a relational, or I-Thou, ethic based on the friends archetype.

Besides following the primitive hostile brothers archetype, Milton the apologist's decision to make rebellious will the origin of sin follows a common Christian pattern. The religion began as a solace for slaves, Nietzsche observed with more psychological than sociological truth. By the time of Constantine, however, the masters realized that if they could define sin as rebellion and make its remedy obedience, Christianity could become a powerful tool for controlling the masses.[83] Far from giving men freedom, post-Constantinian Christianity, when it defines sin as rebellion, enslaves men by instilling guilt at freedom's exercise. And, what is equally pernicious, sin as rebellion undermines *caritas*. Suffering results from rebellion against God, the masters say, which excuses their not acting to relieve it, induces guilt in the sufferers, and inhibits protest. Free will, a notion never preached by Jesus, became the master's "catch 22" to the Golden Rule. There is no more telling example of free will as a "catch 22" than Milton's God's using it to defend his master mentality toward Adam and Eve.

Freedom, Nietzsche taught, begins when we embrace our inner fate or authentic selves.[84] The choice between Nietzschean freedom on one hand and Christian free will and obedience on the other is a choice between the archetypes of Prometheus-Lucifer and the Jobean Son of theology (not to be confused with Jesus, a figure of wholeness who balances Promethean and Jobean attributes). Promethean defiance, the aggressive brother's opposition to the tyrant father, is ethically more advanced than the docile brother's Job-Son obedience inasmuch as it entails tragic insight. Nonetheless, the stance of Prometheus needs to be surmounted with a metastance or overview that accedes supremacy to no single stance. Nietzsche called the overview *amor fati*, Spinoza called it seeing things *natura naturans*, and Jung referred to it as wholeness and harmony with the *unus mundus*. All share one basic assumption: we attain mature freedom upon transcending the need to believe in any Truth, particularly that Truth of Free Will the followers of the Christian ego-God proclaim to rationalize enslaving men to sin and guilt.

What precipitates sin, or satanic and human rebellion, in *Paradise Lost*? As I argued in the preceding chapter, Milton the artist, in a metadramatic subversion of Christian orthodoxy, reveals the true catalyst to be not the creature's defective love, but God's defective love evident in His inflated claim to being an absolutely self-sufficient *Summum Bonum*. God's inflation inevitably alienates his creation, stifles love, and prompts rebellion.

All depend upon God, teaches Augustine, following the most influential philosopher of the era, Plotinus. Jung's great advance over Augustine is *interdependence:* as the creature depends on the Creator so also does the Creator depend on his creation—to realize consciousness and love. Without interdependence the creature has no power and no dignity. Wherefore, the creator has neither shown nor can show the creature love. In rejecting the *Summum Bonum*'s "sinless" perfection to embrace interdependence and mutual responsibility, Jung's God shows genuine love by becoming vulnerable.

Milton the apologist and much of Protestantism, under the sway of a God whose *summum bonum* identity embodies patriarchy's inflated ideal of moral invulnerability, anticipated and, with the doctrine of free will, repudiated interdependence and mutual responsibility for sin. Attempting to make God morally invulnerable, they succeeded in making him like the part of themselves that seeks invulnerability, like a self-fed, self-consumed, inflated ego denying interdependence. If men alienate and diminish themselves by denying their dependence on God, so also do they make God alien and diminish his love by denying his interdependence with men to assert instead his freedom from responsibility for their sins and suffering.

Decision, Character, Muse. If Jung is right, there is ultimately only one decision for all men and all gods: whether to follow the self toward individuated wholeness and interdependence with the *unus mundus* or to withdraw into inflation and alienation. By repudiating, through the doctrine of free will, mutual responsibility for the sins of his creatures, *Paradise Lost*'s God, no less than Satan, opts for alienation. Men depend on God for meaning and God has the selfsame dependence on his creation. Both are free to recognize interdependence or deny it. To recognize interdependence shows love, to deny it shows inflation. Men who understand their choice and rightly choose interdependence over alienated "freedom" also envision a deity who chooses rightly. Deciding our identity decides the identity of the God image we envision.

In Adam and Eve's case they decide the identity of not just themselves, but of their progeny as well—or so we are told. About man's first sin there is something quite odd. The oddness lies in the elusive way Milton presents it. To understand Milton's technique we must review his dilemma. Orthodoxy specifies that the penalty for Adam and Eve's disobedience falls also upon their progeny. Condemning their descendants makes ethical sense only if Adam and Eve are universal types who epitomize human nature so perfectly that any other normal human couple in their place would have chosen as they did and likewise brought the race to ruin. However, making them universal types and granting universality to their choices implies that God created the species with a proclivity to sin and so must bear responsibility for that proclivity and the suffering it causes.

God and the narrator rule out any bent toward sin by assuring us Adam and Eve were made sufficient to withstand Satan's temptation. Their free will lies at fault, we are told. Notwithstanding, free will by itself is insufficient to make them accountable let alone to condemn their descendants. One course remains open to Milton: for Adam and Eve to be justly held accountable, their defect must be attributed to their character. Moreover the problem of condemning their descendants must be ignored since it admits no solution.

Milton draws our attention to the crucial role of character when he has Adam counsel the departing Eve, "relie / On what thou hast of vertue, summon all" (IX 373-74). Character or, to use the Renaissance term, "vertue" comprises that ballast of habit, judgment, and inner discipline accrued through identity defining decisions. Character, moreover, does not exist in the abstract. Its individual pattern of decisions develops within a social context of family, friends, community, nation, and culture. Character, therefore, requires, in addition to free will, a process of individuation and a social context.

In one respect Adam and Eve are simply not credible. Having universal humanity but lacking the experience needed to develop character, they are like born-yesterday adults. The real world no more contains normal adults with mature character who are total innocents than it contains mermaids. Credibility problems notwithstanding, Milton the apologist treats Adam and Eve as though they possess mature characters whose flaws render them accountable.

But what's odd about Adam and Eve's sin is not that Milton's narrator tacitly blames it on the sinner's characters when they are innocents lacking credible, mature character. Their sin's oddness lies in the way it's presented: that presentation induces readers to overlook the problem of blaming their character.

How are the readers induced to overlook the obvious? This is accomplished, I believe, primarily by making Adam, Eve, and Eden too beautiful to belong to our world. They become "once upon a time" characters in a "never-never land." As the reader adjusts to Eden's make-believe world, his critical intellect falls into abeyance. The abeyance encourages the "fit" reader to breeze over the problem of God's justice in transmitting guilt to descendants. And, what is crucial, abeyance allows him to assume that uxoriousness and feminine insubordination make Adam and Eve blameworthy without asking whether these flaws are culpable defects ingrained in mature character or merely reflect the natural impulse of two inexperienced persons to explore, and so better understand, themselves and each other—in short the impulse to individuate.

Satan too is a creature of make believe. If Adam and Eve are more inexperienced than adults in the real world can ever be, the archfiend with his career spanning aeons and orbs has more ballast of character than any actual human ever acquires. None live so long or see so much as Satan. Satan's ballast of character, however fascinating it may render him, has an unfortunate repercussion for God: it makes the Deity like a demented parent who exposes his two innocent children to a masterful seducer then relentless punishes them for yielding to temptation. In fact, God is worse than the most unconscionable parent, for Adam and Eve are more innocent than any children, and Satan is more callous than the worst human seducer. Nevertheless, Milton's fairy tale so suspends the "fit" reader's critical intellect and inflames him against Satan that he neglects to scrutinize God's responsibility.

However, just as choosing orthodoxy in the seventeenth century has a meaning different from choosing it today when options are different, so different options change the meaning of reader "fitness." And while Milton the apologist speaks to the original "fit" reader, Milton the artist addresses the fit reader of subsequent times and all time. Today's fit readers will not castigate Milton the artist for exposing innocent humans to Satan. This travesty, they will recognize, was thrust upon him by the exigencies of his myth. Rather, they will admire the artist for intuiting the archetypal truths of his myth despite the blinders of Milton the apologist. Indeed, they will conclude, the limitations upon the apologist make possible the artist's extraordinary achievement: by giving the love and innocence of Adam and Eve a ring of truth unique in Eden, Milton the artist creates an epiphany of God's injustice to man at once more poignant, more compelling, and more provocative than any philosopher's attempt to debunk Christian theodicy.

Whence came the artist's inspiration? Where but from the anima wisdom of that "Heaven'ly Muse" whose guidance Milton invokes at the epic's beginning and midpoint and to whom he turns for inspiration in treating the fall?

> Sing Heav'nly Muse, that on the secret top
> Of Oreb, or of Sinai, didst inspire
> That Shepherd, who first taught the chosen Seed
> In the Beginning how the Heav'ns and Earth
> Rose out of Chaos: . . .
>   I thence
> Invoke thy aid to my adventrous Song,
> . . . Thou from the first
> Wast present, and with mighty wings outspread
> Dove-like satst brooding on the vast Abyss
> And mad'st it pregnant: What in me is dark
> Illumin, [I.6-23]

> Descend from Heav'n Urania, by that name
> If rightly thou art call'd, whose Voice divine
> Following, above th' Olympian Hill I soar,

> Above the flight of Pegasean wing,
> The meaning, not the Name I call: for thou
> Nor of the Muses nine, nor on the top
> Of old Olympus dwell'st, but Heav'nlie born,
> Before the Hills appeerd, or Fountain flow'd,
> Thou with Eternal wisdom didst converse,
> Wisdom thy Sister, [VII.1-10]

> my Celestian Patroness, who deignes
> Her nightly visitation unimplor'd,
> And dictates to me slumbring, or inspires
> Easie my unpremeditated Verse: [IX.21-24]

He would fail to do justice to his subject, Milton confesses, if the inspiration "be all mine / Not Hers who brings it nightly to my Ear" (IX.46-47).

Here we have the solution to the problem of the missing feminine in Milton's God: the feminine, repressed at the ego level, reappears as divine anima-muse to guide the artist and lead him to the heaven of heavens. Anima-muse also offers the solution to the problem of freedom in man, artist, and God. For, we realize, all remain trapped in ego's false dream of free will and none achieve the mature freedom of individuated wholeness until they integrate the feminine, the anima-muse whose wisdom brings the truths of self and God.

Urania and Wisdom, her sister, manifest that Divine Anima I have identified with the Holy Spirit as Paraclete. The Paraclete-anima gently supercedes the Father, the Son, and Satan in the full canvas of *Paradise Lost* (see "A note on the Holy Spirit and Milton's Muse" at the end of this chapter for a discussion of the identity of Urania and Milton's muse). In the Father we meet archetypal will power, in the Son archetypal ethical force, and in Satan archetypal rebellious energy. But that neglected Fourth, depreciated in *De Doctrina* and overlooked in the action and theology of *Paradise Lost*, reveals the deepest truths of Godhead and the human psyche in its quiet epiphanies.[85]

Milton chose in the fall of man a subject whose theological trappings concealed its true nature. Following his muse above the theologians, the Divine Anima above God the Father or Son, he intuited a vision of his subject he could not comprehend any way other than through art. Too much we stress conscious, ego intentions. We ought to regard equally those epiphanies from Divine Anima, which transcend not just Milton's cultural canon but also his own ego commitments. By authenticating the love and innocence of Adam and Eve in matchless poetry and by having Adam choose love over obedience and Eve individuation over subordination, Milton as artist penetrated his subject's darkness through inward vision from the anima of God.

<h2 style="text-align:center">MESSIAH'S DECISION</h2>

Why did Milton in *Paradise Regained* depart from soteriological custom to disregard the crucifixion and make the temptation the remedy to the fall? The most obvious explanation is that in both the temptation and the fall everything hinges on an identity-defining decision. The crucifixion simply finalizes the decision Messiah made in the desert at his mission's outset. Lacking a specific identity-defining decision, it cannot reverse man's wrong decision in Eden.

Moreover, according to Jung, in the crucifixion's background stands the Father's decision that he needed a personal sacrifice to remedy his own moral limitations. As I noted in Chapter 1, Milton attempted to come to grips with God's sacrifice but failed.[86] The chief psychological obstacle, I believe, was his exaltation of the Father archetype. The crucifixion proved an unworkable topic for Milton because it forced him to confront the Father's deficiencies.

Yet the temptation forced him to deal with the deficiencies of Messiah, the Son incarnate, and with Messiah's problematic relationship to Satan. Milton's achievement, we shall see, resides less in the apologist's paragon of decisive identity, than in the artist's subversion of that paragon through epiphanies of the archetypes behind the male Persons of Godhead.

Strength to What End? *Paradise Regained* is often viewed as a sequel to *Paradise Lost* and much has been made of the differences that elevate Messiah above Adam.[87] The crucial difference is one of character. Everyone notices that Messiah possesses the stronger character, though few observe that Adam is never granted the experience needed to develop character.

At the opening of *Paradise Regained* Messiah is a mature, fully realized individual with a past substantiated by a mother who frets about him and two disciples who become distressed over his long absence. He partakes of the fabric of society like every experienced person we encounter in real life. The primary devices used to detail Messiah's character and past experience are the long dramatic meditations where he recounts his parentage, birth, youth, and baptism. His detailed character and past give Messiah's decisions weight and credibility lacking in Adam and Eve's decisions.

So thoroughly do Adam and Eve define each other that it's impossible to imagine either without the other. Though Messiah has a mother and disciples, they are far from defining him. What defines Messiah is a network of ties binding him to history and his sense of having a divinely ordained mission that centers the network and history on himself.

Messiah's first meditation indicates a general sense of mission whose particulars he is struggling to discover:

> O what a multitude of thoughts at once
> Awaken'd in me swarm, while I consider
> What from within I feel my self, . . .
> When I was yet a child, no childish play
> To me was pleasing, all my mind was set
> Serious to learn and know, and thence to do
> What might be publick good; my self I thought
> Born to that end, born to promote all truth,
> All righteous things: therefore above my years,
> The Law of God I read, and found it sweet,
> Made it my whole delight, [I.195-208]

Here is a strong, sharply defined, if not endearing, character. Far more thoroughly than Jung's anima and animus direct Adam and Eve, Freud's superego directs Messiah, who at times seems superego personified. Discipline is the salient quality that elevates him above uxorious Adam, discipline particularized in austere independence and an indomitable will to discover and carry out his God given purpose. He is rigid and humorless, not as Milton actually was but as he is sometimes perceived. There is so much strength in Messiah's character no room seems left for the love that distinguished the Gospel Jesus; certainly, there's no place for the human frailties that endear Adam and Eve to Milton's readers.

A cool, single-minded purposiveness is evident in all Messiah does. For example, not even the image of mother distracts him from his mission:

> These growing thoughts my Mother soon perceiving
> By words at times cast forth inly rejoyc'd,
> And said to me apart, high are thy thoughts
> O Son, but nourish them and let them soar
> To what highth sacred vertue and true worth
> Can raise them, though above example high;
> By matchless Deeds express thy matchless Sire.
> For know, thou art no Son of mortal man,
> Though men esteem thee low of Parentage,
> Thy Father is the eternal King, who rules
> All Heav'n and Earth, Angels and Sons of men. [I.227-37]

Mothers are expected to center hope and concern upon their sons; that's what motherhood is about in a patriarchal society. Yet this son would be more likable if he showed a little more softness toward his mother and less concern for himself. Indeed, he lacks those feminine anima qualities essential to human wholeness. Messiah is all logos and no eros. By will and thought alone without aid of feeling he'll overcome Satan and confirm his divine identity. More real than Adam because his character is more fully detailed, he seems less human because he lacks Adam's human vulnerability. Adam, the first man, loved not wisely but too well, not a mistake Messiah will ever make.

He will defeat Satan by dint of greater strength. This fact impels the fit modern reader to ask if the purpose of Messiah's long struggle with Satan is primarily to demonstrate Messiah's superior strength. In only one way, our feelings whisper, can Messiah defeat Satan and simultaneously establish moral superiority to him: Messiah must banish Satan to irrelevance through the power of love. Since God would have banished Satan to irrelevance before Eden were love his overriding motive, we must look elsewhere for the ruling motives of God and of Messiah, his obedient Son incarnate.

We glimpse the quality of these motives when the Father, exposing Messiah to Satan's temptations, speaks like a tyrant-patriarch repudiating his black sheep son:

> let him tempt and now assay
> His utmost subtlity, because he boasts
> And vaunts of his great cunning to the throng
> Of his Apostasie; he might have learnt
> Less over-weening, since he fail'd with Job,
> Whose constant perseverance overcame
> Whate're his cruel malice could invent.
> He shall now know I can produce a man
> Of female Seed, . . .
> Winning by Conquest what the first man lost
> By fallacy surpriz'd. . . .
> That all the Angels and Aetherial Powers,
> They now, and men hereafter may discern,
> From what consummate vertue I have chose
> This perfect Man, by merit call'd my Son, [I.143-55, 163-66]

These words raise doubts that undermine, at the level of metadrama, the orthodox *summum bonum* deity. Does nothing more profound than deified father-son and brother-brother strife, we wonder in dismay, explain human suffering? How psychologically mature is a deity who needs to prove to angels and men the "consumate vertue" of his favorite, "This perfect Man, by merit call'd my Son?" And what are we to conclude of a redemption scenario that revolves around Satan's surprising Adam by fallacy and Messiah's resisting Satan's solicitations to win by conquest what Adam lost through folly? A God who constructs such a scenario seems, upon meta-dramatic reflection, a moral cretin unable to find better employment for his almighty power than sadistic games that show off His superiority to Satan, a being so nugatory any circumspect omnipotent would toss him straightaway into that cosmic trashcan, the bottomless pit, and seal the lid for eternity.

The Two Hostile Brothers.   There is more to *Paradise Regained*'s myth—its three main characters, the Father, the Son, and Satan and its central action, Messiah's decision—than meets the eye. In *Answer to Job* Jung taught us to excavate the archetypes beneath sacred myth to discover myth's graver import. What archetypes dominate *Paradise Regained*? One bifurcate archetype informs the entire action of the brief epic and shapes the identities of its protagonist and antagonist: the archetype of the two hostile brothers.[88]

Orthodoxy inhibited Milton the apologist from consciously recognizing the archetypal ground of his myth. The critics' orthodoxy or their refusal to look beneath professed intentions exercise a similar obscuring influence. By contrast, William Blake, imagination's son and orthodoxy's sworn foe, saw the archetype working metadramatically in the subtle strokes of Milton the artist. Drawing Jesus and Satan as identical save for expression, Blake gives us a transparent image of the hostile brothers.[89]

Blake's docile Savior carries the generally recognized Job archetype subsumed in the hostile brothers archetype. His hard, loveless Satan carries the opposite half of this dual archetype. Whenever the loyal, patiently suffering son, Job-Christ, appears, Blake intuited, the aspiring brother, Prometheus or Satan, must also become constellated. The unwillingness of Milton the apologist to acknowledge the underlying fraternal relationship that Blake saw so clearly in no way alters the archetypal dynamics. These became ineluctable once Milton designated the Book of Job as the model for *Paradise Regained*, because Job is the Old Testament genesis of the hostile brothers archetype that, according to Jung, defines the Christian era.[90]

Milton's preoccupation with Job is obvious. He refers to the character by name six times (I.147, 369, 425; III.64, 67, 95); he makes frequent references to Job's qualities, most notably patience; and he quotes the Book of Job twice (I.33, 368). All the above has been often noted and thoroughly discussed. What is not stressed sufficiently, besides the two

hostile brothers archetype, is that by the criteria of modern biblical schol-
arship Milton as apologist had a very restricted understanding of the Book
of Job. Indeed he seems to have scarcely read it at all, for, rather than
grappling with its dark issues, he remained content with the facile inter-
pretation offered by St. James. Semitic scholar Marvin H. Pope's com-
ments are apropos:

"You have heard of the patience of Job, and you have seen the purpose of the Lord,
how the Lord is merciful and compassionate." This traditional view of the patient
Job, as it is stated in the New Testament Epistle of James (v 11), is familiar to nearly
everyone. It is, however, scarcely a balanced view, since it ignores the thrust of
more than nine tenths of the book and appears to take account only of the
beginning and end of the story. The vehement protests of the supposedly patient
Job will surprise and shock any who expect to find the traditional patient and pious
sufferer throughout. In spite of sporadic attempts of ancient scribes and translators
to soften the impact of some of the near blasphemous tirades, the fact cannot be
mistaken that Job bluntly calls into question divine justice and providence. The
extreme case of Job's unmerited woes, as with every instance of seemingly sense-
less suffering, raises the ultimate questions of divine justice (theodicy) and the
meaning and purpose of life.[91]

In the Book of Job Satan is a function of Yahweh and Job himself incor-
porates both hostile brothers. But the two brothers make separate ap-
pearances in two distinct parts of Job's story and of the Book of Job. Job the
legendary figure of patience and patron saint of the ethic of obedience
appears in the prose account written by a later writer and tacked on to the
beginning and end of the long poem to render it palatable to the pious.
The Job of the poem is rebellious and refuses to submit to injustice;
indeed, we respect and admire him not for any patience but for Prome-
thean protests against divine injustice. His final words issue not from new
faith in divine justice but from surrender to God's awesome power. There
is, nonetheless, a powerful affirmation of God amidst Job's protests, for
their very intensity shows that he truly loves God. But Job's affirmation
remains incomprehensible to those committed to the archetype of the
patient, faithful and submissive son, the legendary Job.[92]
       Milton the apologist, caught up in the Job-son archetype, lacked
objective understanding of the Book of Job and the biblical Satan. Sim-
ilarly, he remained purblind to the Promethean Job in the Gospel hero
seeing only Job-Christ, the Son of theology. These deficiencies in no way
diminish the achievement of Milton the artist; nonetheless, recognition of
them is essential to understanding that achievement and to grasping the
graver import of *Paradise Regained*.
       Considering that Milton the apologist overlooks nine-tenths of the

Book of Job, his leaving unstated the fraternal dynamism between Job-Christ and Prometheus-Satan should not startle anyone. Repression to a subliminal level of the archetype of the two hostile brothers is one of four chief problems with his conscious treatment of Godhead, the others being disinclination to grant a full role to that divine anima, the Paraclete; insistence upon making the Godhead's most primitive member supreme; and reluctance to raise hard questions about divine justice. Repression of his controlling archetype, the two hostile brothers, shapes the other three problems in *Paradise Regained* and forms the key to the brief epic's stance on Godhead.

Religious repressions notwithstanding, the imagination of Milton as artist works subtly through metadrama to subvert the Christian apologist in him. Imagination's metadramatic epiphanies of the archetypal nature of Godhead are evident in four instances where the hostile brothers flicker through the orthodox personae of Messiah and Satan. We see these flickerings in the course of the temptations where a curious intimacy becomes evident between Messiah and Satan. The intimacy makes it seem as though they had long rivaled each other like Jacob and Esau, those archetypal twins bound by fate from earliest beginnings.

We first glimpse their archetypal bond during the interchange sparked by Satan's offer to fulfil prophesy by setting Messiah on David's throne. Messiah replies that before fulfilling the prophesy the Father wishes to build his character trying him in humble state with "tribulations, injuries, insults, / Contempts, and scorns, and snares, and violence. . . . that he may know / What I can suffer, how obey." He concludes:

> who best
> Can suffer, best can do, best raign; who first
> Well hath obey'd; just tryal e're I merit
> My exaltation without change or end.
> But what concerns it thee when I begin
> My everlasting Kingdom, why art thou
> Sollicitous, what moves thy inquisition?
> Know'st thou not that my rising is thy fall,
> And my promotion thy destruction? [III.194-202]

"Let that come when it comes," the tempter replies, introducing a curiously personal tone to a discussion that has so far been intellectual on each side. He continues almost confidingly as one might with an intimate enemy:

> My error was my error, and my crime
> My crime; whatever for it self condemn'd

> And will alike be punish'd; whether thou
> Raign or raign not: though to that gentle brow
> Willingly I could fly, and hope thy raign,
> From that placid aspect and meek regard,
> Rather then aggravate my evil state,
> Would stand between me and thy Father's ire [III.212-19]

These moving words have an emotional authenticity that sets them apart, causing us to wonder about the intimacy, the almost fraternal understanding, wherefrom they appear to flow. Our wondering consumates the first metadramatic epiphany of the hostile brothers archetype.

The second epiphany is subtle to the point of being subliminal. It commences as Messiah himself briefly sounds an intimate, though by no means warm, note in telling Satan:

> My time I told thee (and that time for thee
> Were better farthest off) is not yet come;
> When that comes think not to find me slack
> On my part aught endeavouring, or to need
> Thy politic maxims, or that cumbersome
> Luggage of war there shewn me, argument
> Of human weakness rather than strength. [III.396-402]

Messiah is decidedly more his Father's son than his brother's brother. His hard stance toward Satan, his lost brother, extends, the parallel unfolding the epiphany, to their Father's other lost children, the lost ten tribes of Israel. To Satan's offer for help in securing their return, Messiah replies that they wrought their own captivity by forsaking the Father. He will not concern himself with their liberty but rather leave them to their deserved fate serving enemies until such time as the Father chooses to restore them. Again Messiah silences Satan, but not the narrator, who remarks: "So spake Israel's true King, and to the Fiend / Made answer meet, that made void all his wiles. / So fares it when with truth falsehood contends." (III.441-43). There will be no reconciliation of hostile brothers, no *coincidentia oppositorum* of the ethics of obedience and rebellion. Job-Christ, the relentlessly dutiful Son, will vindicate the Father's Truth against all questioning.

In the third epiphany of the brothers archetype we foray across the frontier of the subliminal into the territory of the suggestive. To discover the identity of Messiah, the precise sense in which he is a "son of God," has been Satan's aim from the onset where he tells his assembled cohorts: "Who this is we must learn, for man he seems / In all his lineaments, though in his face / The glimpses of his Fathers glory shine." (I.91-93).

After all his wiles have been spent, Satan in desperation prepares to spring
his ultimate trick, setting Messiah on the tower of the temple in Jerusalem.
Though he is angry, barely in control, his purpose remains unswerving.

> Then hear, O Son of David, Virgin-born;
> For Son of God to me is yet in doubt,
> Of the Messiah I have heard foretold
> By all the Prophets; of thy berth at length
> Announc't by Gabriel with the first I knew, . . .
> Thenceforth I thought thee worth my nearer view
> And narrower Scrutiny, that I might learn
> In what degree or meaning thou art call'd
> The Son of God, which bears no single sence;
> The Son of God I also am, or was,
> And if I was, I am; relation stands; . . .
> Good reason then, if I before-hand seek
> To understand my Adversary, who
> And what he is; his wisdom, power, intent,
> By parl, or composition, truce, or league
> To win him, or win from him what I can. [IV.500-4, 514-19, 526-30]

Like Messiah, Satan is, or was, a Son of God, which makes them brothers:
the question, then, being in what degree of paternal favor Messiah stands.
Furthermore, they are enemies and Satan wishes to test the strength and
skill of his adversary, tests of strength and skill being standard ritual acts of
hostile brothers.

The tower is Satan's climatic test. The narrator's comment on Satan
and Messiah's struggle sounds the hostile brothers archetype for the crucial
fourth time in an epic simile that links them to Antaeus and Alcides
(Hercules), two hostile cousins who engage in a ritual test of strength:[93]

> As when Earth's Son Antaeus (to compare
> Small things with greatest) in Irassa strove
> With Joves Alcides, and oft foil'd still rose,
> Receiving from his mother Earth new strength,
> Fresh from his fall, and fiercer grapple joyn'd. [IV.563-67]

The whole series of temptations is a ritual test of strength and skill. It
resembles an initiation into manhood (or mature deity for Messiah) with
Satan playing the initiator, a role to which he has grown accustomed having
performed it with Adam and Job. Like every good initiator, Satan adapts
his tests to the strengths and weaknesses of the initiate, resorting to talk,
composition, truce, or league to win him over if he cannot defeat him.[94]

His methods are ever those of the opportunist and shape changer: like them and Antaeus he has a preternatural ability to recover his strength.

On the tower Satan and Messiah at last face each other in their real identities. Messiah shows himself to be the "good son" and "heir" whose loyalty to the Father proves unwavering ("proof against all temptation as a rock of Adamant," Satan acknowledges). And Satan shows himself to be the "black sheep" whose proper roles are henchman and initiator. His initiations have not been confined to Messiah and his types, Adam and Job. "All men are Sons of God," he declares, ready always to initiate every single one of them into the divine darkness. Satan the initiator is also Satan the trickster, for an initiator is inevitably a trickster and vice versa. Because in *Paradise Regained* Satan's tricks fail, the brief epic might be subtitled "The Trickster Foiled" or better "The Trickster Tricked."

Many have remarked upon the tower scene's Oedipus-Sphinx allusion. From a Jungian point of view, this allusion carries the trickster theme.[95] When he tempts Messiah to either stand or cast himself from the tower and be rescued, Satan, like the Sphinx, presents a riddle or trick. (The Sphinx, it should be remembered, is an anima figure, which establishes Satan's identification with evil anima.) The temptation here is to respond at all, which Messiah does not. Smitten by amazement, Satan himself falls:

> So after many a foil the Tempter proud,
> Renewing fresh assaults, amidst his pride
> Fell whence he stood to see his Victor fall.
> And as that Theban Monster that propos'd
> Her riddle, and him, who solv'd it not, devour'd;
> That once found out and solv'd, for grief and spight
> Cast her self headlong from th' Ismenian steep,
> So strook with dread and anguish fell the Fiend, [IV.569-76]

Satan may fall like the Sphinx, but his temptations lack the mystery of her riddles. They all follow the transparent pattern of offering fraudulent material shortcuts to legitimate spiritual goals. Consequently, they are trials of patience—Job's putative virtue—and their effect is cumulative. One of the great dramatic ironies of *Paradise Regained* is that Messiah, having patience to spare, tries and in the end breaks Satan's patience. Messiah foils, tricks, and initiates Satan, initiation being at bottom a trial of patience. Whereupon Messiah ousts Satan from his old office of divine initiator and trickster.

In this final epiphany Milton the artist deepens the Jungian trickster theme with a Freudian dimension when he identifies Messiah with the man who foiled the Sphinx, Oedipus. Never did a son work harder to avoid Oedipus's sin than Milton's indefatigably obedient Messiah! The subtle identification of Messiah, the future redeemer, with Oedipus, a rebellious rather than an obedient son, constitutes a metadramatic allusion to the need to redeem both of the hostile brothers.

The Hero and the Dragon.   In *Paradise Regained* Milton the artist presents metadramatically a profound interpretation of the hostile brothers archetype as manifest in Christian myth: even as the "good" brother is openly allied with the Father, the "bad" brother is metadramatically allied with the uroboric dragon. Milton presents that alliance by combining in Satan the attributes of both the "bad" brother and the dragon, or "bad" mother. Accordingly, in the brief epic the battle of the hostile brothers becomes a battle of the primal parents as its hero champions reason, the conscious ego, and the Father against a Satan who represents passion, the shadow, and devouring uroboros.

Messiah's relationship to the patriarchal sky god and Satan's link to the primal mother are evident in the afore cited Alcides-Antaeus and Sphinx images. Unlike the physical combat of Alcides and Antaeus, Messiah's struggle with Satan is an inner struggle to realize consciously the Father's identity in himself. Satan tempts Messiah with shortcuts to power that, far from achieving identity, will infect him with inflation. Inflation, the dragon the hero should kill, will then devour Messiah. Uroboros mysticism is Erich Neumann's term for the engulfment Satan intends for Messiah: "Uroboros mysticism rejects not only the world, but also man, the ego and consciousness; it negates the experience of a differentiated world creatively formed and with it the differentiation of consciousness . . . In its nihilism creative nothingness is exchanged for the abysmal deathly womb of the Terrible Mother which sucks back the newborn babe before it has ever attained life and independence."[96] Neumann contrasts engulfing uroboros mysticism with nourishing creative mysticism where "not only the world and man are affirmed but also the ego and the historical process in time, for development implies history both for the individual and the collectivity."[97] Here we have the larger meaning of Messiah's rejection of Satan's temptations to power (Parthia, Rome, etc.): he refuses to hurry, deciding instead to subordinate personal ambition to the historical process in which God sets a time and place for everything. Messiah, like the jaded philosopher who penned Ecclesiastes, accepts history and development as natural and good.[98] Had he rejected historical process to take the satanic shortcut, Messiah would have rejected the creative principle he embodies in his full divinity in *Paradise Lost*, for creative growth works only in time and through history.[99]

While Satan fancies himself the God of this world and promises its glories to Messiah, he in fact loathes the world for he seeks to escape its challenge to creative growth and fears what history will ultimately bring. The typical satanic escape is to short-circuit time and history along with the suffering and labor of individuation in order to "win" immediately. Seen psychologically and philosophically, the satanic ploy is an inflation that embraces too easy a solution to the problem of evil. Those who embrace satanic inflation to avoid creative growth through suffering end up engulfed in the womb of the primeval dragon, the uroboric mother.

Satan is not the dragon, only its creature. Accepting history and creative struggle as man's unavoidable lot, Messiah dispels inflation and prepares to fight the dragon Satan represents. Neumann remarks of the dragon fight:

An essential trait of the dragon-fight situation, and one which also constitutes the content of the rites of initiation and puberty, is the union of the ego with the "higher man," with the godhead or ancestor. It is this union which establishes the "divine nature" of the hero as premise and consequence of the fight with the dragon. The myth of the hero and of rebirth culminates in the mystical encounter between ego and self, which releases a divinely strengthened ego, an ego which has itself become numinous and in this numinous character faces the battle of life in the world.[100]

These words could not better describe the situation and challenges Messiah faces had they been written with *Paradise Regained* in mind. (It's unlikely that Milton's brief epic or the temptation were on Neumann's mind, since the only biblical example he cites is David and Goliath.)[101]

In primitive myths (such as David and Goliath) the dragon fight always includes physical combat. St. George slays a fire-breathing monster whose description remains heavily physical, however symbolic the physical attributes may be. One of Milton the artist's supreme achievements in *Paradise Regained* lies in transforming the simple dragon fight into the psychologically subtle and intellectually sophisticated mental duel that comprises Satan's temptation of Messiah. Through the stroke of genius in making the evil hostile brother carry the archetypal impetus of the uroboric maternal dragon, *Paradise Regained* conveys directly and searches deeply the graver import of the dragon fight.

Paradise Regained and *Hamlet* contain Renaissance literature's signal instances of a dragon fight. Hamlet battles the maternal dragon within himself in a struggle for consciousness symbolized by the external struggle with his unthinking mother (Gertrude). Here the brother is either a true friend (Horatio) or when an enemy (Laertes) he is won over by the hero's nobility. The male who plays the dragon's creature, Claudius, is a usurper who has killed the hero's father to marry his mother.[102]

With Messiah, as with Hamlet, the most dangerous temptations are internal. Satan is not the dragon mother, but her son in the guise of Messiah's hostile brother or shadow. Subtly disguised as befits insidious evil, Satan's archetypal link to the dragon mother is no more acknowledged by Milton the apologist than is the Holy Spirit-Paraclete's link to feminine Sophia, that ultimate transcendence of the dragon's inflation. Satan's link to uroboros constitutes yet another example of Milton the visionary artist's metadramatic epiphanies of the true archetypes of Godhead. As a result of these epiphanies, Messiah and his hostile brother gain a fascination and a numinous power unique in Renaissance literature.

The metadrama of *Paradise Regained* shows the Christian Godhead's uroboric, collective shadow and evil *anima*, contaminating Satan, its personal shadow. All Satan's temptations, seeking to entangle Messiah in inflation, are typical products of scheming, evil anima. Satan's bond with evil anima is evident in the allegorical figure of Sin in *Paradise Lost*. Sin is at once Satan's "daughter," his own evil anima, and a variation of the terrible mother.[103] Sin's inflated, uroboric nature is manifest in her womb breeding that bloated devourer, Death, and affirmed in Satan's promise:

> And bring ye to the place where Thou and Death
> Shall dwell at ease, and up and down unseen
> Wing silently the buxom Air, imbalm'd
> With odours; there ye shall be fed and fill'd
> Immeasurably, all things shall be your prey. [II.840-44]

Together with Satan and Death, Satan's "son" and "shadow seem'd" (II.669), Sin becomes the Unholy Spirit of an evil, uroboric trinity.[104] Temptation, Sin's method of snaring her prey, is a feminine form of aggression akin to seduction. Whereas the negative masculine principle seeks direct conquest through violent physical confrontation, the negative feminine principle never announces its aims, but quietly seduces through the tricks, traps, and subtle suggestions that constitute temptation.

According with the anima concern for nourishment, Satan's initial temptations are culinary: in the first Satan, disguised as an impoverished swain, entreats Messiah to feed both of them by turning stones into bread; in the second he offers a lavish banquet. Later Satan becomes Lady Fortune, another version of the destructive mother, when he tells Messiah:

> Therefore, if at great things thou wouldst arrive,
> Get Riches first, get Wealth, and Treasure heap,

> Not difficult, if thou hearken to me,
> Riches are mine, Fortune is in my hand;
> They whom I favour thrive in wealth amain, [II.427-31]

Given to feminine boasts, Satan is likewise given to sharp, abrupt feminine displays of temper, for example:

> With that
> Both Table and Provision vanish'd quite
> With sound of Harpies wings, and Talons heard;
> Only the importune Tempter still remain'd, [II.401-4]

Harpies are of course female, talons connote long feminine nails, and importuning is a vice associated most commonly with nagging wives and mistresses. Furthermore, to combat the male by trying his patience is a standard nag ploy that Satan uses again and again with Messiah.

Satan's affiliation with the terrible mother may explain his rejecting Belial's suggestion (II.153-71) that they tempt Messiah with feminine beauty. Belial displays not the psychology of a seductress, but that of a pimp. Satan chooses instead to tempt with a banquet laid out in sensuous extravagance. While the servers are beautiful, they do not lure with sex but merely add to the seductive beauty of the banquet. Food, much more than sex, is the way mothers seduce.[105] Food of course is oral; all of Satan's temptations are one way or another oral. Once the temptations offering literal food fail, he tempts Messiah verbally with food for pride. Like the devouring Mother, Satan embodies oral evil.

The oral nature of Satan's evil, the connection of mouths, lies, and food, is not lost on Messiah who tells his tempter: "The other service was thy chosen task, / To be a liar in four hundred mouths; / For lying is thy sustenance, thy food." (I.427-29). And, Messiah notes, Satan uses the culinary craft of subtle mixing to make his lies more palatable:

> that hath been thy craft.
> By mixing somewhat true to vent more lies.
> But what have been thy answers, what but dark,
> Ambiguous and with double sense deluding, [I.432-35]

Hell from whence Satan hails and which embodies his true character is often represented in art as having for an entry a gaping mouth. Hell is, in addition, a physical representation of the devouring Mother.[106] Finally, the arrogance Satan displays in telling Messiah to bow down and worship him carries oral aggression to its ultimate extreme. Since Satan has no reason whatsoever to believe Messiah will comply, the demand reveals Satan's possession by uroboric inflation.

In *Paradise Regained* the feminine appears chiefly in the qualities of Satan's evil, scheming anima, in Satan's role as agent of the dragon, and in his uroboric inflation (its other appearance is the ever-subordinate Mary). By contrast, the strength that enables Messiah to win the dragon fight is a one-sided, male ego-strength that identifies with the Father and represses Adam's anima weaknesses. Herein he is less whole than the Son of *Paradise Lost* who has a positive, if subordinate, anima, and distinct feminine creative qualities. Traditionally, the hero wins the dragon fight with the aid of anima in the shape of the heroine. But *Paradise Regained* lacks a heroine, and hero-ego wins the fight without aid of anima.

We do not know when the brief epic was first composed. It is possible that Milton conceived it during a time of marital troubles when woman and anima seemed to lack the redeeming attributes he gives them in *Paradise Lost*. Whatever the circumstances of *Paradise Regained*'s conception, Milton the artist chose to plumb the battle of the hostile brothers' archetypal roots in the dragon fight. Moreover, the hostile brothers archetype tends to limit the feminine to its draconic aspect, since healing anima might transform the hostile brothers into the friends archetype. Christian dogma, of course, dictated that the brothers be enemies. At the same time, we shall see, it put certain suggestive limits upon their enmity.

Satanic Complicity. Whereas Satan inherits the dragon mother's uroboric inflation, Messiah inherits the tyrant Father's logos-inflation manifest in self-righteousness and scorn. For example, when Satan confides that what wounds him most is envy that fallen man can be restored but never Satan, Messiah replies, sternly we are told though his words carry more scorn than sternness:

> Deservedly thou griev'st, compos'd of lies
> From the beginning, and in lies wilt end;
> Who boast'st release from Hell, and leave to come
> Into the Hav'n of Heav'ns; thou com'st indeed,
> As a poor miserable captive thrall
> Comes to the place wher he before had sat
> Among the Prime in Splendour, now depos'd
> Ejected, emptied, gaz'd, unpitied, shun'd,
> A spectacle of ruin or of scorn
> To all the Host of Heav'n; the happy place
> Imparts to thee no happiness, no joy,
> Rather inflames thy torment, representing
> Lost bliss, to thee no more communicable,
> So never more in Hell then when in Heav'n. [I.407-20]

Messiah (once again more Son of the Father than son of Mary) really rubs it in on black sheep Satan. He is deposed, stared at, despised, shunned, a spectacle of ruin and scorn. For him heaven exists only to inflame his inner hell. Messiah's words are full of contempt and empty of that mercy for the unfortunate preached by the more noble-spirited Gospel hero. Indeed, to the psychologically perceptive, fit modern reader they suggest sadistic relishing of an adversary's failure and torment. They suggest, additionally, that Satan embodies Messiah's own shadow. Satan, he declares, is composed of lies. True, of course, Satan carries the projection beautifully, and projection is what it is, for deception runs in Yahweh's family. Messiah's own hard words belie divine claims to mercy and benevolence.

After forty more lines in which Messiah parades a veritable pageant of Satan's failures, he concludes with the promise that God "sends his Spirit of Truth henceforth to dwell / In pious Hearts, an inward Oracle / To all truth requisite for men to know" (I.462-64). The narrator then observes: "but the subtle Fiend, / Though inly stung with anger and disdain, / Dissembl'd, and this Answer smooth return'd." (I.465-67). The phrase "subtle Fiend" provokes a metadramatic question. What subtlety lies behind Satan's (1) overlooking the inflation, scorn, and sadism latent in Messiah's words, and (2) never drawing attention to the hypocrisy of the Father's prolonging humanity's torments while proclaiming himself a God of perfect love and mercy?

Satan's true subtlety lies not in inflated temptations. To grasp it we must examine his cooperativeness. Oddly, Satan becomes as cooperative as a comrade in a purge trial when it comes time to acknowledge his errors and extol his persecutor:

> Thy Father, who is holy, wise and pure,
> Suffers the Hypocrite or Atheous Priest
> To tread his Sacred Courts, and minister
> About his Altar, handling holy things,
> Praying or vowing, and vouchsaf'd his voice
> To Balaam Reprobate, a Prophet yet
> Inspir'd; disdain not such access to me. [I.486-92]

Does Satan really believe the Father holy, wise, and pure? Were absence of doubt proof of belief, the answer would be yes. Nowhere after his defeat in the war in heaven in *Paradise Lost* does he question the Father's moral character. Nowhere does he question God's harsh judgment upon fallen man. And nowhere in *Paradise Regained* does he challenge the necessity of Messiah's mission.

A telling instance of Satan's failure to exploit opportunities occurs when Messiah mentions the trials and suffering the Father plans to inflict upon him as a test of obedience (III.188-96). The problem here, as the Jung of *Answer to Job* might observe, is that the Father in his omniscience already knows what Messiah can suffer and how well obey. What motive can there be for testing him other than the sadist's desire to see him suffer and obey?

Why should Satan, the adversary, be loathe to raise the crucial problem of Messiah's (and mankind's) suffering? Here Satan's silence displays a subtlety so profound it escapes most readers. Yet those who heed *Answer to Job* can apprehend that subtlety's import along with Milton the artist's subversive intent: the devil's seemingly unaccountable silence on theodicy indicates secret complicity.

Satan never questions divine justice because, as the metadrama's archetypal epiphanies reveal, he too is a part of the Godhead, complementing Messiah the way shadow complements ego. Indeed, proving God unjust is the easiest thing in the world: all Satan need do to overthrow the most elaborate theodicies is point to his own continuing existence and activity. His failure to do so ought to be revelatory to anyone who approaches the matter with open eyes.

Satan's disinclination to question divine justice or put his fraternal rival on the defensive by exposing the spiritual pride underneath Messiah's scorn accounts for the miscarriage of his temptations. Satan understands his shadow role. He must put up a strong enough front to be an effective foil, a foil that will make the divine Son-ego's "victory" appear authentic and his heroism seem credible. He knows also that from beginning to end there is only one real loser—mankind.

Though Christians call the Trinity the highest mystery, a more intriguing mystery is Satan's true relationship to the acknowledged Three. Why should theologians take such pains to precisely define the Trinity's Three Persons (subordinationist Milton spends much of *De Doctrina* on just that), but shrink from defining the perpetrator of man's fall and suffering-laden history whose unhampered criminal activity necessitates the scheme of salvation at the heart of the religion? The various theological definitions of the Father, Son, and Holy Spirit do not fundamentally alter either the plan of salvation or its rationale. Yet without Satan Christian orthodoxy can establish neither a need for salvation nor an explanation of human suffering. Orthodoxy's motive for defining Godhead by rigid Trinitarian dogma becomes apparent when we consider what the dogma accomplishes: it precludes investigation of Satan's archetypal bonds to and his complicity with Godhead's acknowledged Three.[107]

Milton the artist unfolds Godhead's true archetypes in metadramatic epiphanies. Many of the critical problems these epiphanies pose arise because Christian orthodoxy has inhibited psychological investigation of Godhead. Hence, to resolve the critical problems we must surmount orthodox inhibitions. To "read Milton in the context of his time" in order to force Milton the artist into the procrustean bed of Milton the apologist precludes understanding of the artist's metadramatic epiphanies in the same manner orthodoxy precludes understanding of Godhead itself. Those who believe that proving the orthodoxy of Milton's vision of Godhead enhances Milton's achievement are sadly misguided. They devalue a quality far superior to mere conventionality: the integrity he shows in allowing his muse her epiphanies of the archetypes of Godhead. Those epiphanies ought not be denied or explained away but prized as glimpses of truths orthodoxy labors to conceal.

Let us, then, view Satan's temptations as metadramatic epiphanies unfolding the true nature of Godhead. The tempter, we observe, has two strategies open to him. Either he can appeal to pride to foment rebellion as Satan does with Eve or he can undermine faith to induce despair. Patience is ever the remedy to the temptation to rebel. Messiah, except when scorning Satan, is a model of patience. Satan always offers Messiah quick and easy shortcuts to the glory he has been promised. Satan offers glory without suffering, learning, or even preparation in an attempt to inflate Messiah's desires to a level where they overwhelm patience. But he never tries to bring the man in Messiah to despair of his divine Father's goodness or of his will to end human suffering. The omission raises a metadramatic question: "why not?"

As Dostoevsky understood so well, for the deeply religious the temptations to pride and rebellion are superficial: the supreme challenge is to resist despair.[108] Yet the man for whom despair poses no challenge is far from being religious. Just the opposite, he proves impervious to suffering and despair because he is uroborically self-contained. Messiah and the Father he represents, if not altogether impervious to human suffering, certainly love men far less than they love power over men, angels, and all creation. In loving men less than they love power they resemble Satan, which reminds us of the complicity of all three in playing down human suffering. That resemblance to Satan and that reminder of complicity form a metadramatic epiphany of the archetypal bonds uniting Father, Son, and their shadow Satan in one Godhead. They form as well an epiphany of the desperate need for a feminine Fourth to bring love, individuated wholeness, and mature freedom to Godhead and mankind.

Messiah's Identity. The Messiah of *Paradise Regained* lacks those redemptive qualities associated with women and anima, most notably compassion. He is cool, self-contained, and even at times a trifle arrogant. It is hard to say what he has in common with the hero of the Gospels beyond a name. He does, however, have a great deal in common with the Satan of *Paradise Regained*. Satan personifies the dark shadow cast by Messiah's righteous ego. All critics acknowledge that Satan is cold, proud, and scornful without, it seems, perceiving how the same traits appear in more elusive guise in Messiah. Besides the afore cited long speech laced with scorn (I.406-64), we have brief eruptions like: "Thy pompous Delicacies I contemn"; the narrator's observation, "Whom thus our Savoir answer'd with disdain" (IV.170); and Messiah's derision of Greek learning and the scholar: "Deep verst in books and shallow in himself" (IV.327). Most noticeable to our democratic sensibilities is Messiah's seemingly meretricious contempt for the masses:

> And what the people but a herd confus'd,
> A miscellaneous rabble, who extol
> Things vulgar, and well weigh'd scarce worth the praise,
> They praise and they admire they know not what;
> And know not whom, but as one leads the other;
> And what delight to be by such extoll'd,
> To live upon thir tongues and be thir talk,
> Of whom to be disprais'd were no small praise? [III.49-56]

What moves Messiah to elaborate scorn of the rabble to such excess? Jung teaches that whenever we smell fulsome scorn we are onto the scent of a projected shadow. Excessive projection is the sign of an immature nature lacking in self-knowledge and the mark of a fanatic. With his contempt, single-mindedness, and self-containment Messiah shows he lacks the insight, flexibility, and healing compassion of the Gospel hero. Scorn was so alien to the Gospel hero that one is hard-pressed to cite a single instance of it. In place of scorn he gives us denunciations of hypocrisy: these indicate his awareness of the harm done when in scorn we project our shadows on scapegoats.

While Messiah does not authentically represent the hero of Gospel myth, he does accurately reflect the theological construct, Christ as logos, of orthodoxy. It is from the theological construct that Messiah draws his scornful arrogance. Arrogance is inherent to a theology that claims God is all-knowing, all-powerful, and all-good in defiance of our experience of the evil and suffering in his creation.

Milton, then, derives the character identity of Messiah chiefly from orthodox Christian theology. That derivation governs the presentation of Messiah's identity in *Paradise Regained*. However, neither the identity Christian theology gives Messiah nor the way Milton presents it is uncomplicated. The complications center on a perplexing theological question: in what respect is Messiah man and in what respect God? To the extent that he is a man, his identity ought to develop and mature in response to Satan's initiatory temptations. To the extent that he manifests the divinity of Christian theology, his identity ought to manifest static "perfection." Countering docetism, Milton attempts to show us divinity unfolding in a character who is both a man and a theological construct.

The unfolding of Messiah's divine identity, unlike the two hostile brothers archetype, works at the level of conscious artistry. Lest anyone doubt the deliberateness, let them consider the following references to Messiah's identity:

> Who this is we must learn, for man he seems
> In all his lineaments, though in his face
> The glimpses of his Fathers glory shine. [I.91-93]

> For know, thou art no Son of Mortal man,
> Though men esteem thee low of Parentage, [I.234-35]

> her Son tracing the Desert wild,
> Sole but with holiest Meditations fed,
> Into himself descended and at once
> All his great works to come before him set;
> How to begin, how to accomplish best
> His end of being on Earth, and mission high: [II.108-11]

> O Son of David, Virgin-born;
> For Son of God to me is yet in doubt, [IV.500-1]

> that I might learn
> In what degree of meaning thou art call'd
> The Son of God, which bears no single sence; [IV.516-17]

> Therefore to know what more thou art then man,
> Worth naming Son of God by voice from Heav'n,
> Another method I must now begin. [IV.538-40]

> Hail Son of the most High, heir of both worlds,
> Queller of Satan, [IV.633-34]

The importance of the identity motif in *Paradise Regained* has not gone unnoted by scholarly critics. One of the most thorough of them, Barbara Lewalski, comments: "The 'identity motif' is not a minor theme, as sometimes suggested, but is of the very substance of dramatic action, for only if Christ comes to understand himself and his work perfectly can he withstand the temptations of Satan, all of which present extremely clever parodies, falsifications, or inadequate statements of that self and that work."[109] Identity is clearly an important motif, but what is its graver import? Viewing *Paradise Regained* metadramatically and in light of Jung's *Answer to Job* can give us the insight we need to apprehend that graver import: while Messiah establishes his divine identity, as interpreted by orthodox Christianity, in the temptation, full understanding of human identity must wait upon the crucifixion.

Milton the apologist fashions Messiah's human identity around the legendary Job's putative patience and obedience. However, patience in Messiah's case is a empty virtue, for while Satan torments Job unto fathomless anguish he merely aggravates Messiah, who responds not with faith so much as with scorn. Behind Milton's reluctance to confront the anguish, protest, and despair of Job and Christ may lie fear of confronting what activates their Promethean side: the tragic nature of human existence. Indeed, Milton gives the temptation a happy ending that not only ignores human tragedy but makes right all of Messiah's rather minor physical sufferings at the hand of Satan:

> strait a fiery Globe
> Of Angels onfull sail of wing flew nigh,
> Who on their plumy Vans receiv'd him soft
> From his uneasie station, and upbore
> As on a floating couch through the blithe Air,
> Then in a flowry valley set him down
> On green bank, and set before him spred
> A table of Celestial Food, Divine,
> Ambrosial, Fruits fetcht from the tree of life,
> And from the fount of life Ambroisial drink,
> That soon refresh'd him wearied, [IV.581-91]

Angelic choirs sing anthems to his victory as he eats, then escort him on the way to his mother's house. It's hard to imagine this same pampered "Son of God" enduring crucifixion—hard for us and evidently impossible for Milton.

Indeed, the pampering, viewed in light of Jung, seems an unconscious attempt to repudiate the crucifixion. At the level of metadrama this attempt causes us to wonder "why was the crucifixion necessary?" Jung's answer is that the crucifixion, far from being alien to the spirit of Christianity, as Blake and possibly Milton thought, is essential to the full manifestation of the Christian Godhead. For only by feeling human anguish, protest, and despair, thereby realizing tragic consciousness, can God attain the Promethean compassion he needs to manifest the Paraclete. The whole point of kenosis is tragic consciousness culminating in that supreme anagnorisis and revelation "Eloi, Eloi, lama, sabachthani?"[110] Like all committed to a dogma that makes Yahweh, the Father, the *Summum Bonum*, Milton the apologist stopped short of both tragic consciousness and understanding of the awesome moral choice the incarnation represents.

Milton the apologist set out to show us the Son of God as his divine identity unfolds. Yet once more orthodoxy worked at cross purposes with artistic integrity. Far from what the narrator intended, although exactly what Milton the artist's unconscious compensating for conscious imbalances intended, the result was a metadramatic epiphany of the theological God-man's desperate need to understand what it means to be a suffering human being. Ironically, *Paradise Regained* shows more pointedly than any great literary work, except The Book of Job and *King Lear,* the divinity's need for that knowledge of humanity only crucifixion could give. *King Lear* unfolds the crucifixion's full archetypal meaning. The relationship of Milton's brief epic to Shakespeare's tragedy resembles that of John the Baptist's role to Jesus's: it prepares the way.

There is no proof that Milton consciously compared *Paradise Regained* with *King Lear.* Nevertheless, Milton undoubtedly knew *King Lear,* and the artist's unconscious does not need permission of his conscious will to shape a work of art. Indeed, whenever powerful archetypes are constellated, it spurns conscious permission. Both *King Lear* and *Paradise Regained* rely heavily on the Book of Job, and the Job archetype shapes the protagonist's identity in each. Both set forth the Promethean archetype. In *Paradise Regained* the negative side of the archetype appears in a Satan who, like Prometheus, is an overreacher and whose temptations are all to overreach. In *King Lear* a beneficial Prometheus inspires Lear's final defiance.

Both works have storm scenes; although the protagonist's attitudes toward their storms are as far apart as their stances toward human suffering. With no storm of anger in himself, Messiah never moves beyond Job's patience to experience his anguish let alone attain Promethean protest. And the archetype Cordelia carries is beyond the grasp of either Messiah or anyone fettered by Christian orthodoxy. Ignorant of human suffering, Messiah understands neither the wrong Yahweh committed against Job nor the necessity of Promethean protest. Satan too, silent on Yahweh's injustices, remains stuck in inflated overreaching, his challenge devoid of Promethean spirit.

Because Satan fails to mount a true Promethean challenge to the Father, he presents no viable alternatives. Hence, Messiah cannot exercise true decisive identity, which requires a choice between real alternatives, one of which consciously advances individuation. Messiah merely unveils a fixed identity to an almost admiring Satan. Satan's temptations try Messiah's strength, patience, and intellectual agility, but, not challenging divine justice, they offer no genuine alternatives, no chance to learn or change, and no opportunity to deepen character through decisive identity.[111]

Those who claim Messiah really changes sometimes assert that the storm-tower temptation sequence, which concludes Satan's tests of Messiah's identity, foreshadows Christ's passion and death, making their literary treatment unnecessary.[112] Such appears to be Milton the apologist's intent. But the ploy falls short, proving to be a formality without emotional substance, since Messiah never really suffers, never experiences what it means to be man. "Mee worse than wet thou findest not," he declares, its sheer oppositeness reminding us of Lear's wrenchingly human response to the storm.

Adam, the Old Testament type to Messiah's antitype, does learn and change, but his great decision antecedes rather than flows from character. Indeed, knowledge of sin is the inception of Adam's character growth. Messiah, by contrast, displays no character growth; in him we see a mere unfolding of divinity. Not once does Messiah make a mistake and initiate the radical leap in consciousness that comes with facing one's errors and, humbled, learning to do things better. Perfection has its handicaps.

CONCLUSION

"We begin to live," Yeats wrote, "when we have conceived of life as a tragedy."[113] To conceive of life as a tragedy is also the beginning of that conscious guidance of individuation called decisive identity. Decisive identity remains an empty ideal for those committed to the doctrine of *summum bonum:* they can no more fully realize decisive identity than their deity, with his inflated claim of moral perfection, can realize credibility. In itself this is tragic, for while moral perfection is an inflated delusion, decisive identity is supremely worth the struggle.

Decisive identity's opposite is inflation. Inflation has many guises, but its apotheosis is the doctrine of *summum bonum* with its claim of metaphysical knowledge of the Deity's perfect moral character. The truth of *summum bonum*, not being empirically verifiable, must be a revelation. But where is it revealed? Certainly not in that repository of Christian myth, Scripture, where we find only the process Godhead Jung describes, a Godhead reflecting the archetype of the self. The actual, though unacknowledged, source is Platonic philosophy with its controlling idea of Eternal Being derived from the uroboros archetype.

The Platonist's assumption that essentialist Truths founded upon Being itself are something man can possess becomes with a little inflation the orthodox theologian's presumption that not only do we possess Truths founded upon Being, these Truths are sacred, and believing them is requisite to salvation. Here begins the zealot's path to that ultimate moral inflation and spiritual tragedy of persecuting all who decline to accept Sacred Truths.

Thus, those who declare God the *Summum Bonum* make the criteria of moral judgment not the identity men create but the "Truths" they profess to believe. Orthodox Christianity's purported ethical aims affirm decisive identity, but its actual methods rely on compulsory belief in Sacred Truths of Eternal Being. Christianity's aims spring from Godhead or the archetype of the self; it fails to achieve its aims because its methods stem from the archetype that is Godhead's negation—the devouring uroboros.

Milton's Messiah, like the theology that shapes his character, lacks the tragic insight necessary to advance individuation through decisive identity. What Messiah demonstrates, in another of Milton the artist's epiphanies, is that his identity, like that of the Son-logos of theology, rests not upon the values of mythic Godhead and its incarnation, the Gospel Jesus, but upon orthodox "Truths." The epiphany is couched in the poem's strongest assertion of theological supremacy, Messiah's rejection of Satan's offer of the wisdom of Greek philosophy:

> Think not but that I know these things, or think
> I know them not; not therefore I am short
> Of knowing what I ought: he who receives
> Light from above, from the fountain of light,
> No other doctrine needs, though granted true;
> But these are false, or little else but dreams,
> Conjectures, fancies, built on nothing firm.
> The first and wisest of them all profess'd
> To know this only, that he nothing knew;
> The next to fabling fell and smooth conceits,
> A third sort doubted all things, though plain sence;
> Others in vertue plac'd felicity,
> But vertue joyn'd with riches and long life,
> In corporal pleasure he, and careless ease,
> The Stoic last in Philosophic pride,
> By him call'd vertue; and his vertuous man,
> Wise, perfect in himself, and all possessing
> Equal to God, oft shames not to prefer,
> As fearing God nor man, contemning all
> Wealth, pleasure, pain, or torment, death and life,
> Which when he lists, he leaves, or boasts he can,

For all his tedious talk is but vain boast,
Or subtle shifts conviction to evade.
Alas what can they teach and not mislead;
Ignorant of themselves, of God much more,
And how the world began, and how man fell
Degraded by himself, on grace depending?
Much of the Soul they talk, but all awrie,
And in themselves seek vertue, and to themselves
All glory arrogate, to God give none, [IV.286-315]

Ironically, far more "Philosophic pride" has gone into Messiah than has the humility of the Gospel hero. From the philosophic quester for certainty defending his Truth, Messiah derives the inflation evident in his scornful tone. Psychologically speaking, the inflation and scorn signify a hidden need to compensate doubt. Jesus may have been refreshingly free of inflation and scorn. Not free because he possessed Truth, but because he had matured beyond the ego need to possess Truth. Those who, through suffering, gain the living truth of decisive identity show a humility that makes inflated claims for certain, essentialist Truths ring hollow. There were inflated men in the time of the Gospel hero too. He had a name for them—hypocrites. His warnings against hypocrisy proved prophetic, for hypocrisy made possible all the evils that would be done by those claiming to possess his Truth.

To speak true is to speak free of inflation and its identifying vice, hypocrisy. Messiah's scornful denunciation of the ancient philosophers is a hypocritical projection since he and the theology he espouses are to a large extent their creature. That very projection unfolds a metadramatic epiphany of the orthodox Son's true nature. The apologist in Milton trumpets orthodox delusions. The artist in Milton reveals those delusions for what they are in subtle epiphanies. It remains for us to choose between the delusions and the epiphanies. Substituting melodramatic vision for tragic vision, Milton as Christian apologist can never give Adam, Eve, Satan, and Messiah decisive identity no matter how hard he tries. Yet Milton as artist strives to present alternatives that can help us develop the decisive identity these characters lack. Where the apologist fails, the artist succeeds.

A NOTE ON
THE HOLY SPIRIT AND MILTON'S MUSE

Although in *De Doctrina* Milton reduced the Holy Spirit to a supernumer-
ary appendix to his monotheistic God, he continued to regard it as the
source of his inspiration. Indeed, he believed that the Holy Spirit inspired
him just as It inspired the writers of scripture. He observes in *De Doctrina*:
"I do not know why God's providence should have committed the contents
of the New Testament to such wayward and uncertain guardians, unless it
was so that this very fact might convince us that the Spirit which is given to
us is a more certain guide than scripture, and that we ought to follow
it."[114] Furthermore, Milton's wife, Masson reports, confirmed that the
Holy Spirit inspired his writing when she declared he "stole from nobody
but the muse that inspired him, and that was God's Holy Spirit."[115]

    Notwithstanding, the view that Milton's muse and the Holy Spirit are
one and the same has not received universal acceptance. William B.
Hunter, for example, has challenged it, contending that Urania cannot be
the Holy Spirit because Milton declares in *De Doctrina* that the Holy Spirit
is never to be invoked.[116] Hunter's view depends upon an assumption that
depth psychology rejects: conscious intentions always determine literary
meaning even in works that are profoundly archetypal.[117]

    Jung maintains that the very nature of an archetype (and the Holy
Spirit is surely this) is to take possession of the visionary artist and set aside
his conscious intentions. Jung observes: "It is a primordial experience
which surpasses man's understanding and to which in his weakness he may
easily succumb. The very enormity of the experience gives it its value and
its shattering impact . . . But the primordial experiences rend from top to
bottom the curtain upon which is painted the picture of an ordered world,
and allow a glimpse into the unfathomable abyss of the unborn and of
things yet to be."[118] In discussing the "feminine-maternal wisdom" of the
unconscious Jung's follower Erich Neumann coincidentally offers a com-
pelling description of Milton's muse: "in the generating and nourishing,
protective and transformative, feminine power of the unconscious, a
wisdom is at work that is infinitely superior to the wisdom of man's waking
consciousness, and that, as source of vision and symbol, of ritual and law,
poetry and vision, intervenes, summoned or unsummoned, to save man
and give direction to his life."[119]

    Hunter assumes, additionally, that *De Doctrina*, written before the
completed *Paradise Lost*, provides a dependable guide to Milton's inten-
tions at the time he was writing the epic. Even if we agree that for Milton
the Holy Spirit cannot be invoked (it is invoked in the Catholic tradition
and Milton does allow for men to call upon God to send his Holy Spirit),

the problem remains of identifying what it could be, other than the Holy Spirit, that Milton means in "Urania, if by that name rightly thou art call'd."

Hunter contends that Urania, the muse, represents Uranian Aphrodite, which, according to Plotinus, is "no other than Mind itself." The Neoplatonic Trinity of One-Mind-Soul may parallel the Christian Father-Son-Spirit. If so, Uranian Aphrodite is equivalent to Neoplatonic Mind, which forms a counterpart to the Son as logos. Wisdom, her sister, is also identified with Christ by St. Paul (1 Cor. 1:24). The two sisters, Urania and Wisdom, Hunter concluded, may be names for two of the Son's manifestations. He cites Tertullian as his source for the tradition that Word and Spirit, or Wisdom and Urania, represent the Son.

The aggregation of "ifs" and "mays" that comprise Hunter's argument lacks compelling logic. Consequently, Hunter is left with a leap not of faith so much as opinion wherein he concludes that in praying to the Spirit Milton prays for the help of the Father manifest in the Son which he addresses variously as Holy Light, as Spirit, and as Urania.

Hunter's argument has serious flaws beyond its logic. He assumes that "Descend from Heav'n Urania," means that Milton is invoking and praying to Urania. Since the Holy Spirit, represented as a dove, traditionally does descend, may not Milton be calling upon God to let His Spirit descend upon him? Poetry cannot spell out everything and remain poetry; it has to leave some things unsaid. Here what may remain unsaid is that the poet calls upon God to send his Spirit. This would not be the same as invoking the Holy Spirit directly, if Milton indeed still felt theological inhibitions about that. In any event Milton's views about invoking the Holy Spirit would seem to be more descriptive of proper Christian practice than proscriptive. Protestants do not ordinarily pray to the Holy Spirit, but they do pray to God for guidance from his Holy Spirit, which is probably what Milton is doing.

Another difficulty with Hunter's position lies in the gender of Urania and Wisdom. Milton repeatedly refers to them as feminine, which would be inappropriate if he saw them as manifestating the Son, not the Holy Spirit. Feminine gender might not, however, be inappropriate with the Godhead's "neuter" Person. Moreover, although the Holy Spirit is officially neuter, in Milton's and Protestant civilization's unconscious, the Holy Spirit would be feminine to compensate the one-sided masculinity of the other members of the Godhead. That Milton unconsciously saw the Holy Spirit as feminine is indicated in Book II of *Paradise Lost* where he presents Satan, Death, and Sin as an evil trinity parodying Father, Son, and Holy Spirit: here Sin is not just unmistakably feminine, she embodies devouring uroboros, Sophia's or Wisdom's feminine archetypal opposite.

Recently, Hunter, collaborating with Stevie Davies, has attempted to deal with some of the above difficulties and acknowledged in part both the femininity of the Holy Spirit and the Spirit's role as Milton's muse. Hunter and Davies note the association of Urania and Milton's muse with the Old Testament wisdom figure of Sophia (Hokmah) and point out that pneuma and Sophia (or Ruah and Hokmah) are linked. These they associate with the Holy Spirit. The muse addressed in Book VII and contemplated in the exordium to Book VII, they contend, is a "poetic refraction of the Holy Spirit"; but, they add, in the muse sophia is coupled with the traditionally male logos.

Hunter and Davies sound almost Jungian in observing of Milton's inspiration: "he offers no prayer for heavenly support but rather observes of Urania that he experiences "Her nightly visitation *unimplored*" (line 22, emphasis added). The state of mind he describes is tantamount to that of daemonic possession." [120] However, although they venture close to identifying Milton's daemon with the Holy Spirit, they shrink from making the identification unequivocal: "in Book VII the aspect of the feminine archetype detached and presented is that of sanctuary, lucid guide, and mediatrix, a sared [sic] version of Calliope in her motherhood of Orpheus (37-38), evoking the role of the Holy Spirit as Paraclete, 'the Comforter which is the Holy Ghost'" (John 14:26).[121] Hunter and Davies are not Jungians, and their basic theological categories and outlook are Trinitarian, not Quaternian. Hence, their view of God remains centered on the Father, or primal parent archetype. While, in apparent deference to feminism, they ambiguously refer to a "bisexuality" in the Deity, they never come to grips with God's anima. Their ignoring the divine anima precludes full understanding of the archetypal basis of the Holy Spirit and Milton's muse.

4

Yahweh Agonistes

Learn as you go seems to be the rule for creative endeavors. It is arguable whether literary criticism can be genuinely creative; the criticism in this chapter at least bears the marks of learning in process. My original conception assumed that *Samson Agonistes*, first published in 1671, was written subsequent to the publication of *Paradise Lost* in 1667. I was aware of the minority scholarly opinion, most forcefully enunciated by Shawcross, Gilbert, and Parker, that it was conceived and first composed much earlier, probably in the mid-1640s, later revised, and finally published much later still.[1] Although their arguments cast the widely accepted chronology into doubt, they did not induce me to embrace their early composition theory. However, as I more carefully scrutinized *Samson Agonistes*, an early composition became more credible and a later less, until I finally became persuaded an early composition date was not just correct but crucial to understanding the archetypes in the poem.

My arguments for early composition blend psychological and aesthetic considerations. No single argument seems decisive in itself, but when we conjoin them and draw in the evidence of Shawcross, Gilbert, and Parker, a compelling case emerges for early composition. Before proffering the arguments and evidence, I shall review briefly what we know about the chronology of Milton's most important poems.

We know that Milton began *Paradise Lost* around 1640, as the Trinity Manuscript shows, and worked on it for a while. If Edward Phillips's biography may be relied on, Milton first drafted Satan's address to the sun in Book IV around 1642. How long he continued the work is uncertain. He probably returned to it several times after 1652 when he became totally blind, putting in substantial effort in 1655-1658 and laboring assiduously from 1660 to 1665. Publication came in 1667, its delay an apparent repercussion of the plague and the great fire. We also know that Milton wrote his masque *Comus* in 1634 and his elegy *Lycidas* in 1637. Of the composition dates of *Samson Agonistes* and *Paradise Regained* we know only that they must have been after 1645 and before 1671.[2]

My first argument for dating *Samson Agonistes* after *Comus* and *Lycidas* but before *Paradise Lost* is that it stands between these early works and the epic in relative complexity and ambition. *Comus* and *Lycidas* are simpler in their ideas and less formidable in their aesthetic objectives than *Paradise Lost;* at the same time they are more harmonious and lack major intellectual shortcomings. Though *Paradise Lost* asserts eternal providence, it fails to provide a sound or convincing theodicy, fails to fulfil its author's theological intent. But other remarkable literary monuments—*Moby Dick, The Brothers Karamazov,* and *Remembrance of Things Past* come to mind—fall short of their author's intellectual ambitions yet, like *Paradise Lost,* achieve a magnificence less aspiring works cannot approach. The movement from *Comus* and *Lycidas* to *Paradise Lost* is a movement from works of comparatively simple ideas and limited ambition to a work of vast conceptions and awesome challenges. It's almost as if Shakespeare wrote *A Midsummer Night's Dream* and jumped into *King Lear* having done nothing between. Still, in respect to ascending complexity and ambition two major works neatly bridge Milton's gap: *Samson Agonistes* and *Paradise Regained.* Knowing as we do that Milton was a fastidious planner, it seems plausible that he would save the completion of his greatest challenge until last and use his other endeavors in preparation.

My second argument for an early dating is that *Samson Agonistes* exhibits the marks of a relatively youthful writer. Samson's opening speech (1-114) is rich in *energia*, the quality Aristotle said was necessary to move drama forward. The speech, Samson, and the drama itself show an superabundance of *energia* that is difficult to account for if we assume the writer an aging valetudinarian. *Samson Agonistes*'s allusions to the most famous drama written in the December of life, *Oedipus at Colonus,* notwithstanding, it lacks the matured emotions and settled resolution of Sophocles' play, which in turn lacks *energia. Samson Agonistes* has too much raw passion, too little disillusionment and its bitterness wants the seasoned qualities of defeated old age. Moreover, its echoes of Elizabethan drama bespeak a youthful Milton with fresh memories of the stage and of reading the great Elizabethans. Finally, we should recall Milton's remark in *Of Education* (1644): the best poetry, he observed, is "simple, sensuous and passionate." Such a preference is typical of a younger man; and it fits the Elizabethans, *Comus, Lycidas,* and *Samson Agonistes* more than it does *Paradise Regained* or *Paradise Lost.*

But what of the notion so popular with biographical critics that the declining Milton of the Restoration represented his own blindness, disillusionment, and defeat in Samson's plight?[3] Appealing though this analogy of Milton to Samson may seem, the objections to it are serious. Most prominent among them is an obvious historical discrepancy: England failed Milton while Samson failed Israel. Recognizing his flaw, Samson declares:

> tell me Friends
> Am I not sung and proverb'd for a Fool
> In every street, do they not say, how well
> Are come upon him his deserts? yet why?
> Immeasurable strength they might behold
> In me, of wisdom nothing more than mean. [202-7]

The unlikelihood of Milton proclaiming his wisdom to be "nothing more than mean" suggests another miscarriage of the analogy: Samson's character is nothing like Milton's since their weaknesses and strengths are totally different. A third miscarriage resides in their fates: while the Philistines are ever watchful of Samson and in the end demand that he exhibit his strength to them, during the years when Milton supposedly wrote *Samson Agonistes* the Restoration monarchy utterly ignored him.[4]

Ignored, Milton had neither hope, nor opportunity, nor, it seems, desire for revenge. A fourth miscarriage lies in the extent of the analogy. Blindness in *Samson Agonistes* is not just a physical defect afflicting Samson; it is also a ubiquitous mental and spiritual malady afflicting the Chorus, Manoa, Dalila, and Harapha no less than Samson. If we assume that in *Samson Agonistes* Milton portrays his own physical blindness, must we not also assume the analogy extends to mental and spiritual blindness as well?

In addition to the above disparaties, the afflictions of the biblical hero and of the poet had totally different causes. Samson suffered blinding because of weakness and folly; Milton sacrificed his sight laboring for what he believed to be England's best interests and God's will.[5] Furthermore, their afflictions were of very different duration. By the late 1660s Milton, blind more than fifteen years, was surely resigned to his dark fate. Wise, faithful resignation lends mature dignity and grace to his personal aside in *Paradise Lost*:

> Thus with the year
> Seasons return, but not to me returns
> Day, or the sweet approach of Ev'n or Morn,
> Or sight of vernal bloom, or Summers Rose
> Or flocks, or heards, or human face divine;
> But cloud instead, and ever-during dark
> Surrounds me, from the chearful wayes of men
> Cut off, and for the Book of knowledge fair
> Presented with a Universal blanc,
> Of Natures works to me expung'd and ras'd
> And wisdom at one entrance quite shut out

> So much rather thou Celestial light
> Shine inward, and the mind through all her powers
> Irradiate, there plant eyes, that I may see and tell
> Of all things invisible to mortal sight. [III.40-55]

Samson's blindness, by contrast, is a fresh torment that he regards not with resignation but with the rough passions of anguish, protest and despair:

> O dark, dark, dark, amid the blaze of noon,
> Irrecoverably dark, total Eclipse
> Without all hope of day!
> O first created Beam, and thou great Word,
> Let there be light, and light there was over all;
> Why am I thus bereav'd thy prime decree?
> The Sun to me is dark
> And silent as the Moon,
> When she deserts the night
> Hid in her vacant interlunar cave.
> Since light so necessary is to life
> And almost life itself, . . .
> To live a life half dead, a living death,
> And buried; but O yet more miserable!
> My self, my Sepulcher, a moving Grave,
> Buried, yet not exempt
> By privilege of death and burial
> From the worst of other evils, pains and wrongs,
> But made hereby obnoxious more
> To all the miseries of life,
> Life in captivity
> Among inhuman foes. [80-109]

Samson's terrible lamentation, despondent and bitter without parallel in any reference to blindness in *Paradise Lost*, is more plausibly seen as revealing the writer's fear or initial horror than as bewailing a state to which he had long ago grown accustomed.

Samson's is the plaint of a man still young enough to enjoy ardently, indeed to desire in excess, life's physical pleasures. Similarly, his violent reactions to Dalila befit a younger man upon whose restive spirit desire, betrayal, and jealousy readily prey. The treatment of Dalila presents marriage at its worst, all lust and no mutual understanding. The treatment of Eve is quite different, not stressing the disunity of the married pair so much as feminine insubordination. Is it not more probable that the caustic, thin, and one-sided portrayal of Dalila was written amidst the disasters of the poet's marriage to Mary Powell (1642-1652) than written recalling those traumas after twenty years and happier marital experiences, after the powerful sonnet "Mee thought I saw my late espous'd saint" and after creating an Eve who, despite her frailties, embodies much of what endears in her sex?[6]

Divergent attitudes toward women give me my third argument for dating *Samson Agonistes* well before *Paradise Lost*. *Samson Agonistes*, like *Paradise Regained*, is a one-sidedly masculine work that shows an urgent need for the woman's part, anima, to bring balance and wholeness. In these works the feminine is either hopelessly deficient, as in Dalila, or wholly subservient to patriarchy, as in Messiah's mother, or diabolical, as in Satan's evil anima. Not until Milton's greatest and last work does the artist in him liberate the feminine by introducing the positive anima with Eve and, essential to the life of his design, his Muse. Since it is psychologically improbable for Milton to regress in his last years from the comparatively balanced and mature attitude toward women and the feminine he achieves in *Paradise Lost*, the absence of this attitude in *Samson Agonistes* and *Paradise Regained* is a powerful argument for assigning these poems earlier dates of initial composition.

A related argument for assuming Dalila the early and Eve the late creation, and my fourth argument for dating *Samson Agonistes* earlier than the epic, is that the portrayal of Eve and her bond with her husband shows more subtle and mature artistry. This comparison of Dalila and Eve holds in respect to the other major portrayals in *Samson Agonistes* and *Paradise Lost*. Similarly, to compare the temptations in Eden and in *Paradise Regained* with those of Manoa, Dalila, and Harapha is to show Milton mastering the dramatist's art of orchestrating and detailing complex scenes. Another sign of mature artistry is inwardness of character, that dimension which distinguishes a Falstaff or a Hamlet from a Gobbo or a Hieronimo. We see real inwardness for the first time in Messiah, and Milton develops it further in Adam, Eve, and the Satan of *Paradise Lost*.

If Messiah, Adam, Eve, and Satan are more nuanced and dimensional than Samson, Dalila, Harapha, and Manoa, they are at the same time more archetypal. But then, in *Paradise Regained* the background workings of archetypes are deeper and more pervasive than in *Samson Agonistes*. *Paradise Lost* advances the trend to show more mature archetypal influence than *Paradise Regained*. Maturity of archetypal influence comprises the last and, for this study, the most compelling argument for assigning an early composition date to *Samson Agonistes*. With Milton, as with Shakespeare, archetypal meanings gained depth and pervasiveness as the artist in him ripened. In our own time Yeats, Joyce, and Thomas Mann exhibit a similar pattern.

BLIND YAHWEH

The validity of my application of archetypal theories to Milton's major poems does not, however, hinge upon dating. Nonetheless, the dating can lend weight to my application and vice versa. My application holds that Milton's major poems contain epiphanies that show the Christian Godhead imaging an individuation process that is four-part in structure and three-fold in staging. The primitive Yahweh archetype that Samson personifies dominates *Samson Agonistes*. The Son-ego dominates *Paradise Regained*; his hostile brother Satan-shadow at times steals the show in *Paradise Lost* only to be quietly superseded by the poet's anima-muse. The archetypes of Godhead, Jung maintains, unfold historically in a definite pattern of individuation: first the rudimentary consciousness of Yahweh emerges, then opposites are fully constellated with Job-Christ and Prometheus-Satan, and finally the Holy Spirit-anima works to make Godhead whole. And that is how they unfold in the chronology of Milton's major poems if Shawcross, Gilbert, and Parker's dating is correct.

In saying that Samson personifies the Yahweh archetype I mean that in certain crucial respects he resembles the Yahweh Jung presented in *Answer to Job*.[7] I do not of course mean that he resembles the Old Testament patriarchal deity as seen through the rose-tinted glasses of orthodoxy or that he mirrors the conceptions of the Father Milton presents in *De Doctrina* and *Paradise Lost*. Jung's archetypal Yahweh includes psychological realities of Godhead and self that orthodox theology excludes with its rigid dogmas. Like Jung's Yahweh, Samson embodies blind power, understands himself poorly, knows no moderation in his emotions, and suffers from his lack of moderation. Nonetheless, he realizes that he is eaten up with passion and caught in maelstroms of affect. Although this realization proves painful, Samson, like Yahweh, continues to strive for self-understanding. Both are deeply flawed, and Samson compounds Yahweh's flaws with self-pity.

Another analogue is Lear who, more conclusively than Samson, manifests the numinous qualities of Yahweh. Partly because of the blinders orthodoxy imposes, partly because he conceived *Samson Agonistes* before the artist in him had ripened, Milton failed to develop his Yahweh figure with the insight we find in Shakespeare. Nevertheless, the figure is present, and it constitutes Milton's most direct and honest exploration of the Yahweh archetype.

Samson's blindness was a prime reason why Milton lighted upon him as a Yahweh figure. Yahweh, Jung maintains, is above all blind—not evil, but lacking the inward vision of consciousness. Milton the artist intuited Yahweh's mental blindness, even though orthodoxy censored its recognition. Since that blindness had to be dealt with indirectly, Samson, a character that neither Milton nor anyone else in the seventeenth century would consciously identify with Yahweh, provided a perfect vehicle. Mental blindness also characterizes the Yahweh figures in *King Lear* where Lear and Gloucester must recognize that they have been blind to others, Gloucester through literal blinding like Samson, before they can see inwardly. Given that the paramount exemplars of Greek and Elizabethan tragedy, *Oedipus Rex* and *King Lear*, made mental blindness and physical blinding salient themes, given the tragic blindness of Yahweh in his dealings with men and the blind power of the Father-Yahweh archetype in Milton's psyche, he hardly needed the spur of personal blindness to choose the Samson story for his attempt at a biblical tragedy.

Blindness pervades *Samson Agonistes*. Samson's blindness is mirrored and amplified in the other major characters as well as in the Chorus which in Greek drama often presents a more insightful outlook: "For inward light alas / Puts forth no visual beam" (163-64), it declares, characteristically undervaluing the inward vision of reflection. Manoa is hardly more perspicacious than the Chorus and Dalila is much less. Irene Samuel has observed that Dalila is the most harebrained woman to have gotten herself involved in a major tragedy.[8] Dalila carries the projection of Samson's trifling anima; the shallowness she exhibits in her blind sensuality made the projection appropriate and so reinforced his attraction to her. Moreover, his own shallowness of mind fostered a mental blindness that led directly to his physical blinding.

Samson's sole insight upon himself is recognition of his shallowness:

> Immeasurable strength they might behold
> In me, of wisdom nothing more than mean;
> This with the other should, at least, have paird,
> These two proportiond ill drove me transverse. [206-9]

Ironically, there's more than a touch of superficiality in his recognition. Wisdom is something one earns: never is it merely given the way physical strength and beauty are given. Samson's mental blindness prevents him from seeing what wisdom is let alone attaining it.

Milton both accentuates and interprets Samson's mental blindness by depriving him of that source of divine wisdom, the Holy Spirit. In the Biblical account, whenever Samson does something requiring power the stock phrase is, "and the Spirit of the Lord came upon him." Milton, in a notable epiphany, conspicuously omits references to "the Spirit of the Lord" and never mentions the Spirit coming to Samson's mother. While the inspired mother is ignored, we are given Manoa, the bumbling father.

Cumulatively, these changes downplay the traditional identification of Samson as a type of Christ, born of the Spirit coming to Mary, and identify Samson instead with the mentally blind Yahweh.

Like Lear in his Yahweh stage, Samson's attempts to probe deeper questions always abort into shallow self-commiseration:

> the next I took to Wife
> (O that I never had! fond wish too late)
> Was in the vale of Sorec, Dalila,
> That specious Monster, my accomplisht snare.
> . . . of what I now suffer
> She was not the prime cause, but I myself,
> Who vanquisht with a peal of words (O weakness!)
> Gave up my fort of silence to a Woman. [227-36]

Dalila, we later learn, was far from an accomplisht snare, her victory due to mere pertinacity. Despite his eagerness to blame her, Samson realizes that the prime cause of his fall was not Dalila but rather he himself. Others might find in that realization a key to self. For Samson it affords yet another opportunity to bemoan his weakness.

Samson's ease in brushing aside all deeper questions is mirrored in the Chorus's facility in summoning platitude. They display collectively his mental blindness. Theirs is a particularly deliberate blindness, a closing of the eyes to avoid what's staring them in the face. The critics have often noted their imperceptiveness. What passes unremarked is that the Chorus's imperceptiveness belongs in part to Milton the apologist, although his results from the blinders orthodoxy imposes. We see both their blindness and the apologist's blinders in their pat dismissal of atheism:

> Just are the ways of God,
> And justifiable to Men;
> Unless there be who think not God at all,
> If any be, they walk obscure;
> For such Doctrine never there was School,
> But the heart of the Fool,
> And no man therein Doctor but himself.
>   Yet there be who doubt his ways not just,
> As to his own edicts, found contradicting,
> Then they give the rains to wandring thought,
> Regardless of his glories diminution;
> Till by thir own perplexities involv'd
> They ravel more, still less resolv'd,
> But never find self-satisfying solution. [293-306]

The Chorus's and Milton the apologist's blindspot is divine justice, a matter that ever proves central to the graver import of genuine tragedy. Content with glib evasions, the Chorus demands of Yahweh no more introspection than it demands of Samson or of itself. Milton, I suspect, gradually became dissatisfied with glibness. Out of that dissatisfaction may have emerged the deep, subtle vision of his Muse in *Paradise Lost*.

Samson, though far from self-content, questions the divine justice no more than does the chorus. Manoa does question, but his questioning is as shallow as the Chorus's evasions:

> Alas methinks whom God hath chosen once
> To worthiest deeds, if he through frailty err,
> He should not so o'rewhelm, and as a thrall
> Subject him to so foul indignities,
> Be it for honours sake of former deeds. [368-72]

Samson responds with the sanctimony of Job's comforters rather than the insight of Job. Like the comforters, Samson proves ever ready to truckle to Yahweh:

> Appoint not heav'nly disposition, Father,
> Nothing of all these evils hath befall'n me
> But justly; I myself have brought them on
> Sole Author I, sole cause; if aught seem vile
> As vile hath been my folly, who have profan'd
> The mystery of God giv'n me under pledge
> Of vow, and have betray'd it to a woman,
> A Canaanite, my faithless enemy.
> This well I knew, nor was at all surpris'd,
> But warn'd by oft experience: [373-80]

The first three lines suffice to establish the theological superficiality Samson shares with the Chorus, Manoa, and Job's comforters. I quote the remainder to illustrate Samson's garrulity ("Sole Author I, sole cause"; "if aught seem vile / As vile hath been"; "under pledge / Of vow"; "faithless enemy"; and "This well I knew, nor was at all surpris'd"). Garrulity fosters shallow thought and mental blindness, since it diffuses every potential insight. Garrulity is, significantly, a flaw Samson shares with the repetitive Yahweh Jung discerned in the Book of Job.

If Dalila is the most shallow woman ever to precipitate a major tragedy, Samson is the most shallowly garrulous of tragic heroes.[9] His only rival for loquacity is Hamlet. Talk, for Hamlet, far from being a aspect of super-ficiality, becomes a relentless self-examination toward ever deepening insight. Deepened insight tempers hubris enabling us to expiate our wrongs and achieve transformation. Typically, Samson's recognition of his fatal garrulity expatiates upon rather than expiates the flaw:

> Spare the proposal, Father, spare the trouble
> Of that sollicitation; let me here
> As I deserve, pay on my punishment;
> And expiate, if possible my crime,
> Shameful garrulity. To have reveal'd
> Secrets of men, the secrets of a friend,
> How hainous had the fact been, how deserving
> Contempt, and scorn of all, to be excluded
> All friendship, and avoided as a blab,
> The mark of fool set on his front! But I
> Gods counsel have not kept, his holy secret
> Presumptuously have publish'd, impiously,
> Weakly at least, and shamefully: [487-9]

Here Milton elaborates the biblical account's simple vice of divulging secrets to make Samson garrulous almost to the point of caricature. Why? Is it amateurism marring a early attempt to create character?—not likely, since even though *Samson Agonistes* appears to be, after *Comus*, only his second serious dramatic poem, Milton doubtless revised it later. Samson's trifling garrulity is surely not Milton's own. In fact, its glaring presence constitutes startling testimony against the theory that Milton is portraying himself. If Milton intended garrulity to be Samson's hamartia, it is an odd flaw for a tragic hero and an inappropriate one insofar as it thrusts him toward the boundary of comedy. The hero ought to be flawed by great passion as Hamlet, Lear, Othello, and Coriolanus are. But when that flaw is a passion for blabbing, it can undermine the dignity the hero also ought to have. Only if we see Samson's garrulity as a verbal inflation that evades all insight does it begin to assume a tragic character. Its true function and compatibility with greatness become apparent when we recognize its ground in the mental blindness of the Yahweh archetype.

The Yahweh archetype worked, as archetypes do, at an unconscious level. At a conscious level Milton may have been reflecting on how garrulous mental habits diffuse insight in a flood of words, the immemorial vice of theologians. The profusion of scriptural citations aside, Milton was notably pithy in *De Doctrina*. And the cool, austere Messiah of *Paradise Regained*, Milton's ideal, personifies the laconic. Milton doubtless realized that garrulity's power to diffuse insight (garrulity is linguistic diffusion) makes it one of the most effective of Satan's snares. Indeed, Messiah's success against Satan often hinges upon his ability to resist the temptation to say more than he need say. Restraint, it should be remembered, forms an important element of Messiah's superiority to Yahweh and validates his claim to identity with logos. In God's plan there is a time and a place for everything. And every word.

Like Jung's Yahweh and Shakespeare's Lear, Samson senses that he has been foolish and blind, yet he persists in his folly with the trifling garrulity that spoils his very confession of the flaw. Samson's self-knowledge, if it can be called that, is defective, garrulous, and decidedly ironic:

> Fearless of danger, like a petty God
> I walk'd about admir'd of all and dreaded
> On hostile ground, none daring my affront
> Then swollen with pride into the snare I fell
> Of fair fallacious looks, venereal trains,
> Soft'n'd with pleasure and voluptuous life;
> At length to lay my head and hallow'd pledge
> Of all my strength in the lascivious lap
> Of a deceitful Concubine [529-38]

Reminiscent of Richard III's "the lascivious pleasing of a lute," the veritable orgy of lewd "l"s in the four endmost lines relish the vice described even as the initial lines exhibit inflation in the very act of deploring it. The favored vehicle of Samson's hubris is thus the shallow garrulity through which he revels in his follies and sucks upon the stale candies of vainglory. He is a verbal sybarite!

If Samson's garrulity indulges hedonism, it also caters to masochism. His masochism becomes apparent as he dwells on being shaved:

> who shore me
> Like a tame Weather, all my precious fleece,
> Then turn'd me out ridiculous, despoil'd,
> Shav'n and disarm'd [536-40]

Hair symbolizes masculine pride and virility. Ever the glutton for sensation, Samson cannot resist an opportunity to experience the sensation of being despoiled of his hair and what it symbolizes. Why else marry a Dalila or tell her the secret of his strength when he knows full well the probable outcome? There is certainly no deception involved since the Dalila Milton portrays is too harebrained to deceive any other than herself. Samson asked to be shaved for the sensation of it.

But what, besides masochistic loss of virility, are the psychological components of that fateful sensation?[10] Among other things hair is a garment and, as the keepers of Auschwitz well knew, no one is fully naked until he has been shorn. In alchemical myths, Jung notes, the hero sometimes must undergo a humiliating loss of hair in preparation for self-knowledge.[11] The hero encounters, thereby, what Lear called the "bare, fork'd animal." Behind Samson's secret desire to have his head shaved is an impulse to know essential humanity that he shares with a Lear who in equal, purposeful folly gives everything to his wicked daughters. By becoming conscious of essential humanity, they can advance beyond the mental blindness of the Yahweh archetype to attain the ethical vision of Job. Samson asked to be shaved and Lear to be plundered in just the manner that the unthinking Yahweh of the Book of Job asked to become Christ crucified when in an act of hubris he let Satan, his adversarial aspect, subject the innocent Job to a sadistic ordeal.

Yahweh is what Samson has been and Job-Christ is what he's becoming. Samson, however, never completes the transition to the Job archetype, for he fails to attain Job's ethical vision.[12] Samson is unable to actualize the Job-Christ archetype because, in a Christian theological context, that is not possible before Christ's sacrifice and the new dispensation it inaugurates. Hence, he comes to recognize in himself Yahweh's mental blindness without actualizing its remedy, the ethical vision of the Job-Christ archetype. Critics speak of his redemption and regeneration; but redemption is out of the question and regeneration is misleading since he fails to realize the Job-Christ archetype.[13] Samson's achievement lies not in regeneration so much as in surmounting the despair that comes upon recognition of the Yahweh archetype's inadequacy.

To think of despair solely as a spiritual nadir can be misleading. Like adversity, despair has its uses. For Samson the only effective purgative of hubris and shallow garrulity is despair:

> All otherwise to me my thoughts portend,
> That these dark orbs no more shall treat with light,
> Nor th' other light of life continue long,
> But to yield to double darkness nigh at hand;
> So much I feel my genial spirits droop,
> My hopes all flat, nature within me seems
> In all her functions weary of her self; [590-96]

Samson's bluster, like Lear's after the storm, gives way to despair. And just as Lear moves from invoking the gods to doubting them, Samson proclaims his sense of "heaven's dissertion" and deems his losses "irreparable." The Chorus's subsequent calls for patience trumpet a virtue that cannot be fully realized until the Job-like Messiah of *Paradise Regained*. What ultimately rescues Samson from despair is not any Jobean patience, but purgation of hubris to renew the strengths of the Yahweh archetype. This restoration of identity, "Samson acquits himself as Samson," Manoa later remarks, is prompted by the visits of Dalila and Harapha. Dalila and Harapha parody the mental blindness that made possible Samson's physical blinding. By parodying his flaw they provoke overreactions. These overreactions shake him out of despair as despair gives way to Yahwehistic wrath.

YAHWEH'S ANIMA

Dalila, D.C. Allen has pointed out, is not exactly the poisonous bosom snake Samson calls her.[14] Tormenting him is not among the purposes of her visit; sadism seems too heavy a motive for her frail mind to support. Indeed, a thin vein of genuine remorse glints through her trifling words. Though the Philistines have probably sent her to discover whether Samson's strength has returned, her truest personal motive is simple animal lust. Himself too simple to readily fathom the Philistine purpose and too bitter to pardon her treachery, Samson greets her dubious offers of penitence and recompense with misogynistic rage:

> Out, out Hyena; these are thy wonted arts,
> And arts of every woman false like thee,
> To break all faith, all vows, deceive, betray,
> Then as repentant to submit, beseech, . . .
> That wisest and best men full oft beguil'd
> With goodness principl'd not to reject
> The penitent, but ever to forgive,
> Are drawn to wear out miserable days,
> Entangl'd with a poysnous bosom snake, [748-63]

Here we see Samson's inflation and self-delusion stoked to full roar. Hardly can he be numbered among the "wisest and best men." If he were, he'd understand that such men are unlikely to "wear out miserable days, / Entang'd with a poysnous bosom snake." And Dalila, far from being artful, is almost pathetic in her transparency. Mere persistence won her his secret. Persistence with no little aid, we can be sure, from Samson's inclination to blab, his fatal garrulity. Samson's attributing to Dalila arts too substantial to take berth in the shallow shoal of her mind is a ruse to obscure his folly and stupidity and a projection of his own anima, which, repressed into shadow, turns to vindictive scheming.

Although Samson is unable to acknowledge to her face responsibility for his own fall, he admits to Manoa that he has brought destruction upon himself and reveals how his bride of Timna also wrested secrets from him. The bride of Timna's success ought to have left him wary and wise. But rather than putting the new bride in her wifely place, Samson, bowing to scheming anima, chose to play games with her:

> Thrice she assay'd with flattering prayers and sighs,
> And amorous reproaches to win from me
> My capital secret, in what part my strength
> Lay stored, in what part summ'd, that she might know:
> Thrice I deluded her, and turn'd to sport
> Her importunity, each time perceiving
> How openly, and with what impudence
> She propos'd to betray me [392-99]

So ineffective a temptress was Dalila that Samson deluded her three times, each time relishing, it appears, his anima-inspired cleverness and never asserting masculine authority to stop the game. The game and their connubial activities, we infer, were thoroughly entangled. Hers was not a triumph of feminine wile over masculine reason but of a strumpet's impudence over lechery grown weary:

> Yet the fourth time, when mustring all her wiles,
> With blandisht parlies, feminine assaults,
> Tongue-batteries, she surceas'd not day nor night
> To storm me over-watch'd, and wearied out.
> At times when men seek most repose and rest
> I yielded, and unlock'd her all my heart,
> Who with a grain of manhood well resolv'd
> Might easily have shook off all her snares:
> But foul effeminacy held me yok't
> Her bond slave; [402-411]

"Foul effeminacy" is an apt term for Samson's festering anima. Often in men with a braggart persona and an ego that identifies with persona, anima, repressed into shadow, will make a fool of persona through games, riddles, and intrigues. Such an anima-shadow festers for an opportunity to take center stage in a cat fight with a real woman like Dalila. While Samson can acknowledge his weakness to Manoa, when Dalila appears admission becomes impossible because she riles his anima, who demands a cat fight. He is truly a bond slave, but Dalila is not his master. Samson's own repressed anima, grown impudent and vindictive, holds him in bondage. The crucial symptom of that bondage is Samson's mental blindness.[15]

What he finds so maddening about Dalila is that lust and her receiving, albeit sometimes inappropriately, his anima projection gives her power to overwhelm his common sense.[16] Milton too, I believe, found Dalila maddening, not because she received his anima projection, a task left for the much more sympathetic Eve, but because she reminded him of repressed anima's power to take vengeance by cutting off the imaginal world and so inducing mental blindness. Indeed, repression of anima and consequent fear of her revenge in the form of blinding are prime causes of misogynistic bias in Milton, in Samson, and in patriarchal males in general.[17]

Samson, we should remember, is not alone in altering Dalila to fit personal biases. Just as Samson's convenient image of the wily Dalila differs sharply from the character Milton portrays, so the character differs from its biblical source. In the Bible Samson never marries her: notwithstanding, Milton makes her a second wife. Nowhere does the Bible suggest that she loved or even lusted after him. She was a Philistine tool from the moment it became known that Samson desired her. Far from impudent and harebrained, Dalilah (Milton even altered her name) is clever and single-mindedly traitorous from start to finish. While Samson changes Dalila to excuse his own weaknesses, Milton the artist changes her to develop and illuminate the anima weaknesses, especially the mental blindness, of the temperamental, unreflective character Samson derives from the Yahweh archetype.

Dalila's final appeal to Samson is simple lust almost moving in its naivete: "Let me at least touch thy hand." Her sudden, unabashed desire for intimacy riles the inexorable hatred suppurating in his wounded masculine spirit: "Not for thy life, lest fierce rembrance wake / My sudden rage to tear thee joint by joint. / At distance I forgive thee, go with that;" (951-53). Reminding Samson of the intimacy they once shared, Dalila reminds him of the power that intimacy gave her. He can partially forgive her folly and treachery because he partially accepts responsibility for being a fool and a traitor to himself in yielding to her. But he cannot forgive Dalila's power because he still fears the part of himself he projects upon her, his brazen anima scheming to blind him.

Samson dimly realizes that he has a blinding, emasculating anima yet never achieves tragic recognition of the problem. Why? The explanation, I believe, again resides in the Yahweh archetype.[18] Yahweh's encounter with Job, Jung maintains, compels him to recover his positive anima and later develop it as Wisdom or Sophia.[19] Jung assumes that Yahweh simply follows his ego's shadow, Satan. Yet anima remains active in every psyche. In Yahweh's psyche patriarchal ego represses anima into shadow where, rebelling, it allies with Satan (the way Eve's repressed animus allies with the serpent) to bring about mental blindness. Job does not compel Yahweh to remember anima, as Jung thought, so much as to liberate her feminine wisdom and thereby gain the inner vision repressed anima's league with Satan forced upon Job.

The so-called wisdom literature, particularly the Book of Proverbs, attempts to deal with the divine anima. Proverbs 7:4-27 presents in the heart of its salute to wise Sophia an intriguing sketch of the treacherous harlot. Chapters 5, 7, and 9 contrast this Dalila-like figure to Sophia. We must turn to Hebrew lore, however, to find a complete portrait of Yahweh's anima. Here the good and evil, the seeing and the blinding, sides of the divine feminine essence, are personified and richly developed in the Shekhinah and Lilith. Invariably the brazen seductress, Lilith's most familiar form was as a lavishly adorned harlot. She began her long career of lust as Adam's first wife; he could find no happiness living with her insolence so God created the more modest Eve. Later she married Samael, another name for Satan, and together they became the androgynous image of sexual evil. When Shekhinah, or Wisdom, left Yahweh to go into exile with Israel, trifling Lilith became his consort. The Gnostic Kabbalists went further to speculate that in the very days of creation Yahweh fell into sin by coupling with Lilith. Thus, while Satan-Samael embodied Yahweh's destructive shadow, Lilith embodied the side of his anima that encouraged frivolity and mental blindness. The messianic days were thought to mark the end of frivolous Lilith and the triumphant return of wise Shekhinah.[20]

While Lear may be a better representation of Yahweh than Samson, there is no better literary personification of Yahweh's repressed Lilith-anima than Dalila. If need to atone for the wrongs of his minimally conscious patriarchal ego forced Yahweh to realize a Christ-ego, then the shallowness and treachery of his Lilith-anima compelled him to realize a wise and faithful anima or Sophia in the Holy Spirit. In Goneril Shakespeare personified Yahweh's satanic shadow. In Cordelia he gave us the Sophia-anima, leaving it for Milton to show with Dalila how Yahweh's mental blindness arises from the treacherous and trivial Lilith-anima Jung missed.

As Dalila parodies Samson's residually shallow anima, so Harapha parodies his inflated persona. With Harapha Milton judiciously avoids stretching parody to the extreme of caricature. Although Harapha, true to his characonym, is a windy *miles gloriosus*, he proves to be neither crude nor evil. More a catalyst to Samson's faults than a purposeful tempter, the hubristic Philistine giant goads Samson to counter with inflation. "The way to know were not to see but taste," Samson replies to Harapha's opening volley with the masculine elan of one primed to meet a rival blow for blow. A boasting match ensues that calls to mind *Samson Agonistes*'s Elizabethan antecedents. Comparing gods with Harapha the way small boys boast "my dad can beat up your dad!" Samson vaunts:

> if Dagon be thy god,
> Go to his Temple, invoke his aid
> With solemnest devotion, spread before him
> How highly it concerns his glory now
> To frustrate and dissolve his Magic spells
> Which I to be the power of Israel's God
> Avow, and challenge Dagon to the test,
> Offering to combat thee his Champion bold,
> With th' utmost of his Godhead seconded:
> Then thou shalt see, or rather to thy sorrow
> Soon feel, whose God is strongest, thine or mine. [1145-55]

To which the blustery Harapha retorts

> Presume not on thy God, what e're he be,
> Thee he regards not, owns not, hath cut off
> Quite from his people, and deliver'd up
> Into thy Enemies hand, permitted them
> To put out both thine eyes, and fetter'd send thee
> Into the common Prison, there to grind
> Among the Slaves and Asses thy comrades,
> As good for nothing else [1156-63]

The verbal volleys blast back and forth until Samson calls Harapha's bluff by challenging him to physical combat. Deflated, his "Giantship" withdraws in a "sultrie chafe."

The episode with Harapha reveals a side of Samson that does not surprise us, given his military fame, even though we haven't directly encountered it before. Despite his posing, boasting masculinity, Harapha fails to incite Samson to anger the way Dalila does, which provides further evidence that repressed anima is Samson's fundamental problem. Anima takes revenge against his inflated, masculine persona through scheming that redounds on his head making a mockery of his bombast. In contrast to anima, which Samson cannot control, he controls persona so well that the instant Harapha leaves he dispels every trace of bombast to coolly analyze the threat the Chorus fears in the Philistine giant's bluster:

> He must allege some cause, and offer'd fight
> Will not dare mention, lest a question rise
> Whether he durst accept the offer or not
> And that he durst not plain enough appear'd. [1253-56]

Dismissing Harapha's threat, Samson masters inflation along with its symptom, garrulity, and prepares to face death with dignity: "But come what will, my deadliest foe will prove / My speediest friend, by death to rid me hence, / The worst that he can give, to me the best." (1262-64). Like Kent in *King Lear*, in whom antagonists bring out soldierly braggadocio, upon his foe's departure Samson hones his words to fit his tragic situation.

The change involves no change of character, for with the third Philistine's appearance Samson's inflated garrulity returns. But the garrulity has grown so mechanical, virtually a Pavlovian response to the presence of a Philistine, it seems more humorous than tragic. Indeed, Samson raises comedy's banner by invoking the image of a circus:

> *Officer.* This answer, be assur'd, will not content them.
> *Samson.* Have they not Sword-players, and ev'ry sort
> Of Gymnic Artists, Wrestlers, Riders, Runners,
> Juglers and Dancers, Antics, Mummers, Mimics,
> But they must pick me out with shackles tir'd,
> And over-labour'd at their publick Mill
> To make them sport with blind activity? [1322-28]

The officer, a sober, laconic fellow who meets Samson's verbal indulgences with single-sentence replies, eventually induces pith in Samson: "*Officer.* I am sorry what this stoutness will produce. / *Samson.* Perhaps thou shalt have cause to sorrow indeed." (1346-47). His final remarks to the officer flash the old hubris, then yield to sober realism:

> I could be well content to try their Art,
> Which to no few of them would prove pernicious.
> Yet knowing thir advantages too many,
> Because they shall not trail me through thir streets
> Like a wild Beast, I am content to go. [1399-1403]

What are we to conclude of Samson's three Philistine visitors, each decidedly less offensive than his predecessor? Of Dalila and Harapha it may be observed that Milton could have made them worse. Milton gave Dalila a demitasse of genuine feeling for Samson that helps humanize her treachery, triviality, and impudence. And though he made Harapha empty and flatulent, he did not make him the sadistic or absurd bully he could have been. Neither of them can be intended to set off Samson's regenerating virtue. The Philistine officer, moreover, is much kinder and more courteous than might be expected.

The encounters with the three Philistines demonstrate that Samson reacts to everything, often with blind, garrulous inflation, and never initiates anything. His inflated outbursts, both physical and verbal, habitually substitute for authentic action. Authentic action entails reflection, which must be severely limited in one whose anima is so shallow a Dalila best carries her projection. Yahweh too is passive save for outbursts and so unreflecting he needs others' reactions to prove to himself that he is real. Perhaps we should be thankful that he lacks a full-fledged consort, since what we know of his masculine surface indicates she might have resembled Dalila, or worse, Lilith.

The Philistines, to be sure, are foils to Samson, though none are the kind that make his virtues shine all the brighter. While they are not subtle characterizations, their effects on Samson show Milton the artist's skill in giving psychological weight to Samson's character while illumining the inner dynamics of the Yahweh archetype.

TRAGIC GODHEAD

After bidding his companions farewell, Samson departs, resigned to fate. We learn nothing of that fate until the messenger launches his classical presentation of the catastrophe. Samson, he discloses, went patient but undaunted where the Philistines led him, the Jobean note again signaling the archetypal identity Samson moves toward. Still, we hear little of Job in Samson's last words:

> Hitherto, Lords, what your commands impos'd
> I have perform'd, as reason was, obeying,
> Not without wonder or delight beheld.
> Now of my own accord such other tryal
> I mean to shew you of my strength, yet greater;
> As with amaze shall strike all who behold. [1640-45]

There follows the destruction of the temple along with the Philistine lords and Samson. Some have detected hubris in the riddle-pun playing on the word "strike."[21] However, the element of hubris is so muted it can be dismissed as a residual mannerism.

The act of self-sacrifice is crucial. What does it reveal about Samson, about Milton's understanding of tragic sacrifice, and about the tragic effect of *Samson Agonistes*?

Samson. The Chorus and Manoa, ever the voices of conventional piety, supply the conventional answers. Samson, Manoa assures us, has died a national hero deserving a monument that he proposes to build:

> Thither shall all the valiant youth resort,
> And from his memory inflame thir breasts
> To matchless valour, and adventures high:
> The Virgins also shall on feast days
> Visit his tomb with flowers, only bewailing
> His lot unfortunate in nuptial choice,
> From whence captivity and loss of eyes. [1738-44]

To Manoa Samson remains an essentially unflawed hero whose successes were compromised by an unfortunate nuptial choice. Manoa's phrasing makes it appear as though Samson's choice of Dalila, like an accidental drawing of a bad lot, does not reflect upon his character. Such tact is excusable coming from a father who has lost a beloved son; but it belies the Samson the poem presents.

The Samson the reader or audience knows has, along with the martial virtues of strength and courage, a deep hamartia that, impairing his entire character, determines his grim fate. Like the hamartia of Yahweh, it is a shallowness of mind or mental blindness rooted in repression of anima. Their shallowness makes them boast and blab thoughtlessly while rendering them quick-tempered and blind to repressed anima's schemes to turn everything into a game. In Yahweh's case the games are sadistic exercises that serve little purpose beyond satisfying puerile curiosity: he tortures Job the way small boys torture flies, almost, it seems, for sport. But Yahweh is omnipotent. Samson begins with an illusory omnipotence that can be lost as easily as his hair. Only Yahweh can long afford to play Yahweh. For men possessed by the Yahweh archetype, as Lear and Samson learn, the game soon becomes an exercise in masochism. The same eventually holds for Yahweh too, if Jung is right, since Yahweh cannot attain the depth of consciousness he forces upon suffering Job except by electing to suffer himself.

Samson, like Lear and Yahweh, is woefully deficient in insight. Feeding the self-destructive folly of all three is a hidden drive to realize the inward vision that develops through ego suffering and mediation of anima. But we have little reason to believe that the tragic enlightenment that comes to Yahweh turned Christ and Lear reunited with Cordelia ever comes to Samson offstage when no signs of it appear onstage. Despite his self-sacrifice, then, Samson is not tragic in the sense of full *anagnorisis* we see in Lear but only in the limited sense of folly bringing irreparable loss that he shares with those lesser tragic figures Brutus and Julius Caesar.

Two explanations for the failure of Samson's self-sacrifice to yield tragic insight come to mind. The first is that, *Samson Agonistes* being an early work, Milton's skills had not matured enough to present authentic tragic learning. Though undoubtedly true in part, such an explanation does little to advance our understanding.

The second, and more productive, explanation rests on the theory of typology. Samson is a type for Christ's antitype; according to seventeenth-century typological theory, the meaning of a type cannot be known until it is fulfilled in the antitype.[22] Samson cannot achieve tragic enlightenment because, being a embryonic Christ yet to emerge from the Yahweh archetype, he must illustrate with his mental blindness the need for Christ's inward vision and, like Yahweh, make the need acute through acts of blind folly. In that function Samson became an essential part of the Christ myth from early Christianity onward.

Milton's Understanding of Tragic Sacrifice.   Orthodoxy, when it embraced the doctrine of *summum bonum*, permitted an ossified ideal to supplant the vital myth of blind Yahweh and self-sacrificing Christ. In so doing, Jung maintained, orthodoxy deprived Christianity of its archetypal purpose, God's attainment of inward vision through suffering himself the afflictions he blindly visits upon men. The archetypal God Jung portrays in *Answer to Job* is profoundly tragic. The development of anima-Sophia or inward vision in him shows that individuation must inevitably be a tragic process, a sacrifice, or crucifixion of ego. Moreover, recognizing the suffering he inflicts on mankind and suffering tragedy himself in order to understand it, he shows a Godlike nobility that raises him far above the deity of theology who claims perfect goodness while behaving like a Roman tyrant.

Christ's crucifixion, being Godhead's tragedy, is the supreme tragic experience. But the greatest tragedy ever written is *King Lear:* that is one matter of opinion where most critics agree. Why does *King Lear* enjoy such preeminence? The basic reasons are two. First, Shakespeare was overall the most able of those who have penned a tragedy, and he wrote *King Lear* at the height of his powers. Second, he seems to have possessed a unique intuitive apprehension of the graver import of tragic sacrifice. What Shakespeare intuited, long before modern psychology and philosophy grasped it intellectually, was that tragic sacrifice is an inescapable feature of the individuation of Godhead. This very unorthodox and un-Aristotelian intuition undergirds the Gospel myth and *King Lear. King Lear* is not just the greatest tragedy, it is our most powerful work of literature. It moves us as no other work can by letting us glimpse through myth and symbol truths about the self and our Western image of self, the Christian Godhead, that are too overwhelming for us to accept directly. Orthodoxy, by contrast, attempts to evade these truths.

Orthodox in most respects, Milton balked at acknowledging that tragic sacrifice is necessary for Godhead to manifest inward vision and individuate its wholeness. He possessed, notwithstanding, rare intelligence and integrity. Consequently, he showed a concern few theologians have shown for the difficulties posed by the orthodox evasion of the divine tragedy. His salient departures from strict orthodoxy—Pelagian tendencies, subordinationism, mortalism, and his apparent aversion to the bloody crucifixion—can be seen as indirect and, I'm afraid, ineffectual attempts to deal with the divine tragedy. Indeed, from *Samson Agonistes* through *De Doctrina* and *Paradise Regained* to *Paradise Lost* Milton endeavors to examine, then to solve, and finally to diminish those elusive problems with Christianity's tragic Godhead, which Shakespeare projected on the scrims of myth in his transcendent tragedy *King Lear* but which were not fully articulated until Jung's *Answer to Job. Samson Agonistes*, if I am correct, was Milton's first serious try at these problems and that try, he realized, raised more questions than it answered. Hence the need to continue wrestling with the problems in *De Doctrina, Paradise Regained*, and *Paradise Lost.*[23]

Nevertheless, *Samson Agonistes* remains an authentic tragedy, although of a type quite different from *King Lear.* The difference does not reside entirely in disparate treatments of tragic sacrifice, although the disparity proves blatant. Milton, I believe, was attempting to write a tragedy based on Greek models and conforming to Aristotle's rules.[24] As R.C. Jebb points out, his understanding of Greek tragedy is not ours.[25] Yet the essential consideration is not how well Milton the scholar understood the Greeks, but how close Milton the artist came to apprehending the significance of tragic sacrifice to Godhead.

An intriguing clue appears in his forward, "OF THAT SORT OF DRAMATIC POEM WHICH IS CALL'D TRAGEDY," in an aside often overlooked amidst the critical ado about Aristotelian definitions: "Gregory Nazianzen a Father of the Church, thought it not unbeseaming the sanctity of his person to write a Tragedy, which he entitl'd Christ suffering. This is mentioned to vindicate Tragedy from the small esteem or rather infamy, which in the account of many it undergoes to this day with other common Interludes, hap'ning through the Poets error of intermixing Comic stuff with Tragic sadness and gravity; or introducing trivial and vulgar persons which by all judicious hath been counted absurd; and brought in without discretion corruptly to gratifie the people." The reference to Gregory Nazianzen indicates that Milton consciously saw the crucifixion as a tragic subject. His purpose in mentioning Nazianzen, he declares, is to vindicate tragedy from the infamy fallen upon it because of intermixing comic and tragic effects and introducing trivial and vulgar persons. If Milton is not referring specifically to *King Lear* with the Fool, Oswald, Kent, and Edgar in his madman disguise, he certainly must have been subliminally aware that his criticism applied to it.[26] What is most striking is that Milton couples a oblique reference to *King Lear* with a direct reference to Christ's passion in an aside from his main argument. These coupled references indicate that Milton the artist's apprehension of the tragic vision of Godhead in *King Lear* and the Gospel myth influenced tragic sacrifice in *Samson Agonistes*.[27]

The Tragic Effect of Samson Agonistes.   *Samson Agonistes* raises, yet fails to resolve, questions about Samson's tragic sacrifice and about the need for sacrifice in the Yahweh archetype that Samson represents. At this early juncture Milton seems to have been content to silence disturbing questions with a distinctly Christian call to faith. For his purpose the Chorus, that voice of convention undistracted by insight into either Samson or the mystery of tragic sacrifice, stands primed:

> All is best, though we oft doubt,
> What th' unsearchable dispose
> Of highest wisdom brings about
> And ever found best in the close.
> Oft he seems to hide his face,
> But unexpectedly returns
> And to his faithful Champion hath in place
> Bore witness gloriously; whence Gaza mourns
> And all that band them to resist
> His uncontroulable intent;
> His servants he with new acquist
> Of true experience from this great event
> With peace and consolation hath dismist,
> And calm of mind all passion spent. [1745-58]

Why all should be best and ever found best in the close is something *Samson Agonistes* never dramatizes or explains; *Paradise Lost* doesn't either, but it does make a grander and more thorough attempt to search the unsearchable. For the Chorus to call Samson a faithful champion is difficult to justify other than by the convention of speaking kindly of the recently deceased. His act of self-immolation in Gaza, in light of his inflated character, seems more a final self-assertion than a submission to divine will. Samson quits himself as Samson by reestablishing the identity of a strongman-hero and by reversion to the Yahweh archetype. Pious wishful thinking accounts for the Chorus's assumption that they learned something—"new acquist / Of true experience"—and will leave wiser than they came. Doubtless they will leave with peace and consolation in calm of mind, all passion spent. But they owe their tranquility to construing events as they want them to be, not to seeing events as they are.

Though the Chorus's reassuring lines give the play an unforgettable close, they show little understanding and less capacity to perceive. Consequently, they are a faulty and inadequate summary of what the perceptive reader thinks and feels at the end. The perceptive reader, I believe, remains with a puzzlement that is Milton's own. Behind the puzzlement over what good purpose Samson's tragic sacrifice may have served (beyond a political gain for Israel) when neither Samson, nor Manoa, nor the Chorus learn anything lurks a question so disturbing none in Milton's time gave it voice—what good purpose did its antitype, Christ's tragic sacrifice, serve if neither God nor man learns anything from it? Milton's failure to confront the question in *Samson Agonistes* led to his attempts to supercede the crucifixion with the temptation in *Paradise Regained* and finally to diminish, indeed to loose, God's tragedy, in the vast canvas of *Paradise Lost*. Correlative to these are the awkward attempts in *De Doctrina* to obscure the fact of Very God suffering on the cross by making Christ's divinity subordinate.

The above observations in no way imply that *Samson Agonistes* fails artistically. Far from it, Milton set out to write a tragedy and succeeded in writing one with the crucial elements: a hero of flawed greatness, sacrifice, irreparable loss, and beauty of execution. Its faults are not aesthetic so much as philosophic. The philosophic faults spring not from Milton's art but from his theological commitments. The result is that the poem, like its theology, raises questions it cannot answer, leaving us puzzled. At the same time our puzzlement gives birth to a sense of mystery that enhances the poem's tragic effect. Moreover, it sets up expectations for bigger works that will grapple with questions *Samson Agonistes* hints at without attempting to resolve.

Samson Agonistes's puzzlement and mystery are like windows that open the poem into a larger world beyond the small, enclosed spaces of Greek tragedy. Samson himself resembles a Greek tragic hero in that hubris brings destruction upon his head. Nonetheless, he remains unique and mysterious, for while conforming to a classic tragic formula he simultaneously manifests the primitive Yahweh archetype and in his self-sacrifice moves toward that of Job-Christ. The mystery of *Samson Agonistes* thus becomes the mystery at the heart of the Christian Godhead, the mystery of the divinity's tragic sacrifice.

Heroic Artistry. We like to believe that our greatest artists have the courage to see things as they are. One may not care all that much about the vision of a Kyd or a Heywood, but the thought of a Shakespeare or a Milton darkening his eyes to truth distresses us profoundly. It would seem to indicate that humanity, even at its best, is fated to grope in darkness.

Nevertheless, many whom we deem great have blinded themselves for orthodoxy—faith, they call it. Previously, I observed that Shakespeare was able to write our greatest tragedy because he possessed preeminent talent and insight. There is a third reason, and that strictly moral. Shakespeare was able to write *King Lear* because he had the moral courage to refuse to blind himself for orthodoxy. He wrote what he saw, not what he ought to say.

Milton the apologist did blind himself for orthodoxy, but Milton the artist refused to darken his inner sight. The basic direction of the artist's career is a slow, painful movement away from the blindness of youthful orthodoxy, a ceaseless struggle to perceive the archetypal realities behind Christian Godhead. Viewing *Samson Agonistes* in the context of Milton's entire career, its most crucial agon is not Samson's but Milton's own grappling with the facile assurances of the Chorus and Manoa. Samson himself does look deeper than they, although not very much deeper. The play's unresolved questions suggest that Milton the artist was looking deeper still, but could not make manifest what he as yet dimly perceived. *Samson Agonistes* marks the beginning of the artist's struggle to search God's unsearchable ordering and probe his uncontrollable intent. The artist's eye is ever on Godhead itself, his concern ever with the problem of evil and the question of individual decision. The apologist's determination to hold up the blinders of orthodoxy prevented him from attaining in *Paradise Lost* the soaring vision of Godhead Shakespeare attains in *King Lear.* Notwithstanding, Milton the artist's inner eye perceived the rough outlines of *King Lear*'s vision and revealed in metadramatic epiphanies truths the orthodox Milton resists.

The struggle for that inward vision called consciousness is the quintessential heroic quest. Samson remains ever the blind man groping for consciousness in the night of his hubris, but he does struggle on. Without the struggle for consciousness he would not be heroic. On the other hand were he successful, as Prospero is, he would not be tragic. To struggle in darkness is Samson's tragic fate. It was also Milton the apologist's fate. Samson-Yahweh could not see his own full nature because its next stage waited to unfold in his antitype Christ. Similarly, Milton the apologist could not see the full nature of Godhead because he was not ready for full revelations of the anima function of the Holy Spirit or of the ego-shadow dynamic between Christ and his hostile brother, Satan. Yet Milton the artist struggled heroically on to create the epiphanies of *Paradise Regained* and *Paradise Lost*, which, though they may lack *King Lear*'s soaring vision, in their subtle way unfold Godhead to consciousness.

Glossary of Jungian Terms

Unlike most glossaries of Jungian terms, which are clinically oriented, this glossary is tailored to literary criticism and psychology of religion. Readers not well versed in Jung may profit by initially perusing all the entries and referring back from time to time; readers with broad knowledge of Jung will nonetheless want to scrutinize the entries on criticism and religion. Throughout, the definitions reflect new insights, like those of feminist scholars. The glossary as a whole sketches the theoretical underpinnings of *The Unfolding God of Jung and Milton*.

ALCHEMY.   Jung believed that alchemists projected psychic contents into matter and thereby employed alchemy to work on the psyche. Hence, alchemy forms a repository of evidence about and insight into psychic processes, particularly individuation. The alchemists arranged the elements used in their experiments in pairs of opposites, their objective being to make from the conjunction of opposites new elements. Just as alchemy sought to differentiate the elements through work with opposites, so Jung's psychotherapy seeks to differentiate psyche through work with opposites. The goal of alchemy, the philosopher's stone, symbolizes the goal of therapy, wholeness.

ALIENATION.   While currently associated more with Marxian than Jungian thought, this fundamental concept goes back to Augustine and Greek tragedy. Alienation, dependence, and interdependence define the spectrum of possible relationships of individual to God and of ego to self. In traditional views that render God wholly other (e.g., Eriugena) sin is a metaphor for the alienation from God that exists in the cosmos. In Marxian ideologies alienation from historical necessity and the collective induces betrayal or bad faith, the Marxian equivalent of sin. For Jung initial alienation of ego from unconscious oneness is necessary to individuation, but permanent alienation of ego from self and *unus mundus* generates a sickness of soul whose symptoms are despair and meaninglessness. Alienation and inflation, as the internal and external facets of uroboric regression, are symbiotic evils. Alienation feeds inflation, especially in the forms of pride and scorn, and inflation always alienates: their presence ever stifles love. The remedy to alienation and inflation is love or interdependence with others, self, and *unus mundus*.

AMPLIFICATION.   A method of interpreting symbols and myths that makes their meaning ample by drawing upon their cultural and mythological context. For example, consider how Greek culture and mythology can amplify the Oedipus myth. The gods, the Greeks believed, are the driving forces of myths; Jung would tell us that gods represent archetypes and the god or gods in each myth tells us which archetypes are active. The active god-archetype driving the Oedipus myth is Poseidon. Poseidon carries archetypal feeling, as his brother Zeus carries archetypal thinking. The Oedipus myth began not with Oedipus's crime but much earlier with Poseidon in his role as erastes to mortal Pelops' eremenos. Afterwards, when the mature Pelops needed help securing a bride from a destructive senex, Poseidon, remembering his joy in Pelops, came to the man's aid: thus Poseidon and Pelops established an archetypal, ideal erastes-eremenos relationship. The offspring of Pelops's marriage was Chrysipus. Laius, visiting Pelops, lusted for Chrysipus, stole the boy by force, and violated his honor and dignity, causing his death. By his disregard of feeling, Laius became an archetypal insensitive, destructive erastes contrasting with Poseidon's sensitive, beneficial erastes. The disasters that befell the house of Laius through his offspring Oedipus, who symbolizes thought divorced from feeling, can be seen as a retribution of Fate (and Poseidon) against Laius's unfeeling violence. Thus, Jungian amplification discovers in the Oedipus myth a wider range of meanings than Freud found: it makes the rivalry of father and son for the mother a destructive effect of the damage to the feeling function that results when erastes-eremenos male bonding is violated.

ANIMA.   In Jungian psychology the term has acquired two distinct meanings. The earliest sense of anima refers to the contrasexual element in the male psyche that, appearing as a single figure, plays mediatrix to the collective unconscious. However, anima also means soul, and as soul it carries the eros or love function that involves us with others, with the inner, imaginal life of the psyche, and with nature. Carrying the eros function, anima appears in tandem or coupled with another archetype; most often it couples with animus to form the androgynous syzygy. Jung, imbued with patriarchal values, at times blamed the contrasexual "inner woman" or anima for men's weaknesses. Such scapegoating implicitly bolstered the myth of male superiority and inhibited recognition that both men and women have anima in the sense of soul just as both have egos. In either sex ego as spirit tends to behave in an active, assertive manner conventionally identified as masculine. Likewise, while the protean anima is technically androgynous, in Western culture its subtle, "feminine," nurturing qualities tend to predominate. The differences between the two sexes on anima and animus are differences of identification: the male ego usually identifies with animus or spirit and feels separate from anima, while the female ego often associates with anima and dissociates from animus. Taken together anima and animus form the yin and the yang of androgynous wholeness. Anima gives soul, animus gives spirit, and shadow gives substance in both sexes and all sexual orientations. In either sex anima supplies the guiding, healing, nourishing imagination that puts us in touch with the inner world of myth, dream, and fantasy, and with nature; when anima is repressed, intellect, deprived of imaginal nourishment, becomes desiccated and shallow. The muse, that inspired guide and voice of imagination, is anima herself. Feeling and especially intuition tend to fall within the domain of this illusive archetype.

ANIMUS.   In its general sense, refers to the energetic, independent spirit present in either sex, most commonly as assertiveness, initiative, and curiosity or the exploratory drive. Being independent, animus functions differently in every individual. Jung, however, made animus the contrasexual part of the female psyche and chauvinistically associated it with a stereotyped willful opinionatedness. Jung's view of animus fails to recognize that patriarchal repression of logos or thinking in women drives animus into the shadow giving it the negative qualities he mistakenly attributes to animus itself. If women freely live out logos-animus, it will not become a foolish or destructive parody of a man, it will become an integral part of the feminine ego. Possession by an animus or anima that has been repressed into shadow, however, gives a person the negative qualities associated with the opposite sex. Such is the case with Milton's Eve when, deceived by the serpent personifying her repressed animus grown insubordinate, she strives for mastery over Adam. In contrast to the contrasexual anima of man, with which it stands paired in the syzygy, the woman's animus appears not as a single figure but as a multivoiced group. Sexual orientation, no less than sex, influences the ways anima and animus are manifest in individuals. As heterosexual men tend to project anima on women, so homosexual men tend to project animus, in the form of energy and initiative, on men they admire. While heterosexual women usually project animus on admired men, lesbians often project both animus and anima on admired women. Animus and anima, or spirit and soul, can be viewed as complementary aspects of a single archetype of androgyny; accordingly, in Latin the two terms were used interchangeably. Both aspects are thus present in each sex and sexual orientation, but the degree of conscious identification or projection varies with individuals.

ARCHETYPES.   Inherent possibilities of psychic functioning derived from inherited neuropsychic structures. They come in two principal forms: (1) personified archetypes such as anima, shadow, the mother, and the wiseman; (2) archetypes of transformation, which involve a basic situation or pattern like birth, *conjunctio*, initiation, and quest. Though archetypes appear embedded in images, they themselves are not images but psychic predispositions to form and organize images. Archetypes differ from animal instincts in that men, having the gift of reflection, can consciously oppose, tame, direct, and transform archetypal energies. Furthermore, archetypes combine and interface so that manifestations of particular archetypes are always modified by the other archetypes constellated in the individual's psyche and in his social situation or cultural milieu. For example, the shadow, as other archetypes influence it, will become Satanic in one manifestation, Promethean in a second, Mercurial in a third, and merely clownish in a fourth. Only a limited number of archetypes are constellated in a person at any one time; the rest remain potentials of the collective unconscious. The psyche tends to constellate those archetypes that compensate for conscious imbalances. Thus the purpose of constellating an archetype is to transform the psyche that constellates it. When archetypes are constellated psychic energy flows to them making them ordering forces like magnetic fields. At such times archetypes become so powerful they gain a will of their own, which can take possession of ego itself. Balance returns as we become aware of the archetype's power. It must be remembered that manifestations of archetypes, whether historical such as Jesus and Buddha, mythic like Lucifer and Dionysus, or conceptual like the One of Plotinus and the Logos of orthodoxy, never exhaust the possibilities of the archetypes that transcend their manifestations. Finally, archetypes are more like Kantian categories than like Platonic forms: being numinous and vital psychic forces, they transcend and generate our conscious ideas.

ART.   A means the self uses to send forth imagistic messages through anima. Anima's role as channel for images explains why the poet's muse is feminine. The types of written art that most readily serve the self's purposes are primitive myths, fairy tales, and visionary literature. Here characters are often more rewardingly approached as archetypes than as real people. Wherever the archetypal element is pronounced, even in highly complex works like *Paradise Lost* and *King Lear,* this observation holds true. Archetypes in art always compensate one-sidedness in the conscious attitude or cultural canon in order to advance wholeness. Art is, therefore, one of the self's great teaching and healing tools.

COINCIDENTIA OPPOSITORUM (sometimes *complexio oppositorum*).   The principle that opposites contain, generate, and eventually join each other, fundamental to Jung's thought. Recognizing *coincidentia oppositorum* or interdependence of opposites, Jung theorized, enables us to cope with duality, resolve divisive conflicts, and resist one-sided ego commitments. *Coincidentia oppositorum* indicates that attributing a quality to God necessarily posits its opposite: i.e., you cannot make God light without giving him his dark side as well. *Coincidentia oppositorum* is closely related to *unio oppositorum*, both terms supplying alternatives to the *summum bonum* notion of deity. *Coincidentia oppositorum* and *unio oppositorum*, Jung held, explain the dynamic nature of the Deity—its power to transform conflicting opposites into a synthesis or homeostasis that preserves their essential tension and energy yet generates new meaning. Unlike the *summum bonum, coincidentia oppositorum* can account for evil without the pitfalls of dualism, of blaming man for all evil, or of denying evil's reality. Jung held, moreover, that accepting the principle of *coincidentia oppositorum* could encourage integration of shadow and discourage the corrupting hypocrisy, scapegoating, and alienation that occur when we repress and project shadow. Furthermore, *coincidentia oppositorum* represents Jung's psychological and ethical ideals of (1) a balanced wholeness that utilizes opposites while maintaining their vital tensions and (2) an interdependence that ends alienation while maintaining respect for the autonomy of others. Jung's ideals contrast to the Christian ideal of a one-sided, willed goodness or purity achieved by splitting opposites apart, embracing one and repressing the other. Unlike willed purity, wholeness and interdependence recognize that energies contained in opposites generate the psyche and are necessary to its life. The eros function of the syzygy, or androgynous pairing of anima and animus, manifests and realizes *coincidentia oppositorum* among the archetypes of the psyche. *Coincidentia oppositorum* means that pairs of archetypal opposites, when truly understood, become complementary faces of integral archetypes.

COLLECTIVE UNCONSCIOUS.   As distinguished from the personal unconscious, a repository of inherited archetypes common to all humanity. While it comprises much of the total psyche, it is not the whole and should not be confused with the self or that image of self we call God. However, being the seat of the archetypes, the collective unconscious is the source and rough equivalent of the polytheistic pantheon.

COLLECTIVITY and COLLECTIVE THINKING. Project God upon the collective, which is usually imaged after the father archetype. They are evident in the herd behavior and totalitarian mentality common among twentieth-century men (Jung called them "provisional men") and in mass movements, especially religious ones, during previous ages. Such mass behavior and thinking, Jung believed, proves inimical to the individuation process, which is unavoidably an individual struggle. Mitigating against the authentic, individual decisions that form the basis of ethical conduct, collectivity and collective thinking bear a heavy responsibility for the moral and political crisis of modern man and for his spiritual drift and despair. The remedy, Jung insisted, is to seek God within the self rather than following the collective and projecting God on church, party, or state.

COMPENSATION. Activates repressed or neglected opposites to achieve *coincidentia oppositorum* and enact psychic transformation. An archetypal perspective always sees events in pairings of compensatory opposites. The tendency of unconscious emergents in dreams, symbols, visions, and of visionary art to compensate for one-sided imbalances in conscious attitudes or the cultural canon provides a fundamental guideline for Jungian literary criticism.

COMPLEX. Constitutes a feeling toned group of psychic representations usually centered around some dominant archetype, e.g., the father complex, and lodged in the personal unconscious and often the shadow. When complexes split off from the ego and become autonomous, like alternate psyches, they threaten the integrity of the entire personality.

CONJUNCTIO. An alchemical term for a metaphoric sexual union involving transformation of paired opposites into a new element manifesting a new meaning. The opposites are often anima and animus and the new element the androgyne. *Conjunctio* also symbolizes the process of raising opposites from the unconscious to unite them in consciousness whereby the psyche achieves oneness with itself. Being a transpsychic process, *conjunctio* is not in principle amenable to scientific explanation.

CONSCIOUSNESS. That part of the psychic realm that ego perceives and upon which it acts; consciousness stands opposed to the unconscious, which remains hidden to ego. Consciousness mediates between the outer and the inner world through the four functions of thinking, feeling, intuition, and sensation. And by differentiating opposites, it individuates the psyche. The objective of Jungian analysis should be to foster consciousness and bring its unifying center, the ego, into harmony with the greater self. While consciousness is usually associated with ego, anima, shadow, and other archetypes can acquire their own peculiar consciousness.

CONSTELLATE. Literally, to shine forth as a star in a constellation shines forth against the dark background of the sky. It is Jung's figurative term for the activation of an archetype against its unconscious background.

CULTURAL CANON. The sum of consciously inculcated beliefs, dogmas, and authoritative traditions that, while maintaining stable cultural identity by resisting change, tend to make a culture ill-adapted and one-sided. For that reason, the cultural canon is constantly challenged by compensatory unconscious emergents. In the West, Christian orthodoxy has long been the mainstay of the cultural canon.

DECISIVE IDENTITY. That truth to self, or authenticity, wherein decisions at once flow from and further shape identity so that one consciously decides, and thus creates, what one becomes. This requires mature character and discipline, unflinching awareness of alternatives and possible consequences, and the courage to conceive of life as a tragedy. Decisive identity makes us accountable for what we become and allows us to realize the mature freedom needed to consciously guide the individuation process.

DUALISM. Resists interdependence of opposites and *coincidentia oppositorum* by making opposites, especially good and evil, into absolute, irreducible dualities. Though orthodox Christianity rejected the explicit dualism of its rival Manichaeanism by declaring evil a mere *privatio boni,* implicit dualism crept back into its theology with the notion of free will, which makes free agents first causes along with God. Ironically, free will was deemed essential to protect God from the accusation of creating evil. Jung's dismissal of free will as a conceit of ego reflects the incompatibility of his thought with dualism. For Jung, opposites touch, conjoin, and even become each other; they are never irreducible or irreconcilable. The function of anima is to conjoin and transform opposites and so manifest the self in individuated wholeness. Dualism reflects a psychology that, locked in the ego-shadow stage of development, depends on repression and cannot accept either mediation from anima or the individuated wholeness of the self. While Jung borrowed much from Gnosticism, he never embraced its dualistic tendencies.

EGO. For Jung, subordinate to self. Jung offered a self-based psychology in contradistinction to the ego-based psychology Freud propounds and Christian orthodoxy, with its hypertrophied ego-God, assumes. The ego, Jung maintained, is only the subject of one's consciousness, whereas the self is the subject of the entire psyche, which includes the unconscious. Ego, as the active center of will and identity, constructs the persona, stands paired with anima, possesses a shadow, and must cope with the social world, the cultural canon, and collective morality. Standing between the self and its collective shadow, the uroboros, ego must learn to follow self toward individuated wholeness and resist uroboros and its temptation to withdraw into inflated alienation. Among women in Western culture ego tends to be diffuse and identified with eros; whereas among men it is often more focused and identified with logos, animus, or spirit. Just as anima often acts as a feminine presence in each sex, so ego often acts as a masculine presence in each. In women, however, ego attaches to one of the principal feminine archetypes: i.e., mother, daughter-virgin, mistress, wise-woman. Being the seat of the will and responsible for maintaining identity in both sexes, ego constantly seeks strength, security, certainty, and a sense of freedom. These goals are ever sacrificed and the ego ever crucified by the self in its quest for individuated wholeness. Though ego strives for security, because of the self, it achieves instead individuation through suffering. Hence, ego, desiring to play the hero in a comedy, is fated to a tragic role.

ENANTIODROMIO. A tendency for things to change over time into their opposites, an example being the highly spiritual Christian culture of the Middle Ages becoming the extremely materialistic Western culture of today. Jung derived *enantiodromio* from the philosophy of Heraclitus and made it the basis of his principle of compensation.

EPIPHANY. The term's modern meaning owes as much to James Joyce as to Jung. For Joyce an epiphany is a sudden manifestation of a thing's essential nature or, in Jungian nomenclature, its underlying archetype. Epiphanies, thus, can be regarded as glimpses of archetypes (for the ancients they were encounters with gods). Hence, we can see as epiphanies Milton the artist's brief glimpses of the true archetypes of Godhead. Only brief glimpses, usually conveyed through metadrama, could slip though the censor of Milton the apologist. Nevertheless, these glimpses taken together form, like Job's full theophany, signal advances in consciousness of Godhead.

ETHIC OF REBELLION. Arises in reaction to the excesses and defects of the old ethic. The egos of rebels, rejecting traditional values and authority, embrace feelings that have been relegated to the shadow. The rebels, however, suffer from the same inflated perfectionism afflicting those committed to the old ethic: for example, while the orthodox insist, in defiance of human experience, that God is perfectly good, the rebels reject him for falling short of perfection. The clash of the old ethic and the ethic of rebellion characterizes the hostile brothers stage of individuation with its dualist archetype of the Son and Satan and its conflicts of ego and shadow, thought and feeling, stasis and flux. These conflicts are transcended through anima-mediated inward vision.

EVIL. The term is ever surrounded with confusion. Confusion notwithstanding, in post-medieval Western culture there are but three principal visions of evil: evil as impurity, the most primitive of the visions; *privatio boni*, or evil as passive deprivation of good; and uroboric evil, or evil as inflated alienation that actively opposes good. These visions support three basic stances toward evil: (1) One can repress it in oneself and project it onto scapegoats—the position of those Christians who teach will to purity and emphasize the eternal damnation of Satan and his incorrigible followers. This stance is compatible with flux philosophy and leads ultimately to dualism. (2) One can, in effect, deny evil reality, the stance of Plotinus, stasis, and the doctrine of *privatio boni*. (3) One can admit that evil is real in the world, oneself, and God, and set to work transforming it into new good infused with consciousness, the stance of process philosophy and of Jung in his doctrine of *coincidentia oppositorum*. For the third stance evil is not a reason to question God's love but evidence for it: God allows evil so that through love we might co-create with him a new and more conscious good and thereby know the supreme joy of creating consciousness. Evils that we can transform into new good, like the contents of the shadow, are operative evils. Evils that we fail to transform because of uroboric regression, love's opposite, become moral evils. The only absolute evil is the uroboric counterforce to the self's (or God's) individuation drive to transform operative evil, usually in the forms of shadow and suffering, into a new and more conscious good. While the uroboric counterforce to self, being an absolute, can never achieve a *conjunctio oppositorum* with self, it is not a dualistic evil to be overcome at the end of time. The continuing struggle against it is necessary to realization of the absolute goods of individuated consciousness in self and God. The uroboric counterforce is analogous to gravity in significant respects: (1) we are fated to struggle against it; (2) if it triumphs totally, as in a black hole, it becomes totally destructive; (3) without struggling against it we cannot develop strength and substance.

FATHER, YAHWEH (the Great Mother and Mary represent the female aspect). The male aspect of the primal parent, the most rudimentary archetype of the Jungian Quaternity. However, by repressing the mother and daughter, dominating the sons to create oedipal conflicts, and turning them against each other through favoritism, the Father determines the basic archetypal patterns in monotheistic cultures. Generally speaking, the Father manifests herd thinking, collective values, and animus or spirit. Its Yahweh form resembles a patriarchal tyrant, or even a demiurge, in whom conscious ego is immature, anima is rudimentary, opposites have not been fully constellated, and only the sensation function has been differentiated. The quaternal Godhead unfolds to compensate for Yahweh's deficient awareness.

FEELING,   thinking, intuition, and sensation. Comprise the four basic modes of conscious activity. Feeling, a judging activity concerned with values and timing, stands opposite thinking, which judges logically: feeling is associated with anima and eros, and thinking with animus and logos. Feeling gives substance to value and moral judgments just as sensation gives substance to physical judgments. Suffering and evil develop feeling, which finds its supreme expression in tragedy. To the thinking function life is a comedy; to the feeling function life is a tragedy. In Christian theology, where the thinking function has ruled and feeling has been repressed or sentimentalized, evil and tragedy are repudiated in a final comedic affirmation. Feeling or pathos is personified in Prometheus-Lucifer-Satan and also in the Son as the suffering Christ. In Greek mythology feeling's premier embodiment is feminine: the goddess Aphrodite.

FLUX.   Along with process and stasis, forms the three basic philosophical positions. A flux universe is pluralistic, temporal, irrational, and imperfect. Flux bolsters the Satan-Lucifer-Prometheus and shadow archetypes, the feeling function, reductive thought, relativism, alienation, the ethic of rebellion, an ironic outlook, and the basically dualistic attitude that evil is an impurity localized in scapegoats. Flux leads to polytheism even as stasis leads to monotheism.

FREEDOM.   Defined by three concepts: (1) free will, the ego's power to act free of external interference, which is a necessary though not a sufficient condition for (2) responsibility for the consequences of one's acts and 3) mature freedom. Mature freedom or individuated wholeness is a state in which ego and self work in harmony, no single archetype dominates, and decisions flow from the whole self. The androgynous wiseperson archetype is constellated in those who achieve mature freedom. Free will alone cannot make one responsible or give decisive identity. These entail at the very least the character maturity to exercise self-discipline, understand alternatives, and heed consequences. In the West the problems of freedom and the feminine are closely related, since mature freedom requires ending patriarchy's social, psychological, and religious repression of the feminine.

FREUD and Freudian psychology. Stand to Jung and Jungian psychology, Jungians believe, as Ptolemy and the geocentric theory stand to Copernicus and the heliocentric theory. Freud made ego the regulating center of the psyche. Jung saw ego as but one of many subordinate archetypes in a psyche whose ultimate arbiter is the self. Similarly, Jung saw in the oedipal complex one of many archetypal patterns, not the single dominant pattern Freud saw. Jung's psychology is revolutionary not only in respect to Freudianism but also in relation to most Western philosophies and orthodox theology, both of which make ego values supreme and pattern the Deity upon ego. What Freud called the superego, Jung identified with the Father archetype and collective thinking. Freud's id can partake of Jung's shadow, although the shadow is potentially a more creative and more conscious function than the id. Freud's theory of libido reduced all energy to sexual energy, whereas for Jung the sex drive was only one manifestation of psychic energy. Freud's psychology is oriented toward the masculine and men, particularly in their roles as fathers and sons: consequently, it neglects the feminine and women, magnifies the oedipal complex, ignores anima and animus, and rejects the ideal of androgyny. The crucial absence of an overarching, regulating self archetype in Freud reinforces and expresses his atheism and his reductivism.

GODHEAD. For Jung, refers to the unfolding quaternal totality of the Western divinity. It encompasses the Father, Son, and Holy Spirit or Paraclete along with a repressed Fourth figure whom Jung in different phases of his thought speculated must be either Lucifer or Mary. While Godhead's structure mirrors the four-part structure of psyche, its activity manifests the three stages of the dialectic of individuation: the Father or the rude beginnings of divine individuation; the polarized opposites of the dual archetype of the two hostile brothers, Christ and Lucifer; and the consummation of the process in the Paraclete who epitomizes God the Artist. The Paraclete as anima and Father-Son-Satan as animus form the yin and the yang of that divine androgyne and symbol of the self that is Godhead. Godhead's efficacy in imaging the self and its individuation accounts for its tremendous historical dynamism. As an image of the individuating self, Godhead finds its counterforce and collective shadow in the devouring uroboros. Seen philosophically, Godhead can represent the Universal Self or Supreme Identity.

GREAT MOTHER. An all-encompassing archetype of maternity with a distinct positive and negative polarity. The positive Great Mother, embodied in the Virgin Mary and the Mother Church, is a distinguishing archetype of Catholicism. Reacting against Catholicism, radical Protestants, like Milton, focused upon the seductive, entwining, and devouring aspects of the negative Great Mother, which they unconsciously connected with the uroboros. While Protestants rejected the Great Mother and exalted the Father, the feminine quietly returned to them in a different archetype, the wisewoman, to shape the role of the Paraclete as spiritual guide and Divine Anima. Divine Anima furthers life process through nurturing movement, breath (spirit), growth, transformation, and creation. Her negation, the devouring uroboros or evil anima personified in Medusa, demands the permanence, repression, certainty, and perfection that turns life to stone. Just as the Paraclete forms the anima of Godhead, so the devourer forms the collective shadow of Godhead. Together they manifest the Great Mother for good and for evil.

HEROES. Develop in two stages. In the first stage the hero symbolically establishes ego independence from the devouring mother (the uroboros) in the dragon fight and wins the heroine (anima). In the second stage the hero encounters the world, realizes the larger self, and assumes the identity of the father. Typically, this requires a journey involving sacrifice, or deflation of ego, and a quest for a sacred object (e.g., the Grail) that symbolizes the self.

HIEROSGAMOS or sacred marriage. An alchemical metaphor for a transformation achieved through a *conjunctio* of male-female pairs who embody animus and anima or spirit and soul. The pairs are commonly represented by a king and queen, a god and goddess, or Adam and Eve. Jung sought to internalize *hierosgamos* in a single quaternal deity. Hence, he introduced a fourth feminine Person, or anima, who would unify or transform warring opposites to create androgynous wholeness. Jung's internalized *hierosgamos* is personified in the alchemical syzygy or divine androgyne. The internal *hierosgamos* and the androgyne archetype represent the psyche's union with itself or wholeness.

HOLY SPIRIT or Paraclete (literally, companion). The neglected fourth member of the Godhead who arises to resolve the dualistic conflicts of the two hostile brothers in a *coincidentia oppositorum* that consciously individuates the whole. Its guiding, healing, and motivating work parallels that of the transcendent function, intuition and eros. Being closely associated with Greek Sophia, the Old Testament wisdom figure and the wisewoman archetype, and playing the roles of guide, comforter, and inspirer, it is predominantly feminine in function. Indeed the terms "spirit" or "pneuma" are misapplied since the Paraclete acts as the anima or yin of God, who brings individuated wholeness to Godhead through *conjunctio* with the yang or multi-voiced animus-spirits of Father-Son-Satan: thereby the Divine Androgyne is formed. As anima of God, the Paraclete manifests God as artist and the *lumen naturae*, which explains why Milton intuitively identified his muse with it. Largely ignored by orthodoxy, the Paraclete personifies the neglected soul of Western culture and may provide the keys to its transformation and full individuation. Jung speculated that the future of Christianity depends upon transcendence of the strife of hostile brothers (ego and shadow / Christ and Satan / Logos and Pathos / form and substance) through activation (as Eros and Sophia) of the Paraclete.

IMAGE. Furnishes a context and medium for archetypes. Jung discovered that archetypes and psyche itself operate imagistically through symbol, myth, and metaphor. Consequently, archetypes and the psyche are best approached and understood by imagination. Furthermore, for Jung, imagination is primary to and a precondition of thought and sense.

IMAGO DEI. According to Jung, who followed Kant rather than Plato, we cannot know God as metaphysical entity or *ousia*—that is, essential being. Unto the unknowable entity we call God we project archetypes that form our *imago dei*. From the self, the supreme archetype, we derive the idea of God; and the self provides our most adequate image or metaphor of God. However, other archetypes are projected unto the divine unknowable, for example the entire collective unconscious in elaborate pagan pantheons, or the paternal ego in Christian, Jewish, and Islamic monotheism. These polytheistic and monotheistic divine images form partial, and therefore inadequate, metaphors of the uniplural self. Jung saw the psychic imbalances, dysfunctions and diseases that afflict civilizations as symptoms of the inadequacy of their *imago dei*.

INDIVIDUATION. A dialectical movement from split and partial consciousness toward a harmonized, fully differentiated consciousness that gives mature freedom. Individuation works against the counterforce of devouring uroboros. Spurred by the self, individuation proceeds by raising opposites from the unconscious and eventually conjoining them in order to manifest, give substance to, and finally harmonize the diverse parts of the psyche. In the individuation process ego becomes aware of (1) its separation from the unconscious uroboric state, (2) its function as the center of consciousness through identification with the hero archetype, (3) its need for substance through opposition from the shadow, 4) its limited power through tragic experience, and finally, (5) through the work of anima, aware of its interdependence with the whole self, thus realizing the wiseperson archetype. Individuation, moreover, can be viewed as a drama with the psyche its theatre and the self, as dramatist, orchestrating the archetypal players: ego plays the protagonist, shadow the antagonist or comrade, and anima the heroine. Like life and like drama, individuation is a dynamic process of continuous transformation and unfolding wholeness that would cease were it ever to permanently achieve a final, static goal. While the process varies among individuals, images of transformation, e.g., the journey, death, and rebirth, invariably signal its presence. An alternative view of individuation emphasizes not a transformation process directed toward wholeness but an inner deepening where anima enables self to enter and enrich consciousness though epiphany, initiation, tragic sacrifice, and catharsis. In either case individuation by opening ego consciousness to self also opens it to God. When we project self onto *imago dei*, we simultaneously project the individuation process; and as culture matures or individuates so does its *imago dei*. The climatic stage of divine individuation in Western culture is the incarnation and crucifixion; but its full maturity lies in the future with the full manifestation of the Paraclete.

INFLATION. The inflated ego aggressively expands its role within the psyche, which alienates it from other psychic functions such as anima and shadow. Just as the self prompts individuation so the self's antipode, devouring uroboros, prompts inflation. The ultimate inflation, uroboric evil, occurs when ego denies all dependence on self and *unus mundus* to become a totally alienated, self-fed, self-consumed entity like a black hole. Uroboric evil makes the *imago dei* a likeness of a hypertrophied ego, thereby fashioning ego deities such as the *Summum Bonum*. In the less grandiose forms of inflation ego attempts to counter its fears of death and, more often, of failure in life. Inflation seeks security and certainty but actually generates alienation and obsession, which prepare the way for inflation's opposite, deflation or despair. Inflation can be seen as ego sinning against self, others, and cosmos. The remedy to the "sin" of inflation is not repentance but a humbling transformation of ego that opens it to shadow, anima, and self, recognizes interdependence, and gives the faith or *pistis* to accept life and live fully. In Renaissance literature alienation and inflation commonly reveal themselves in envy and malice. Inflation is central to the psychology of all comedy and tragedy. Comedy deflates ridiculous inflation. Tragic inflation may arise from flawed virtue in the hero or from inflated malice in the villian; tragic catharsis allows a purging of ego inflation to release the whole self.

INITIATION.   Enacts transformation. Instigated by the self, initiations begin with the death of a limited ego identity no longer adapted to life's challenges and end with rebirth into a more comprehensive awareness. The initiate is typically accompanied by an initiator who mediates with the spirit realm—usually a shaman, priest, doctor, trickster, or saint—and who carries the projection of what the initiate will become. The psychoanalytic process is analogous to traditional ritualistic initiation. Hermes is the god of initiation.

INTERDEPENDENCE.   A fundamental assumption of Jungian thought. Though Jung explicitly stresses only the interdependence of temporal events in synchronicity, interdependence is implicit in many other central Jungian conceptions. Wholeness can be viewed as the harmonious interdependence or homeostasis of parts within an organism, while individuation is the selfsame interdependence among the archetypes of the self. Likewise, androgyny realizes interdependence or syzygy of individuated male and female elements, *coincidentia oppositorum* realizes interdependence of opposites, and *unus mundus* realizes interdependence of physical and psychical. From a Christian perspective, interdependence requires and manifests love and combats alienating inflation. Interdependence is the ideal relationship of man to God and of ego to self as they work to co-create consciousness. Quaternity implies the interdependence of the archetypes of Godhead. Like Quaternity, interdependence entails uniplurality and a philosophy of process. Moreover, it stands opposed to the alienation latent in uroboric monism or stasis, and active in radical pluralism or flux.

INTUITION.   The psychic function that explores the liminal, determines inherent possibilities, grasps relationships among parts, synthesizes opposites, and sees things whole. Intuition, through metaphor, finds new links between previously (and logically) unconnected ideas. Though Jung does not stress the synergy, intuition's reliance on metaphor and its power to connect parts into wholes makes it synergistic with imagination. Intuition, through imagination, generates visionary poetry. All vision, in the sense of prophetic vision, philosophic vision, or artistic vision, is largely a product of intuition. The inward vision manifest in Jungian psychology and associated with the Holy Spirit's archetype relies on intuition. Identified with the god Hermes, intuition, an intellectual quicksilver, moves swiftly from idea to idea skipping logical connectives to leave the more ponderous thinking function far behind. As mystic channel to the realm of the archetypes, intuition is as essential to psychic and spiritual development as thinking is to intellectual development. Jungian psychology in its effort to map the psyche relies on intuition no less than on thinking.

INWARD VISION.   In its most basic sense, designates man's second sight of consciousness. Seen philosophically, it contrasts to the old ethic of obedience and the ethic of rebellion. Inward vision realizes transformation by reconciling opposites, discerning new patterns, and linking parts to make wholes. The goals of inward vision are understanding in place of obedience, persuasion in place of command, mature freedom or individuated wholeness in place of free will, and metastance (or overview) in place of commitment. Some of its associations are: the Holy Spirit, intuition, the wiseman or wisewoman archetype, anima, *conjunctio oppositorum*, interdependence, Kierkegaardean inwardness, Jung's analytic psychology, and process philosophy.

LOVE, or Eros.   To anima what logos is to ego and pathos to shadow. Love moves us toward an ideal interdependence based on full awareness of self and other. Hence, love encourages dialogue, precludes projection and scapegoating, and curbs inflation and alienation. Love, creating interdependence, is the way anima confers value on others and the world. Though love works through anima, its ultimate source is the self's desire for harmony with the *unus mundus* or God.

LUCIFER.   Denominates the additional fourth member of the heterodox Jungian Quaternity. Manifesting the dark half of the dualist archetype, or the hostile brothers, Lucifer incorporates features of the rebel, the trickster, Dionysus, and the alchemical Mercurius. His creative and destructive sides are PROMETHEUS and SATAN. He stands dialectically opposite the Son or the divine ego confronting his obedient logos and ethereal spirituality with a shadow (or dark counter ego) of rebellious pathos and instinctive animal drives. Viewed externally he is God's scapegoat, but understood by Jungian psychology he is God's potentially creative shadow, which orthodoxy, through its perfectionist doctrine of *summum bonum*, insists upon repudiating and projecting on a putatively external scapegoat.

MANDALA.   Taking a squared circle for its standard visual image, symbolizes the quaternity or interdependent wholeness of the total psyche. In the West the Quaternal Godhead forms the supreme mandala.

METADRAMA.   Orchestrates, often by indirections, juxtapositions, and reverberations or through metaphor and symbol, our subtle responses to and delayed reflections upon the main drama. Creating multiple viewpoints and a tension between role playing and real identity, metadrama spurs doubt and reevaluation. The artist may introduce metadrama either consciously or unconsciously. When metadrama is unconscious, it subverts the main drama with metadramatic epiphanies. Metadramatic epiphanies occur when the artist's unconscious orchestration causes us to question what the artist's conscious ego wants to believe. These epiphanies are commonly of archetypes of Godhead whose true nature cannot be acknowledged. Metadramatic epiphanies constellate archetypes that compensate conscious one-sidedness, especially the one-sidedness of orthodoxy.

MYTHS.   In their primitive or natural form, stories containing archetypal encounters, patterns, symbols, and figures. By bringing the activity of archetypes into consciousness they release us from their compulsive hold and allow ego to tap their energies. Myths can be seen as metaphoric statements by the psyche about itself: God, like the psyche, reveals his or her Self through myth. Consciousness can deepen and amplify myths and create new mythologems with which to restructure our perception of reality. Whether our myths are primitive or sophisticated, religious, political, scientific, or artistic, we unavoidably perceive reality through the categories of myth.

NUMINOUS.   Derives from numen or spirit and carries the meaning of "spiritual" without the baggage of its connotations. It can also imply holiness. Symbols are numinous, meaning that they are mysterious and cannot be precisely defined.

OEDIPUS COMPLEX.   In Freudian psychology, the primary pattern shaping male ego development. In Jungian psychology it becomes secondary to the relationship with the mother; indeed, one of Jung's chief criticisms of Freud is that he recognized only one myth and one archetype: Oedipus. For Jung the Oedipus archetype can be seen as shaping that stage of development where ego identifies with shadow to rebel against the Father or primal parent. Being central to the relationship of father and son or senex and puer, Oedipus is also central to the relationship of God the Father and his two sons, Christ and Satan. The obedient Christ symbolizes repression of oedipal impulses and the rebellious Satan symbolizes living them. Protestant Milton's efforts to subordinate the Son to the Father can be viewed as a theological extension of his strong repression of oedipal impulses. Jewish Freud's efforts to make the oedipal complex primary can be seen as an unconscious attempt to repress Christianity and repudiate its theology: the oedipal complex shows the harmony of Father and Son to be impossible.

OLD ETHIC.   Relies on repression, obedience to the commands of authority, and adherence to orthodox belief to maintain social order and personal sanity. Its controlling archetype is ego, which appears first personified in God the Father and later becomes embodied in the Son as Logos. The old ethic protects ego in its immature development while simultaneously introducing a rigidity that divorces its values from their human purposes. When discontented egos turn to the shadow for an alternative, the ethic of rebellion is born. The two hostile ethics, with their tools of contempt and envy, guilt and justice, perpetuate cycles of sado-masochistic manipulation that are broken only when inward vision develops. The old ethic, the ethic of rebellion, and inward vision are linked to the fundamental philosophic stances of stasis, flux and process.

ORTHODOXY.   The theological mainstream of Christian belief defined by dogmas accepted by the Catholic Church, Eastern Orthodox churches, and most of Protestantism. At the core of orthodox dogma is the Nicene Creed, which holds

Christ fully God and fully human, the doctrine of the Trinity, and the view that God is the *Summum Bonum*. *Privatio boni* is also essential to orthodox belief, even though Christians are not officially required to believe it. Despite the Trinity dogma, orthodoxy is archetypally ruled by the Son-Logos and the Father. Ego, stasis, the old ethic, and the thinking function also dominate orthodoxy. Orthodoxy, following logos, purges the feminine and intuition from the Holy Spirit and redefines it as an aspect of the Son and the Father. Jung sought to go beyond orthodoxy to revitalize Christianity's myths and archetypes with his teaching that God is a quaternity, not a trinity. Jung's heterodox Quaternity restores psychic balance and wholeness to Godhead.

PARACLETE.   Jung often used this term when referring to his heterodox conception of the Holy Spirit. Its simple literal meaning of companion eliminates the Trinitarian theological baggage freighted on the term "Holy Spirit" and readily connotes the Quaternitarian feminine aspects of the Deity, particularly the Old Testament wisdom figure. As companion, the Paraclete carries the archetype of anima and the function of divine soul.

PERSONA.   The mask ego constructs and the roles it assumes to make specific impressions upon others, protect its privacy, and conceal its shadow. The darker the shadow, the brighter the persona must be to conceal it; and the weaker, or less individuated, the ego the stronger the persona. Persona and anima are contraries, the persona being concerned with the external and collective and the anima with the internal and individual. In orthodox theology the doctrines of *summum bonum*, *privatio boni*, and the Trinity form the persona of God. Insight and individuation require facing the activated archetypes persona conceals.

PISTIS.   A type of faith that contrasts to faith as blind submission to an external authority or faith as willed belief in doctrine. For Jung *pistis* refers to a conscious trust in the creative, sustaining abilities of the self, or, to use his phrase, "fidelity to the law of one's own being." Seen in a specifically Christian light, it expresses the authentic love that comes not from ego but from self.

PLEROMA.   The fullness of being encompassing creation and nothingness, a Gnostic notion of a oneness, a *unus mundus*, in which all opposites are subsumed. Mystical states involve perception of the *pleroma*. *Pleroma* also refers to the timeless realm of the archetypes. Jung's predilection for the term is one of many indications of the profound influence of Gnosticism on his thought.

PRIVATIO BONI.   The doctrine that evil is merely deprivation of good, promulgated by Augustine and others to give an explanation of evil that does not compromise the perfect goodness or absolute power of God. It assumes the identity of Being and the Good thereby making the Supreme Being the *Summum Bonum*. *Privatio boni* is one of three basic solutions to the problem of evil; the others are (1) absolute dualism and (2) *coincidentia oppositorum*, which means that a single principle accommodates interdependent good and evil held in dynamic tension. An advocate of *coincidentia oppositorum*, Jung rejected *privatio boni* on the grounds that good becomes unreal when *privatio boni* deprives its opposite, evil, of substance. Jung's rejection of *privatio boni* links him to Freud and the existentialists through shared belief in tragedy and the irrational. Loath to recognize the causes and ramifications of that rejection, many Jungians dismiss or downplay it. They fail to see that Jung's rejection of *privatio boni* for *coincidentia oppositorum* results not from his idiosyncrasies but from his theory of consciousness: consciousness develops as opposites are constellated from the unconscious, differentiated into real alternatives, and eventually (if the counterforce of uroboric unconsciousness is overcome) joined in a conscious *conjunctio oppositorum*.

PROCESS. Transcends the duality of stasis and flux through *conjunctio oppositorum*. Process assumes the universe eschatological and developmental; it entails uniplurality, transformation, interdependence, homeostasis, and *coincidentia oppositorum*. It is associated with the Paraclete in the unfolding Quaternity, individuation, the anima and self archetypes, the intuitive function, synthetic thinking, inward vision, and the tragic outlook. Uroboric evil is for process the prime evil. The characteristic philosophical stance of Jung and of Milton as artist is process.

PROJECTION. In the psyche, works rather like a slide projector projecting images upon a screen; however, the screen is usually another person, and the image projected is associated with an archetype activated in the psyche. For example, a man will often project his shadow upon an enemy or his anima upon his wife or lover, seeing in another his own unintegrated negative or positive characteristics and complexes. Individuation requires withdrawal of projections so we can consciously integrate the archetypes and see others as they are. Projection can also occur between parts of the psyche as in the case of Milton's Eve, where animus is projected onto shadow.

PSYCHE. In its restrictive meaning, refers to anima or soul. In the broader meaning Jung ordinarily employs, psyche encompasses all archetypes, psychic activities, processes, and possibilities both realized and unrealized, conscious and unconscious. It subsumes both the self and its uroboric counterforce. The ego and the conscious personality are only a small part of the total psyche. While ego identifies with one sex or the other, the psyche itself is always androgynous. It is from the regulating, unifying center of the total psyche, the self, that we obtain the idea of God.

QUATERNITY. For Jung, the psychological reality of the unfolding Divine Self that the orthodox dogma of Trinity, working like a persona, conceals. It involves a heterodox four-part *imago dei*, or Godhead, reflecting the four-part totality of psyche and self. Jung sought in Quaternity a truly uniplural *imago dei* that incorporates the psychological, philosophical, and theological advantages of both monism and pluralism (or monotheism and polytheism) while avoiding the pitfalls of each. Quaternity gives wholeness to deity by restoring the feminine with the Paraclete-anima, the material and the instinctive with Satan-shadow, and by recognizing the potential for evil and irrationality. Early Christians had great difficulties with their Trinitarian Godhead because it offers a psychologically simplistic *imago dei* that presents the Persons of Godhead as similar to three egos within one being. Quaternity, by presenting the Persons as separate archetypal functions and stages (primal parent, ego, shadow, and anima) within a homeostatic Divine Self, can dispel the confusion, obscurity, and alienating incomprehensibility that surround the Trinity. Quaternity can also order the chaos of polytheism when we realize that the lesser gods or archetypes are subsumed under the four prime archetypes, parent, ego, shadow, and anima, of the unfolding four-part self.

SELF.   In its most general meaning, psychic totality. In its more restrictive sense, self refers to the psyche's superordinate, transconscious regulating function that activates archeypes, works toward the *coincidentia oppsitorum* or psychic homeostasis, combats uroboros with its temptation to inflate, and thrusts ego down the path of individuation. The self in its wholeness is both an ultimate goal and the dynamism impelling us toward that goal. Self and *imago dei* are interdependent so that as awareness of self develops the image of God more and more reflects the self. In Jung's psychology the self is the energetic center of the psyche; self stands to ego as sun to Earth. This means that Jung follows a paradigm radically different from that of Freud (and most traditional Western thought), for whom ego is paramount. The paradigm shift from ego to self (Jung's Copernican revolution), along with its controversial implication of an androgynous rather than a single-sexed psyche, account for the difficulty Jungian psychology encounters in gaining acceptance.

SENSATION.   Perceiving what is actual and physically substantive rather than possible or apparent, the psychic function opposite intuition. The most basic and primitive of the functions, sensation is the first aspect of consciousness to become differentiated. It is associated with the Father and the animus in Hebrew myth; in Greek myth it is most commonly linked to Artemis and other feminine nature deities.

SHADOW.   Should not be taken literally, since shadow is nothing but a deprivation of light. The term is a metaphor for a realm of the psyche cloaked in shadow and for the archetype ruling that realm. The shadow contains energies that ego has difficulty accepting or developing and therefore relegates to the personal unconscious. In contrast to the contrasexual anima-animus, shadow is the same sex as ego and includes qualities that could give strength and substance to ego. For example, the shadow often incorporates that Promethean-Luciferian protest and anger necessary for healthy reactions to intolerable situations. Sometimes, shadow contains the playfulness repressed by that overdevelopment of ego Freud called superego; examples are the trickster and the prodigal son. And shadow has a largely ignored light side manifest in the sense of humor. Ego either engages shadow in a dialectic and, through mediation of anima, transforms and integrates its protest and playful energies thereby moving toward individuated wholeness, or it deliberately represses shadow. Repressed shadow can break from its prison cell and take possession of ego. Ego, possessed by shadow, embraces an ethic of rebellion that turns the old ethic upside down by calling good whatever was formerly deemed evil. If shadow remains repressed, ego will project it upon those regarded as alien or enemies who then become scapegoats. Projected upon scapegoats, the shadow can be warred against. Projection of shadow explains most personal antipathies as well as most prejudice and persecution. For Jung the healthy way to deal with shadow is not repression but a creative transformation that gives substance to ego by rendering shadow more conscious. In addition to the ego's personal shadow, the self has a counterforce, the devouring uroboros, which contains its collective shadow and impersonal, evil anima. Unlike the personal shadow whose evil is operative, the uroboric counterforce holds no repressed elements that can be transformed into new, conscious good. Rather it is a regressive pull opposing the self's drive for individuated consciousness. Because, resisting and negating consciousness, it never submits to transformation, the uroboric counterforce is an absolute evil.

SIN.   For Jung, violates the self by choosing lesser over greater, part over whole. Sin in a religious sense is an idolatry that defines God not as he truly reveals himself to us, through the self, but through one of its subsidiary archetypes, most commonly the ego. This Jungian view differs from traditional views, such as Milton's, where God is a projection not of self but of ego and sin is impurity or, most commonly, disobedience. Alienation and inflation are the prime symptoms of Jungian sin. Jung was more concerned with healing the alienation, inflation, and other psychic imbalances that come of putting part before whole than he was concerned with soteriology. Orthodox Christian soteriology posits an ego-God whose inflated anger at the "sin" of disobedience must be placated by sacrifice; Jung declared that it fell to him to heal the victims of Christianity's inflated *Summum Bonum* by guiding them toward wholeness.

SON, Messiah, Jesus, Christ.   The second Person of the Godhead in his general form, during his earthly mission, and after crucifixion. Orthodox theology identifies the Son with the light of logos, which embodies the rational ego function of deity. The Son, Jung believed, is an inadequate symbol of wholeness since, sacrificing instinct to law and substance to form, it looses the passional and elemental side of the psyche associated with Lucifer and Mercurius. Both halves of the brothers archetype, the Son and Lucifer, are needed for wholeness. By emphasizing the light half of the psyche and of the brothers archetype, Christians activated the destructiveness of the other half, which set up an unacknowledged dualism. The Job archetype in legend and literature, epitomizing perfect faith and obedience, inspires the orthodox Son.

STASIS.   Views the universe as fundamentally static, monistic, eternal, rational, and perfect. It is compatible with the Son as Logos, the ego, the thinking function, deductive thought, absolutism, monotheism, the ethic of obedience to authority, Christian orthodoxy, the comedic outlook, and the doctrines of *summum bonum* and *privatio boni*. A one-sided philosophic commitment to stasis tends to force its opposite, flux, into shadow where it undermines stasis with covert dualism.

SUBORDINATIONISM.   A nonstandard form of Trinitarianism espoused by Milton and sometimes labeled Arian by scholars of Milton. Minimizing the independent functions and persons of the Son and the Holy Spirit, subordinationism highlights the Father's supremacy. Subordinationism finds its theological opposite in modalism, which reduces Father, Son, and Holy Spirit to mere modes of one transcendent God. Against subordinationism and modalism, orthodoxy argues that the Son must be at once fully God and fully human for his sacrifice to work. For Jung theological statements about Godhead must be understood as statements about archetypes projected on Godhead. Accordingly, attitudes toward the psyche underlie theological positions like Trinitarianism, Arianism, Docetism, subordinationism, and modalism. Since for Milton the Father carries the projection of the patriarchal ego, his subordinationism asserts patriarchal ego's supremacy over the entire self. Milton also applies subordinationism to the sexes making woman (anima) subordinate to man (ego) as man is to God (patriarchal supreme ego). In Milton's schema the divine shadow becomes less than subordinate, for it is repressed into the unconscious and from there projected onto the scapegoat Satan.

SUBSTANTIATION.   The process of making good real through a *coincidentia oppositorum* with the operative evils of shadow and suffering. Without shadow and suffering to substantiate good (and the ego) by building moral substance, the good remains an empty ideal or an unfulfilled potential. Moreover, unless substantiation anchors ego in reality, ego easily falls prey to uroboros and drifts into alienated inflation. Substantiation is, therefore, a basic feature of individuation. The alchemical term for substantiation is *coagulatio*. As shadow and suffering substantiate ego, so encounters with death substantiate the soul.

SUMMUM BONUM or supreme good.   A conception of divinity stemming from Platonism and adopted by the Church fathers who sought to establish the moral perfection of the Christian deity. The belief that God is the omnipotent *Summum Bonum* makes it logically necessary to reduce evil to *privatio boni*. Jung condemned the doctrine of *summum bonum* as a projection of inflated, hypertrophied ego upon the *imago dei*. For Jung God is the *Summum Coincidentia Oppositorum* that encompasses everything and its opposite in a single interdependent reality and strives not for one-sided goodness but for plenary consciousness. Jung blamed the *summum bonum* doctrine for setting impossible standards of perfection that induce guilt and despair and thereby incapacitate us for dealing with real evils. The doctrine lies behind the popular and deleterious expression, *"omne bonum a Deo, omne malum ab homine"* (all good is from God, all evil is from man). Therein God gets credit for everything good, and man, with no good of his own, takes the blame for all evil. Jung's rejection of the *summum bonum* doctrine decidedly places him outside orthodoxy and aligns him with the Gnostic tradition.

SYMBOLS.   Manifest the archetypal structures and energies of the unconscious whence they spontaneously arise. Unlike elements of consciousness, they relate to the whole psychic system, conscious and unconscious, not just the ego. True symbols, being essentially ambiguous, elucidate something unknown by more or less apt analogies in order to compensate for and ultimately transform conscious one-sidedness with a *coincidentia oppositorum*. Since their peculiar function is to compensate for the inadequacy of rational concepts, once they are fully translated into rational terms they cease to be symbols and become mere signs. Symbols are most effectively approached through amplification of the images wherein they are embedded.

SYZYGY.   A Gnostic term for the divine androgyne and for the pairings of each creative emanation. Jung often appropriated it to refer to the *coincidentia oppositorum* of anima and animus or soul and spirit. Syzygy consciousness, which sees everything in interdependent pairs or wholes, contrasts with one-sided ego consciousness, which denies interdependence for dominance and dependence among alienated parts.

THINKING FUNCTION.   Seeks to comprehend and judge the world by means of logical inferences and rational analysis. It is associated with ego, animus, the ethic of obedience to authority, orthodoxy, the gods Zeus and Apollo, logos, stasis, and the Son.

TRANSCENDENT FUNCTION.   Jung's use of the term "function" is unfortunate here since it creates a confusion with the thinking, feeling, sensation, and intuitive functions. Most often operating through the anima, the transcendent function works to achieve transformation and psychic homeostasis by activating elements from the unconscious or by casting up unifying symbols that enable the ego to transcend destructive, one-sided attachments as compensatory opposites enter consciousness. The transcendent function thus allows opposites to dialogue with each other and mediates them to overcome their dualism in a *coincidentia oppositorum*. The Paraclete, providing inward vision and self-tuned conscience, constitutes the religious manifestation of the transcendent function. Whether called Paraclete, anima, or transcendent function, its objectives, psychic depth, and individuated wholeness are opposed to the one-sided perfectionism sought by the old ethic of obedience to traditional authority and belief in orthodoxy.

TRANSFORMATION.   A developmental process by which opposites are constellated in archetypal symbols and then consciously united, thus unfolding self to ego. The symbolism of transformation is found in initiation rites, alchemy, myth, and religious ritual. Transformation begins with an inflated ego alienated from self and shadow and proceeds through symbolic ego-death, or deflation, to an anima-mediated rebirth into a new consciousness that incorporates creative and substantial elements from the shadow. In transformation we confront evil and darkness. The ultimate transformation and darkness is death; through confronting death we deepen our souls. Man has an instinctive drive toward transformations that realize wholeness and depth: Jung calls this drive individuation. Transformation of evil and shadow into a conscious good is the constructive way to deal with their darkness, the destructive way being to deny shadow and project it upon scapegoats. Transformation, rather than perfection, is for Jung the essence of divinity.

TRICKSTER archetype.   Appears in rebellious hero figures like Satan and Prometheus or in playful shape-changers like Mercurius and the prodigal son. Embodying the shadow, it is often associated with the dark member of the two hostile brothers who champions individuality against the collectivity of the father archetype and compensates imbalanced conscious attitudes. By upsetting established order, the trickster releases creative energies along with chaos and destruction. The trickster symbolically manifests phallos.

TWINS as TWO HOSTILE BROTHERS or as FRIENDS.   (feminine examples are the harlot and the virgin, and the mistress and the wife). Dark and light symbol of same sexed psychic opposites. These pairs exemplify the interdependence of opposites necessary to wholeness and the tension of opposites essential to individuation. Ego and shadow, thinking and feeling, are the two sets of opposites most often associated with the rival brothers, whose signal mythic exemplars are Abel and Cain, Christ and Satan. Just as the Great Mother has a nurturing Madonna side and a devouring uroboric side, this archetype can come as either the supportive friends or the combative enemies. Christianity emphasizes antagonism and rivalry between the brothers, while Greek paganism emphasizes dialogue and friendship. The result is two very different attitudes toward the ego-shadow relationship and toward homosexuality. The ego that represses its shadow inevitably projects and scapegoats it on others of the same sex, fostering distrust of same sex bonds. The ego that dialogues with shadow, seeks its cooperation, and learns to use its energy will put a high value on same sex bonds. In the religious sphere the orthodox Christian emphasis on the brothers' antagonism creates an implicit dualism between Christ and Satan.

UNCONSCIOUS.   A general term for those mental contents not readily accessible to the ego, it also refers to a psychic domain with a nature and laws different from the conscious domain and divided into a collective, or inherited, archetypal sphere and a personal sphere. Both the collective and the personal unconscious are independent of ego. The shadow connects ego with the personal unconscious, and anima connects it with the collective unconscious. For Jung God does not coincide with the unconscious, as in polytheism, but with the psyche's unifying center, the archetype of the self.

UNIO MYSTICA.   A Western alchemical analogue to the *tao*, *samadhi*, and *satori*, which in Jungian psychology represent that supreme form of integration in which the ego is subsumed in a self filled with consciousness. It can also refer to a union of self, cosmos, and God. Whether this ideal can actually be attained remains problematic.

UNUS MUNDUS.   An alchemical term, denominates that inherent unity or interconnectedness of the world and that ground of all empirical being (Brahman) sometimes symbolized by the *anthropos* or cosmic man and finding contemporary expression in the idea of Gaia. Known intuitively rather than through reason or sensation, it provides a metaphoric background for acausal theories of meaning such as synchronicity, implicate order, teleology, and mysticism. For Jung, healing, or restoring wholeness to the psyche, involves establishing its interdependence with the *unus mundus*. Wholeness brings knowledge of God whom we encounter first in the self and who ultimately unfolds in the *unus mundus*.

UROBOROS.   Takes for its image a single snake eating its tail, which contrasts with the interdependent energies of the yin/yang or tao, imaged as two snakes eating each other's tails. In its most primitive form the uroboros is simply the "Great Round" where all elements, male and female, good and bad, and promotive of and inimical to consciousness are mingled: as such, uroboros is the encompassing deity of the polytheistic pantheon. Epitomizing total self-sufficiency, uroboros images the archetype from which Plato derived the notion of *ousia* or being. The self constellates opposites to create consciousness and thus spur ego to emerge from uroboros, to advance individuation, and, ultimately, to achieve interdependence with the *unus mundus*. However, when uroboros exerts a regressive pull after ego's emergence, it becomes the devourer (or dragon) archetype that subverts consciousness and interdependence while promoting alienation and inflation. Moreover, devouring uroboros, functioning like a Freudian death wish, incites those destructive autonomous complexes, or psychoses, which find their definitive symbol in the unbearable image of Medusa. It is the devourer who, under the inflated guise of a quest for perfection and purity, tempts the ego of man and God to withdraw from interdependence with the *unus mundus* into alienated self-fed, self-consumed uroboric evil. In this role it becomes the evil anima, collective shadow and archetypal counterforce (symbolized by Leviathan) to Godhead and self. Although the self seeks conscious union of its inner opposites, union with the self's archetypal counterforce negates consciousness and the self's essential drive for individuation. Thus, the devouring uroboros is an implacable enemy to the self, and its evil is, unlike the operative evil of the personal shadow, absolute. Absolutely evil though it may be, uroboros is neither a useless privation nor a dualistic opponent. Overcoming its archetypal counterforce proves indispensable to the self's (and God's) task of individuating consciousness. Since devouring uroboros is necessary to the growth of that individuated consciousness, which characterizes the good and God in a self-based system, there can be no question of why a good God allows it.

VOICE or *vox dei*. Functions like conscience except that it reflects the inner wisdom of the larger self rather than ego commitments to external authority. Though Jung's patriarchal biases inhibited him from recognizing it, the voice often works through anima, as in the case of Milton's muse.

WHOLENESS AND INDIVIDUATED WHOLENESS. Like mature freedom, denote a state in which ego, through anima-mediated integration of shadow, incorporates the whole psyche in its balanced, fully differentiated, and essentially androgynous consciousness. Individuated wholeness does not eliminate conflicting opposites, for tension is essential to life; it encompasses them in an interdependent, homeostatic system symbolized in alchemy by the *hierosgamos*. Because it requires interdependence, individuated wholeness is better understood as uniplurality than as simple unity. The ripening of the individuation process, individuated wholeness stands immediately below *unio mystica* as the highest state possible for man. Like *unio mystica*, its value as a goal for the individuation process resides in our inability to realize it permanently.

Notes

Note: Epigraphs from Aristotle, *Poetics*, in *The Basic Works of Aristotle*, ed. Richard McKeon, trans. Ingram Bywater (New York: Random House, 1941), 1464; and Samuel Taylor Coleridge, "Lecture on Milton and the Paradise Lost" [at the Crown and Anchor], March 4, 1819, from *The Romantics on Milton*, ed. Joseph Anthony Wittreich (Cleveland: Case Western Reserve Univ. Press, 1970).

CHAPTER 1. SOMETHING OF GRAVER IMPORT

1. I refer particularly to those critics and scholars who assume either that orthodox Christian doctrine constitutes Truth or that it must be treated as Truth if we are to understand Milton, who is presumed to believe that Truth. The two seminal critical works proclaiming this outlook are: C.S. Lewis, *A Preface to Paradise Lost* (Oxford: Oxford Univ. Press, 1942), and Douglas Bush, *Paradise Lost in Our Time* (Ithaca: Cornell Univ. Press, 1945). For a more contemporary Christian approach see Dennis Danielson, *Milton's Good God* (Cambridge: Cambridge Univ. Press, 1982). In discussing the traditional approach I will rely often on Stanley Fish, *Surprised by Sin* (Berkeley: Univ. of California Press, 1971). Unlike Lewis, Bush, and Danielson, Fish does not assert his personal belief in Christian doctrine. He asserts only that we must follow Milton's orthodox beliefs to read his poems correctly.

2. Imaginative suspension of disbelief is a widely accepted requirement set down by Coleridge for understanding poetry.

3. Rivkah S. Klugar, *Satan in the Old Testament*, trans. Hildegard Nagel (Evanston: Northwestern Univ. Press, 1967), 64-65.

4. Jung, "Psychology and Literature," in *The Collected Works of C.G. Jung*, 20 vols., ed. Herbert Read, Michael Fordham, and Gerhard Adler, trans. R.F.C. Hull (Princeton: Princeton Univ. Press, 1966), 15:104.

5. For Jungian treatments of literary art as a form of consciously created dream see Mary Watkins, *Waking Dreams* (New York: Harper and Row, 1976); and James Hillman, *Healing Fiction*. (Barrystown, N.Y.: Station Hill, 1983).

6. Anne Ferry, *Milton's Epic Voice* (Chicago: Univ. of Chicago Press, 1983), distinguishes her own view of Milton's narrative voice from Fish's view: "This description of the narrative voice differs from recent ones which find that the poet's mode of speaking is typically to harass and rebuke us, that it is intended to make us feel angry and humiliated. Such a view that the narrator speaks in a superior and hostile way holds also that he uses rhetoric as a strategy of taunts and accusations to trick us into accepting his judgments, thus defining the relationship of narrator to reader as that of Satan to his followers" (xii).

7. Jungian psychology assumes that timeless archetypes link past, present, and future in a single interdependent reality or *unus mundus*. The Jungian belief in teleological causation finds its theoretical basis in the concepts of *unus mundus* or implicate order and synchronicity. For accounts of these concepts see Jung, "Synchronicity: An Acausal Connecting Principle," in *Collected Works*, 16; *Mysterium Coniunctionis*, in *Collected Works* 14; Marie

Louise Von Franz, *On Divination and Synchronicity*, trans. Una Thomas (Toronto: Inner City, 1880); Von Franz, *Number and Time*, trans. Andrea Dykes (Evanston: Northwestern Univ. Press, 1974); and Claude Curling, "Physics and the Psyche," in *In the Wake of Jung*, ed. Molly Tuby (London: Coventure, 1983), 147-60.

8. Jung develops his views on the visionary artist in *"Ulysses:* A Monologue," "Psychology and Literature," and "On the Relation of Analytic Psychology to Poetry," in *Collected Works* 15. Neumann develops his views in *Art and the Creative Unconscious,* trans. Ralph Mannheim (Princeton: Princeton Univ. Press, 1959); and *Creative Man,* trans. Eugene Rolfe (Princeton: Princeton Univ. Press, 1979).

9. There are several parallels between Fish and Kierkegaard. Fish's theory that Milton persuasively develops false positions to force us to reject them and discover the truth or move to something higher underlines a technique Kierkegaard uses with great effect and eloquence in *Either Or, Philosophical Fragments, Repetition,* and *Fear and Trembling.* The technique is implicit in Tertullian as well as in mystical teachings about the cloud of unknowing. I know of no evidence that Milton knew the mystical teachings, but he obviously knew Tertullian since he frequently cited him in the Commonplace Book. There has been no detailed study of Milton and Tertullian.

10. Milton develops the view that God cannot contradict himself in *De Doctrina Christiana,* in *The Complete Prose Works of John Milton,* ed. Maurice Kelley, trans. John Carey (New Haven: Yale Univ. Press, 1955), 4:156-61. Denis Saurat, *Milton: Man and Thinker* (London: Dent, 1944), observes, citing Milton's *De Doctrina:* "The only principle which allows human reason to venture into the study of God is this same principle of non-contradiction: '. . . He can do nothing which involves a contradiction.' Milton uses this idea frequently; for instance, to prove that 'God is not able to annihilate anything altogether, because by creating nothing He would create and not create at the same time, which involves a contradiction.'" (pp. 95-96).

11. Saurat, *Milton: Man and Thinker,* notes the similarity of Milton to nineteenth-century absolutism, 166-68; he treats regeneration through reason in *Paradise Regained,* 146-50.

12. A restrained existential interpretation of Milton is Roland M. Frye, *God, Man, and Satan* (Princeton: Princeton Univ. Press, 1964). Frye avoids viewing as explicit in Milton assumptions, such as radical faith, that are at best implicit.

13. Modern authors do, of course, deliberately use psychological theory to shape their work, as Eugene O'Neil does with Freudian theory or Hermann Hesse with Jung. However, in modern literature as in premodern, the unconscious produces more interesting and enduring results when it is left free to operate unconsciously, as appears to be the case in Kafka's work.

14. See T.S. Eliot, *On Poetry and Poets* (London: Faber and Faber, 1957), 156-83. The idea also contributes to the ideological basis of Eliot's most important poems.

15. Walter Kaufmann, *Without Guilt and Justice* (New York: Delta, 1973), 49.

16. Coleridge observed of Milton's theme and purpose: "Milton's object . . . was to justify the ways of God to man! The controversial spirit observable in many parts of [*Paradise Lost*] . . . is immediately attributable to the great controversy of that age, origination of evil. (*The Complete Works of Samuel Taylor Coleridge,* ed. W.G.T. Shedd [New York, 1853], 4:303.)

17. For a contemporary treatment of Milton's theodicy, see Danielson, *Milton's Good God,* who founds his defense of Milton's theodicy on a defense of the orthodoxy it consciously reinforces. Although Danielson is generally thorough, neglect of modern philosophical and pyschological criticisms of orthodoxy limits his work. He fails to respond to the analytic, pragmatic, and process philosophers and never mentions Jung, who has given us the most influential and original twentieth-century work on theodicy.

18. Milton never calls God the *summum bonum* in his "Of God," *De Doctrina Christiana*, chap. 2. He does say, however, that the will of God is "supremely pure and holy," "supremely kind," and "true and faithful," from which it may reasonably be inferred that Milton's God is essentially the same as the *summum bonum* of orthodox theology.

19. For modern perspectives upon theodicy and free will see Anthony Flew, ed., *New Essays in Philosophical Theology* (London: SMC, 1955); J.L. Mackie, "Evil and Omnipotence," *Mind* 64, no. 256 (1955) :321-40; H.J. McCloskey, "God and Evil," *The Philosophical Quarterly* 10, no. 39 (1960) :111-27; Frithjof Bergmann, *On Being Free* (Notre Dame: Univ. of Notre Dame Press, 1977); Henri Bergson, *Time and Free Will*, trans. F.L. Pogson (London: George Allen & Unwin, 1950); Phillipa Foot, "Free Will as Involving Determinism," *Philosophical Review* 66, (1957); Sydney Hook, ed. *Determinism and Freedom* (New York: New York Univ. Press, 1958); A.I. Melden, *Free Action* (London: Routledge and Kegan Paul, 1961); Jean-Paul Sartre, *Being and Nothingness*, trans. Hazel Barnes (New York: Philosophical Library, 1956); Yves R. Simon, *Freedom of Choice* (New York: Fordham Univ. Press, 1969); and Robert Young, *Freedom, Responsibility and God* (New York: Harper and Row, 1975).

20. Milton does refer to man's "spontaneous fall" in *De Doctrina*, written around 1647. But, perhaps grown wiser with age, he never uses the term when he dramatizes the fall in *Paradise Lost*.

21. Fish, *Surprised by Sin*, 240.

22. Danielson, *Milton's Good God*, 82-163, offers an extended treatment of the historical background to what he sees as Milton's basically Arminian conception of free will. Milton, Danielson points out, rejects compatibilism for a more radical form of free will. See also John Tanner, "'Say First What Cause': Ricoeur and the Etiology of Evil in *Paradise Lost*," *PMLA* 103 (1988): 45-56, for a perceptive account of Milton's use of that ancient version of spontaneous freedom, Pelagian free will.

23. Boethius, *Consolations of Philosophy*, book 5, argues that because he is outside time, God's knowledge is *scientia* rather than *praescentia*. Milton appears to voice the same conception when he has Satan observe of God: "who can deceive his mind, whose eye / Views all things with one view?" (2.189-90).

24. See C.A. Patrides, *Milton and Christian Doctrine* (Oxford: Clarendon, 1966), 130-42, for a detailed discussion of atonement.

25. The notion of epiphanies has a long and complex history upon which Milton draws consciously and unconsciously. For a review of the essential Greek phase of that history see Robin Lane Fox, *Pagans and Christians* (New York: Knopf, 1987), 102-67.

26. The view that Adam's fall was a *felix culpa* comes from A.O. Lovejoy, "Milton and the Paradox of the Fortunate Fall," *ELH* 4, no. 3 (1937): 161-79. For several decades it enjoyed considerable vogue. Recently, Danielson has argued that the doctrine is Catholic in origin, was picked up by the Calvinists and rejected by the Arminian sector of Protestantism, including Milton. *Milton's Good God*, 202-27.

27. Here my interpretation deliberately exphasizes the conflicting opposites within Godhead in order to manifest the contrasting positions of Milton the apologist and Milton the artist. Michael Lieb takes a different approach emphasizing the *coincidentia oppositorium* within Godhead. "Milton and the *Odium Dei*," ELH 53 (Fall 1986): 519-40. I stress the immanent opposition of opposites while Lieb stresses their transcendent unity. Lieb's is the higher, more profound perspective, but that does not invalidate the perspective I develop here and which Jung develops in *Answer to Job*. Immanent conflict makes possible transcendent unity, and we can only truly understand and value the transcendent unity if we are first made aware of the immanent conflict.

28. See Milton, *De Doctrina Christiana*, 229-325. Milton follows Plotinus rather than mainline orthodoxy, which usually espouses *creatio ex nihilo*.

29. See E.M.W. Tillyard, *Milton* (London: Chatto and Windus, 1930); and Saurat, *Milton: Man and Thinker,* 231-67, which traces Kabalistic and Hermetic influences on Milton. Saurat's views, it should be noted, have not won general acceptance.

30. Teilhard de Chardin, *The Phenomenon of Man*, trans. Bernard Woll (New York: Harper and Row, 1961), presents the best known modern example of process theology. For other influential examples see the work of Charles Hartshorne, particularly *The Divine Relativity* (New Haven: Yale Univ. Press, 1948); Shubert Ogden, *The Reality of God* (New York: Harper and Row, 1963); John B. Cobb, Jr., *A Christian Natural Theology* (Philadelphia: Westminster, 1969); and A.N. Whitehead, *Process and Reality* (London: Macmillan, 1929).

31. Jungian thinker Edward F. Edinger develops this idea, which is implicit in Jung's *Answer to Job*, in *The Creation of Consciousness* (Toronto: Inner City, 1984).

32. Some Renaissance thinkers whose ideas at times anticipate the process God are: Robert Fludd, John Dee, Jacob Boehme, and Giordano Bruno. Francis Yates, *Giordano Bruno and the Hermetic Tradition* (New York: Random House, 1964), forms an invaluable introduction to this trend in Renaissance thought.

33. Nelson Pike, "Hume on Evil," *Philosophical Review* 72, no. 2 (1963): 121-35.

34. Pike does not use logic in the sense of laws that govern what's possible but as a metaphor for the laws that describe either metaphysical truth or empirical reality. $E = MC^2$ is an example the "logic of the universe" taken to mean the laws of empirical reality. Einstein's law may not be true in all times and conditions, for example, in the early stages of the big bang. It is hardly the same sort of statement as $A = A$, which cannot be falsified empirically or even conceived of as untrue.

35. Such is the point of Kierkegaard's *Fear and Trembling.*

36. One might compare orthodox theodicy's added twists and turns to the ever more complex array of epicycles that were added to the Ptolemaic model in order to make its theory account for recalcitrant astronomical data.

37. For a provocative contemporary study of this element in Calvin, see William J. Bouwsma, *John Calvin* (Oxford: Oxford Univ. Press, 1988), 86-109, 162-76.

38. Calvin comes close to Augustine in this, but he departs from the position of the Catholic church, which assumes that Augustine went too far in the direction of predestination. The Church follows, instead, the more modern notions of St. Thomas.

39. From Job, *The Anchor Bible*, trans. Marvin H. Pope (Garden City: Doubleday, 1965), 15:316-36.

40. For Jung's views on Manichean influence on Christianity see *Aion, Collected Works* 9:36-60; and *Mysterium Coniunctionis, Collected Works* 14:79.

41. Jeffrey Burton Russell, *Satan* (Ithaca: Cornell Univ. Press, 1981), 149-218, offers a historical survey of these developments.

42. Augustine's long struggle with Manichaeanism doubtless made him particularly sensitive to and wary of dualism in all its subtle guises. Unlike the other Patristic thinkers, Augustine understood the threat radical free will poses to God as first cause. Thus, he attempted to circumvent that threat by stressing man's alienation and affirming predestination.

43. It is important to remember that Jung is concerned only with the psychological reality of Godhead. The metaphysical reality, the transcendent deity that may stand behind the deity that reveals itself immanently through the psyche, remains unknown and unknowable. When it comes to metaphysics Jung is a Kantian, not a Platonist. Jung observes in *Two Essays on Analytic Psychology*, in *Collected Works* 7:71: "The idea of God is an absolutely necessary psychological function of an irrational nature, which has nothing whatever to do with the question of God's existence. The human intellect can never answer this question, still less give any proof of God. Moreover, such proof is superfluous, for the idea of an all-

powerful divine Being is present everywhere, unconsciously if not consciously, because it is an archetype." For Jung's views on the true archetypes of Godhead see *Aion*, 36-117; see also *Psychological Approach to the Trinity* and *Answer to Job*, both in *Collected Works* 11.

44. This division of Western cultural dynamics around the three archetypes of Christ, the Father, and Satan owes much to Jung, especially his *Answer to Job*. The development and application herein, however, is original.

45. Alan Watts, *The Supreme Identity* (New York: Noonday, 1957), 105-12, posits a "Supreme Identity" similar to what Jung calls the *unus mundus* or the implicit order of being. Multiple first causes, Watts points out following St. Thomas, set up dualism.

46. John T. Shawcross, "Stasis, and John Milton and the Myths of Time," *Cithara* (1981): 3-17, gives a perceptive analysis of stasis in Milton. The case for regarding the Son as the nonhuman or supernal hero of *Paradise Lost* is presented in Shawcross, "The Son in His Ascendancy: A Reading of *Paradise Lost*," *MLQ* 27 (1966): 388-401. Contemporary critics usually settle upon one of three choices for the hero: man, the reader, or Adam. Shawcross, in *With Mortal Voice* (Lexington: Univ. Press of Kentucky, 1982), 41, observes of the hero: "The hero of *Paradise Lost*, is thus not just an ordinary hero of literature, not a specific personage within the work, but rather every man who follows the path, who learns like Adam the sum of wisdom."

47. For Kierkegaard's minimizing the role of logos see "The Subjective Truth, Inwardness; Truth is Subjectivity," in *Concluding Unscientific Postscript*, trans. David F. Swenson, (Princeton: Princeton Univ. Press, 1941), 169-282.

48. Walter Kaufmann's introduction to Kierkegaard's, *The Present Age* (New York: Harper and Row, 1962), offers a sound critique of Kierkegaard's assertion that modern man needs passion.

49. Fish, *Surprised by Sin*, 336-39, offers the stock orthodox argument, particularly popular in medieval times, that Satan is merely *privatio boni*. Jeffrey Burton Russell, *Lucifer* (Ithaca: Cornell Univ. Press, 1984), 194-99, 217-26, reviews these arguments in detail and with refreshing acumen.

50. "Knowing the truth of one's self in order to become free" may have been what the hero of the Gospels meant when he said: "Ye shall know the truth and the truth shall make you free." Such at least is John A. Sanford's Jungian interpretation of Christ's teachings in *Evil: The Shadow Side of Reality* (New York: Crossroad, 1986), 67-84; and *The Kingdom Within*, revised ed. (San Francisco: Harper and Row, 1987).

51. The romantics, Shelley most notably, adulated Milton as a political rebel and made a hero of Satan. By contrast, A.J.A. Waldock, *Paradise Lost and Its Critics* (Cambridge: Cambridge Univ. Press, 1947), and John Peter, *A Critique of Paradise Lost* (New York: Columbia Univ. Press, 1960), reacted against Milton's political positions and attempted to depreciate his achievement as a poet. William Empson, *Milton's God* (London: Chatto and Windus, 1961), is often grouped with Peter and Waldock but, unlike them, recognizes Milton's achievements, and his criticisms are much more balanced.

52. Jung expressed this view in different ways many times throughout his life. A typical, though seldom noted, expression is in "Letter to Bernard Lang of 14 June 1957," in *C.G. Jung Letters*, ed. Gerhard Adler, trans R.F.C. Hull (Princeton: Princeton Univ. Press, 1975), vol. 2, 371: "Taking the God-concept as an example, this is demonstrably grounded on archetypal premises corresponding essentially to the instincts. They are given and inherited structures, the instinctual bases of psychic behavior as well as thinking. The structures possess a natural numinosity (i.e. emotional value) and consequently a certain degree of autonomy. When, for instance, a so-called epiphany occurs, it is the projected appearance of this psychic structure, that occurs, that is of an image based on the archetypal structure. Owing to the autonomy and numinosity of the structure it appears as if it had a life

of its own, different from my life. We then say: God has appeared. What can be established is not that God has appeared, but on closer examination the structure of an archetype. Thus far can science go. It cannot cross this threshold and assert that it was God himself. Only belief can do that." Jung, following Kant, denied that we could have knowledge of transcendent things. For a Catholic critique of Jung's rejection of the transcendent deity, a critique that champions historical revelation, see Antonio Moreno, *Jung, Gods and Modern Man*, (Notre Dame: Univ. of Notre Dame Press, 1970).

53. Jung's therapeutic objectives toward Christianity are examined in Murray Stein, *Jung's Treatment of Christianity* (Wilmette, Ill.: Chiron, 1985); and John P. Dourley, *The Illness That We Are: A Jungian Critique of Christianity* (Toronto: Inner City, 1984).

54. John P. Dourley, *The Psyche as Sacrament* (Toronto: Inner City, 1981) offers a comparison of Jung and Tillich.

55. The fourfold nature of the psyche is most clearly explained in Jung's work on mandala symbolism, especially "Concerning Mandala Symbolism," in *Collected Works* 9:355-84; and "The Symbolism of the Mandala," in *Collected Works* 12:95-223. Additionally, it should be pointed out that the original Hebraic Godhead in its most primitive form, the so-called tetragrammaton, *yod he waw he*, is quaternal. Since one of its four letters is duplicated, it's also a triad. (The other Hebraic name for godhead, "elohim," is, likewise, plural.)

56. Jung, *Psychological Approach to the Trinity*, 196.

57. Ibid., 169ff. Jung gives no examples of a religion with the full Godhead in operation. He believed, or hoped, that that religion was yet to come. Specifically, he felt it might arise within the next six hundred years. See Stein, *Jung's Treatment of Christianity*, 179-93.

58. See David L. Miller, *The New Polytheism* (Dallas: Spring, 1981) with James Hillman's appendix, "Psychology: Monotheistic or Polytheistic," 109-42; also Hillman, *The Dream and the Underworld* (New York: Harper and Row, 1979), particularly 91-141. The sociological and political implications of polytheistic or pluralistic psychology are developed by James Ogilvy in *Many Dimensional Man* (New York: Oxford Univ. Press, 1977). Andrew Samuels, "Dethroning the Self," *Spring* (1983), offers a commentary on Hillman and polytheistic trends in contemporary Jungian psychology; Samuels' views are developed fully in *The Plural Psyche* (London: Routledge, 1989). The criticism of Jungian wholeness by Hillman and followers, I believe, fails to take into account the principle of interdependence implicit in the *coincidentia oppositorum*. Basically, Jung rejects polytheism because he believes that the *imago dei* is not just a reflection of the unconscious and all its archetypes, but of a very specific archetype, the self. In *Answer to Job* he observes: "Strictly speaking, the God-image does not coincide with the unconscious as such but with a special content of it, namely the archetype of the self" (469).

59. Tillich, *Systematic Theology* (3 vols. [Chicago: Univ. of Chicago Press, 1956-1964], 1:221), observes: "The concreteness of man's ultimate concern drives him toward polytheistic structures; the reaction of the absolute element against these drives him toward monotheistic structures; and the need for a balance between the concrete and the absolute drives him toward trinitarian structures." Jung, by contrast, held that the mind naturally moves toward structures that reflect its own quaternal nature. Only when something highly significant is repressed does it resort to trinitarian structures. Thus, Christianity's repressions of the shadow and evil, the feminine, and the material, or instinctive, are responsible for its truncated Trinity.

60. Jung, *Psychological Approach to the Trinity*, 168.

61. For example, Jung writes in *Psychological Approach to the Trinity*, 197: "Life, being an energetic process, needs the opposites, for without opposition there is, as we know, no energy. Good and evil are simply the moral aspects of this natural polarity." In support of

Jung's position it may be noted that electrical and atomic energy, along with all chemical bindings, depend on opposites in the form of positive and negative charges.

62. Jung, *Psychological Approach to the Trinity*, 157.

63. Shawcross, "The Son and His Ascendency," points out that the Son stands at the structural center of *Paradise Lost*. This crucial point, unnoted until Shawcross, is readily overlooked because Milton's subordinationism makes the Son appear, theologically, as the Father's willing tool.

64. Jung so recognizes in his *Psychological Approach to the Trinity*, and Edinger develops the idea further in *Ego and Archetype* (New York: Putnam, 1972), 179-93. Edinger's views are challenged by Hillman, who objects to his approach as too "white" because Edinger tends to accept the orthodox persona at face value and to ignore the darker realities hidden beneath. See Hillman's provocative "Notes on White Supremacy," *Spring* (1986): 29-58.

65. See the analogous diagram Jung presents in *Mysterium Coniunctionis*, par. 122: "The cross is by implication the Christian totality symbol: as an instrument of torture it expresses the sufferings on earth of the incarnate God, and as a quaternity it expresses the universe, which also includes the material world. If now we add to this cruciform schema the four protagonists in the divine world-drama—the Father as *auctor rerum*, the Son, his counterpart, the Devil, and the Holy Ghost, we get the following quaternity:

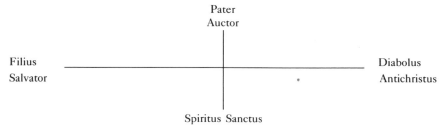

66. See Jung *Psychological Approach to the Trinity*, 175-190.

67. Kierkegaard posits three stages: the aesthetic, the ethical, and the religious or the stage of faith. The Father could be seen as embodying a consciousness similar to Kierke-gaard's aesthetic stage while the Son lies in the ethical stage and the Holy Spirit in the religious stage. Jungian psychology's understanding of these stages is not, of course, Kierke-gaard's. See *Either Or* and *Stages on Life's Way*, trans. Walter Lowrie (Princeton: Princeton Univ. Press, 1945). Significantly, the ethical stage is always one of polarized choices, hence the title *Either Or.*

68. Calvinists and orthodox Marxists with their historical determinism form the important exceptions to this generality. It should be noted that Lenin, himself an unparalled example of the power of individual will, modified Marxist determinism to account for the power of will.

69. Jung, *Psychological Approach to the Trinity*, 176.

70. I use the term "individuated wholeness," even though it is not Jung's term, because the simple term "wholeness" can refer to the unconscious wholeness of the womb. Something more is needed to carry the meaning of conscious wholeness.

71. Jung's development of the four psychic functions first appears in *Psychological Types*, *Collected Works* 6. A more recent work that summarizes and extends Jung's ideas in Marie Louise Von Franz and James Hillman, *Lectures on Jung's Typology* (New York: Spring, 1971).

72. Peter Homans observes of Jung's views on modern man in *Jung in Context* (Chicago: Univ. of Chicago Press, 1979), 174: "I believe Jung's psychology fits lock-and-key with an

enormous and incredibly amorphous body of sociological literature that has been subsumed under the rubric 'the theory of mass society.'" As an example of a theory of mass society paralleling Jung, Homans cites Max Scheler's view that mass man loses individuality and is emotionally unstable, capricious, and hysterical. (David Frisby, *The Alienated Mind* [London: Heineman, 1983], surveys the whole literature on the subject.) Modern man, Jung believed, is characterized by a rigid persona, extraversion, and excessive rationality. As a result he submits totally to the rules of the state. The breakdown of the persona and the emergence of the archetypes is essential to the process of individuation, which alone can counter mass thinking and modern narcissism, instability and hysteria.

73. Erich Neumann, *Depth Psychology and the New Ethic*, trans. Eugene Rolfe (New York: Putnam, 1969), 33. Non-Christian cultures, such as Islam, also have repression-based ethics similar to the old ethic, which is not so much specific to Christianity or Judaism or Islam as it is specific to any religious view that takes ego as a psychological model for deity.

74. The ethic of rebellion is my addition to and qualification of Neumann's schema, which remains limited to the old ethic and what he calls the new ethic or, to use my term, the inward vision. Thomas Sowell, *Conflict of Visions* (New York: William Morrow, 1987) weighs the political aspect of the conflict between the old ethic, which he calls the constrained vision, and the ethic of rebellion, which he calls the unconstrained vision.

75. Neumann calls the new outlook "the new ethic" to accent its basis in self, not in ego, and its guiding rather than proscriptive character. It is more accurate, I believe, to call this new outlook that transcends the opposed ethics of obedience and rebellion a vision rather than an ethic.

76. Kierkegaard, *Either Or,* held that ethics necessarily stands below the higher, religious stage of human consciousness, the stage I call the inward vision. Kierkegaard's most concise and lucid treatment of the religious stage is *Fear and Trembling*.

77. John M. Steadman, *Milton and the Renaissance Hero* (Oxford: Oxford Univ. Press, 1967), particularly 161-201, develops the idea of heroism as obedience to the old ethic.

78. For Jung's views on conscience or *vox dei*, as he sometimes calls it, see "A Psychological View of Conscience," *Collected Works* 10, 437-55. The concept of the voice has been developed more fully by Jungian psychologists than by Jung himself.

79. As the fairy tales show, none can afford to trifle with evil, not even an omnipotent deity. See Marie Louis Von Franz, *Shadow and Evil in Fairy Tales* (Zurich: Spring, 1974).

80. James Hall, *Dictionary of Subjects and Symbols in Art* (New York: Harper and Row, 1974), 80-82, reviews historical images of the suffering Christ.

81. See my account of *King Lear* in *Identity in Shakespearean Drama* (Lewisburg, Pa.: Bucknell Univ. Press, 1983), 123-54.

82. See Stein, *Jung's Treatment of Christianity*, 162-71.

83. The classic treatment of the idea is A.O. Lovejoy's *The Great Chain of Being* (Cambridge: Harvard Univ. Press, 1936). See 160-65 for remarks on Milton.

84. Lewis, *Preface*, (New York: Oxford Univ. Press, 1961), 73-74.

85. Table 3 (next page) is a rough and admittedly speculative attempt to place signal cultural figures mentioned herein among the three fundamental philosophical positions. Elements of all three positions appear in the work of most of these figures; consequently I have located each at the point that seems characteristic of his most influential thoughts. A good example of how thinkers utilize all three positions is found in Marx, who adopts a flux outlook when considering the need for revolution, a modified process view when treating the post-revolutionary period, and a stasis view when formulating the ideal "withering of the state."

86. Neumann, *Depth Psychology,* 101-35.

87. See William Kerrigan, *The Sacred Complex* (Cambridge: Harvard Univ. Press, 1983).

Table 3. Fundamental philosophical positions

Stasis	Process	Flux
Parmenides Plato Aristotle	Bruno	Protagoras Heraclitus
Plotinus Origen	Lactantius Boehme	Pelagius Montaigne
Augustine Aquinas Kant	Hegel	Wittgenstein Mill
Calvin Barth	Tillich Teilhard	Kierkegaard
Spinoza Hobbes	Whitehead James Dewey	Marx Nietzsche Sartre
	Jung	Freud Hillman Kafka
Dante Swift Eliot Tolstoy	Shakespeare	Dostoevsky Melville
Milton (as theologian)	Milton (as artist)	

Christopher Hill, *Milton and the English Revolution* (New York: Viking, 1978); and Andrew Milner, *John Milton and the English Revolution: A Study in the Sociology of Literature* (London: Macmillan, 1981), approach *Paradise Lost* assuming a version of the ethic of rebellion common to contemporary Marxist scholars. Joseph Wittreich, *Feminist Milton* (Ithaca: Cornell Univ. Press, 1987), uses and goes beyond the Marxist ethic of rebellion to show how Milton interacts with, challenges, and revises orthodoxy rather than merely inculcating it. Empson and Shelley also relied on their versions of the ethic of rebellion.

CHAPTER 2. THE SHADOW OF GOD

1. Clement of Alexandria was among the first to posit formally the doctrine that God is the *summa bonum*. He, however, cannot be held responsible for the notion of an all good deity since it was widespread in the culture and found a receptive audience in most postapostolic orthodox theologians. See S. Lilla, *Clement of Alexandria: A Study in Christian Platonism and Gnosticism* (London: 1971); and W.E.G. Floyd, *Clement of Alexandria's Treatment of the Problem of Evil* (New York: 1971). Jung's views on the *summum bonum* appear throughout his work: for a typical example, see "Answers to the Rev. David Cox," *Collected Works* 18: 724-27.

2. Edinger, *The Bible and the Psyche: Individuation Symbolism in the Old Testament* (Toronto: Inner City, 1986), gives a detailed exposition of Yahweh as the self archetype in the Old Testament. Edinger sees Yahweh acting as a self in relation to individuals who are viewed as egos. By contrast, Jung, in *Answer to Job*, often regards Yahweh as like a rather primitive ego.

3. Jung treats the projection of shadow, ego, and self upon *imago dei* in *Aion*, 3-10, 23-94, 222-69.

4. In *Evil*, Sanford remarks on Paul's disavowal of the "sin that dwelleth in me": "This amounts to a refusal on Paul's part to accept the Shadow as an inevitable and legitimate part of his own nature; it leaves as the only possible solution an attempt to find some way to

cut the Shadow off from oneself. As we have seen, this does not solve the problem, but only drives it deeper underground" (70). I would add that polarization of ego and shadow is a key to Paul's personality. We see the effects of polarization in his road to Damascus conversion. Such radical swings, which dramatically illustrate Jung's principle of *enantiodromio*, are possible only when there is no mediating factor, or well developed anima, to bring about a *conjunctio oppositorum*. Paul's exaltation of celibacy and denial of sensual feeling are further evidence of repression of anima.

5. See John Boswell, *Christianity, Social Tolerance, and Homosexuality* (Chicago: Univ. of Chicago Press, 1980); Robert E.L. Masters, *Eros and Evil* (New York: Julian Press, 1962); Joshua Trachtenberg, *The Devil and the Jews* (New Haven: Yale Univ. Press, 1943). Russell, *Satan*, 86, contends that much Christian intolerance stems from the premise that the world is at issue between Christ and Satan.

6. Neumann says the inward vision or new ethic "rejects the hegemony of a partial structure of the personality and postulates the total personality as the basis of ethical conduct." *Depth Psychology*, 92.

7. H.L. Philp, *Jung and the Problem of Evil* (London: Rockcliff, 1958).

8. That Christians are not required to think rigorously is of course Jung's point when he insists that Christian thinkers are often feeling types who exalt excessively their inferior function and its hypostasis, the divine logos. Feeling types have an emotional approach to thinking, which is why so many Christian doctrines, *privatio boni* for example, are logically absurd and must rest upon faith, that prime assertion of feeling over reason.

9. Philp, *Jung and the Problem of Evil* 18-19.

10. Jung to Victor White, 30 Apr. 1952, *Letters* 2:61.

11. Jung to Victor White, 30 June 1952, *Letters* 2:72. I take exception to Jung's notion that God is necessarily Being. The notion gives God metaphysical qualities Jung elsewhere denies that we can know; moreover, it grounds God in the uroboros rather than the self archetype. If our idea of God reflects the self, then God would be like a force running through all being and giving meaning to it.

12. Jung states his view that God is a *coincidentia oppositorum* on many different occasions and in diverse contexts. In *Answer to Job*, 369, for example, he maintains: "Yahweh is not split but an *antimony*—a totality of inner opposites—and this is the indispensable condition for his tremendous dynamism, his omniscience and omnipotence."

13. Homans, *Jung in Context*, 47-73, and Lilianne Frey-Rohn, *From Freud to Jung* (New York: Delta, 1974), develop Jung's link to Freudian irrationalism, which has often been overlooked. For example, Paul Tillich *Dynamics of Faith* (New York: Harper and Rowe, 1956), 4, asserts: "In all these representations of contemporary depth psychology we miss the feeling for the irrational element that we have in Freud and much of existential literature." It may be remarked that Tillich misses Jung's feeling for the irrational shown in his rejection of *privatio boni* and insistence upon absolute evil.

14. For example, Ross Woodman, "Nietzsche's Madness as Soul Building," *Spring* 1986, dismisses out of hand Jung's attacks on *privatio boni*. Woodman writes: "Though Jung made much of the *deus absconditus*, particularly in his *Answer to Job*, he like Job was never persuaded that God's darkness was anything more than his omnipotent light shining in a world that could not comprehend it. . . . Jung's quarrel with Father White over the Catholic view of evil as the *privatio boni* (evil as the absence of good rather than an autonomous force independent of it) was, as Father White always suspected, specious, not really about the nature of evil at all, for both affirmed the omnipotence of love. It was, on the contrary, Jung's deep-rooted Protestantism rebelling against Catholic dogma that placed institutionalized experience of the church above the individual's experience of the will of God. It was, in short, his quarrel with his father" (107-108). Woodman ignores Jung's long (extending over

the last twenty-five years of his life), recurrent (most of it unrelated to Father White) and insistent emphasis on the reality of absolute evil. Moreover, Woodman disregards the possibility that absolute evil might be something more purposive (in the sense that archetypes are purposive) than the chaos of Nietzsche's final insanity. Though Jung never explicitly identified the archetype of absolute evil, an evil absolute in respect to consciousness can be found in the devouring uroboros archetype. Devouring uroboros is not just an absence of consciousness but an active counterforce that holds the potential of total destruction. (See the entries on "evil," "*privatio boni*," and "uroboros" in the glossary). Finally, Woodman's attempt to reduce Jung's opposition to *privatio boni* to a "quarrel with his father" is ill-informed, misleading, and simply wrong. Some of the biographical roots of Jung's hostility to orthodoxy can be traced to his relationship with his pastor father but not to a standard oedipal quarrel. Jung resented orthodoxy because his father's efforts to force himself to believe destroyed him, or so Jung believed. Jung saw his father as a weak, kindly man unable to cope with the cruel, destructive side of the Christian God. Jung's attempt to expose the "evil" within the Divinity grew out of his desire to save others and himself from the tragic fate that befell his father. The world, men, and their Creator, Jung believed, are fraught with evil. By teaching men to pretend that evil is unreal, Christianity incapacitates us for dealing with it and so sets us up for destruction.

15. Jung, *Psychology and Alchemy*, in *Collected Works* 12:20-21.

16. Jung, who customarily made philosophical form bow to psychological fact, presented Godhead as process. All our conscious experience, he contended, subsists in immanent process. This means that we only know God consciously as an immanent process, leaving open the possibility, it would seem, of knowing him in his transcendence by some superconscious means, for example through mystic experience. Jung, however, usually neglects to acknowledge the possibility of mystical cognizance. That neglect constitutes one of the limitations of his theory of the self. (The neglect would be complete were it not for his alchemical work, particularly on the *unio mystica*). How odd it is that Jung's detractors should often accuse him of being mystical when the very neglect of the mystical is a salient deficiency in his theological outlook.

17. Edward C. Whitmont, *Return of the Goddess* (New York: Crossroad, 1986), 91-82.

18. An additional negative consequence of the doctrines of *privatio boni* and *summum bonum* lies in their tendency to encourage unrealistic expectations that produce despair and meaninglessness among the tender-minded and cynicism and hypocrisy among the tough-minded. Marion Woodman, *Addiction to Perfection* (Toronto: Inner City, 1982), analyzes this destructive perfectionism but never traces its roots in Christian doctrine. She attributes perfectionism to repression of the feminine element in the psyche, which in turn takes its revenge by making impossible demands. More fundamental than repression of the feminine is repression of self for ego and the consequent fashioning of God after ego values.

19. See Russell, *Satan*, 107-48.

20. Paul Ricoeur, *The Symbolism of Evil* (Boston: Beacon, 1969), 25-46.

21. Kierkegaard, *Purity of Heart Is to Will One Thing*, trans. Douglas V. Steere (New York: Harper and Row, 1938). For a contemporary philosophical examination of Kierkegaard's edifying discourse, which stresses the concept of commitment, see Jeremy Walker, *To Will One Thing: Reflections on Kierkegaard's Purity of Heart* (Montreal: McGill-Queen's Univ. Press, 1972), especially 111-63.

22. In *Return of the Goddess*, Whitmont observes of modern single-mindedness and its roots in monotheism: "This development sets the pattern for ego's dictatorial use of will to enforce the fiction of being the supreme ruler of the total psyche. The Greek mind still considered it a dangerous hubris to serve one god to the exclusion of others. From the time of the Middle Ages, the modern mind has demanded exclusive loyalty to one god, one way of

seeing things, whether in the name of religion, politics, or psychology. Parochialism, intolerance, and fanaticism are the shadow aspects of mental ego brilliance" (80-81).

23. Elaine Pagels, *Adam, Eve and the Serpent* (New York: Random House, 1988), maintains that early Christians conceived of freedom as a form of autonomy achieved through purity, particularly sexual purity: "For Clement, the "good news" of Christianity meant autonomy: that a Christian could actually defy destiny by mastering bodily impulses. Forces conjured by such names as Aphrodite and Eros, who overpowered their multiple human lovers, must now yield themselves, like beasts before a lion tamer, to the rational will" (84). Thus, the ego achieves autonomy by mastering, that is, repressing into shadow, the "impure" instinctive elements of the psyche.

24. For psychological expositions of manifold-mindedness or psychic pluralism, see James Hillman, *Revisioning Psychology* (New York: Harper and Row, 1975), and *The Dream and the Underworld* (New York: Harper and Row, 1979). James Ogilvy, *The Many Dimensional Self* (Oxford: Oxford Univ. Press, 1977), especially 88-138, examines psychic pluralism from a philosophical perspective.

25. The idea of the final purification of a world in which good and evil have been mixed followed by the destruction of the evil principle is a basic belief of Western dualism. Jeffrey Burton Russell, *The Devil* (Ithaca: Cornell Univ. Press, 1977) 55-174, gives various analogues to the Christian myth of the devil in Near Eastern and classical religions and myths. The clearest analogue, Russell maintains, is in Mithraism: "The dead will rise from their graves, and Mithras will judge them, separating the good from the evil. Ohrmazd will send down an annihilating fire upon the wicked, and upon Ahriman and his demons. An endless reign of happiness and goodness will ensue. The resemblance to Christian eschatology is striking as is the similarity between Ahriman and the Judeo-Christian Satan" (154).

26. Jung's analysis of Christian hypocrisy appears among his comments on the Apocalypse in *Answer to Job*, 434-458.

27. Salient historical examples of the quest for purity appear in ancient dualism. Manichaeanism, for instance, saw the good God as entirely outside the corrupted world, which is ruled by the Devil. The souls of men, which are good, are trapped in material bodies that are evil. The object of spiritual discipline is to escape the world and the body to rejoin the supernal god of light. Henry-Charles Puech, "The Concept of Redemption in Manichaeanism," in *The Mystic Vision*, ed. Joseph Campbell (Princeton: Princeton Univ. Press, 1968), 247-314, gives a detailed account of Manichaean concepts of purification and redemption from the material world.

28. Freud held that ego development requires growing beyond infantile omnipotence and other omnipotence fantasies associated with the womb. He also held that the uroboric impulse to return to the womb is the basic drive motivating religion. Freud's position contrasts sharply with Jung's view that religion arises primarily from the self's drive for conscious wholeness. For Jung the impulse to return to the womb opposes and subverts the true religious impulse. See Sigmund Freud, *The Future of an Illusion*, trans, W.D. Robson-Scott (Garden City: Doubleday, 1964).

29. The classic Jungian studies of uroboros and the Great Mother are: Erich Neumann, *The Origins and History of Consciousness*, trans. R.F.C. Hull (Princeton: Princeton Univ. Press, 1954), 5-101, and *The Great Mother*, 2nd ed., trans. Ralph Mannheim (Princeton: Princeton Univ. Press, 1963). The uroboric Great Mother is the primordial serpent and dragon who has gone by many names, among them Leviathan, Nehushtan, Ophion, Kali, Vasuki, Sata, and the Gnostics' Ouroboros. See S.G.F. Brandon, *Religion in Ancient History* (New York: Scribner, 1969); Robert Graves, *The White Goddess* (New York: Vintage, 1958).

30. The Great Mother appears as a rival to Yahweh in the form of Ishtar, Isis, and other

mother goddesses. See Joan Engelsman, *The Feminine Dimension of the Divine* (Wilmette, Ill.: Chiron, 1987); Robert Graves and Raphael Patai, *Hebrew Myths* (New York: McGraw Hill, 1964); Grant Showerman, *The Great Mother of the Gods* (New York: Argonaut, 1969); and for a cultural comparison see Heinrich Zimmer, "The Indian World Mother," in *Mystic Vision*, 70-102.

31. Northrop Frye, *The Great Code*, (London: Routledge & Kegan Paul, 1982), 190, presents the biblical leviathan as an embodiment of the devouring uroboros archetype.

32. While Jung mentions the uroboros archetype several times, his concept of the uroboros is more general than that postulated in this work. An example of his generalized uroboros appears in *Mysterium Coniunctionis*, par. 513: "In the age old image of the uroboros lies the thought of devouring oneself and turning oneself into a circulatory process. . . . The uroboros is a dramatic symbol for the integration and assimilation of the opposite, i.e., of the shadow." Neumann approaches the uroboros historically rather than theologically in *Great Mother*, 325-35, observing that Sophia, the divine anima, derives from uroboros but does not identify the Hellenic philosophical elements or motivations with the uroboros. Nevertheless, he deals with uroboros's negative aspect in "Mystical Man," in *Mystic Vision*, 375-415.

33. Niel Micklem "The Intolerable Image" *Spring* 1976, 1-18, develops Medusa as the archetype of psychotic fixation. The gist of Medusa is suppression of masculine logos or reflection. Athena, being her reversal, stands close to Medusa. Since Milton's Satan gives birth to Sin the way Zeus gives birth to Athena, the proximity of Athena and Medusa furnishes a direct textual as well as an archetypal reason for linking Satan to the evil anima of the devouring uroboros.

34. Philp, *Jung and the Problem of Evil*, 241.

35. Neumann, "Mystical Man," presents ego's problem somewhat more sympathetically than I do: "The incomplete separation of ego from non-ego characterizes the original uroboros state, which lives in the psyche of mankind as the archetype of paradisiacal wholeness. For the ego, lonely and unhappy in consequence of its necessary development, this image of a lost stage of childhood is a symbol of irreparable loss" (378).

36. Kluger, *Satan in the Old Testament*, 56-76, 139-47, provides an illuminating Jungian analysis of the Malak Satan. Another valuable account, one that relies heavily upon Klugar yet develops its own historical perspective, is Russell, *Devil*, 174-220.

37. For a recent Jungian handling of Satan's exclusion from Yahweh, see Edward F. Edinger, *Encounter with the Self* (Toronto: Inner City, 1986), 55-67.

38. Another influence may have been the Azazel, or scapegoat, whose development in Jewish tradition parallels that of the Malak. Sylvia Brinton Perera, *The Scapegoat Complex* (Toronto: Inner City, 1986), observes: "Azazel then came to stand, psychologically, for the arrogantly pure, condemning, supercritical judge . . . His is the standard that takes no account of the facts of life . . . Azazel, here, has come to be like Satan, the antagonist. As accuser against men, he represents divine Justice separated from divine Mercy" (20).

39. Russell, *Lucifer*, 159-244, ponders the influence of *privatio boni* upon medieval conceptions of the devil.

40. See Sanford, *Evil*, 35-48, 67-83; and Roy Yates, "Jesus and the Demonic in the Synoptic Gospels," *Irish Theological Quarterly* 44 (1977): 39-57.

41. Victor Maag, "The Anti-Christ as a Symbol of Evil," in *Evil*, ed. Curatorium of the C.G. Jung Institute Zurich (Evanston, Ill.: Northwestern Univ. Press, 1967), 57-82, points out that in the New Testament the distinction between Satan and AntiChrist was blurred.

42. Victor Maag, "Anti-Christ," 59-63, for example, denies the Pauline attribution of 2 Thessalonians. Pagels, *Adam, Eve and the Serpent*, 23-25, also denies it, giving a psychosociological explanation for the deutero-Pauline epistles. Their denials reflect the consensus of nonfundamentalist scholars.

43. It should also be noted that the term AntiChrist does not appear in the Apocalypse, whose mythology posits an evil Trinity consisting of Satan, the Beast, and the False Prophet.

44. Russell, *Devil*, 248-49.

45. Michael Fixler, *Milton and the Kingdoms of God* (Evanston, Ill.: Northwestern Univ. Press, 1964). A more recent account of the influence of Revelation upon Milton appears in Joseph Anthony Wittreich, *Visionary Poetics: Milton's Tradition and His Legacy* (San Marino, Ca.: Huntington Library, 1979), 3-78.

46. Jung, *Aion*, 41.

47. Jung, *Aion*, 44, 147-49. The Ebionites believed that God established two beings, Christ and the Devil, committing to the former power over the world to come and to the latter power over this world. Ebionite ethical dualism, Russell comments in *Satan*, 48, bordered on Gnostic cosmic dualism.

48. Kathleen E. Hartwell, *Milton and Lactantius* (Cambridge: Harvard Univ. Press, 1929). Hartwell notes that there are seven entries from Lactantius in Milton's Commonplace Book and two explicit citations in the prose. Milton, she maintains, got from Lactantius the idea that God let Satan remain active in order to test virtue. For Lactantius and Milton, good could not exist without its opposite, and the opposites of good and evil are necessary to man's moral nature. Their emphasis on necessary opposites brings Lactantius and Milton close to Jung's notion of *coincidentia oppositorum*. Jung of course knew of Lactantius, but nowhere in the *Collected Works* does he give him more than incidental mention. Jung appears not to have studied him in depth and seems less than fully cognizant of the similarity between Lactantius's notion of evil and his own. For more on Lactantius's views, see Russell, *Satan*, 149-58.

49. See *The Works of Lactantius*, trans. William Fletcher, 2 vols. (Edinburgh: Clark, 1871). Lactantius writes in *Divine Institutes*, book 5, chapter 7: "For God designed that there should be this distinction between good and evil things, that we may know from that which is evil the quality of the good, and also the quality of the evil from the good. Nor can the nature of the one be understood if the other is taken away. God therefore did not exclude evil, that the nature of virtue might be evident. How could patient endurance retain its meaning and name if there were nothing which we were compelled to endure? How could faith devoted to its God deserve praise, unless there were someone who wished to turn us away from God?"

50. See Russell, *Satan*, 149-60. Lactantius, like many of the church fathers, is a confused and contradictory theologian. Moreover, the texts of his surviving writings may have been corrupted so that we cannot with certainty form definite statements of his positions on specific issues.

51. Jung, *Aion*, 97-172.

52. Ibid, 87.

53. Ibid, 60-61.

54. Jung, *Answer to Job*, 365.

55. Jung saw Kierkegaard's effort to restore transcendence to God as a complex, intellectual neurosis. Though Kierkegaard created a powerful weapon against Hegelian immanence, his transcendent God aborted inner dialogue and alienated him from personal life where the divine, Jung believed, is authentically encountered. In a letter to Arnold Kunzli; 16 March 1943, Jung writes of the Protestant intellectuals who admire Kierkegaard: "To such people his problems and his grizzling are entirely acceptable, because to them it serves the same purpose as it served him: you can settle everything in the study and need not do it in life" (*Letters* 1:332). God appeared to Kierkegaard, Jung maintained, in the person of Regine Olsen to whom Kierkegaard broke off his engagement in order to "serve God." In a letter to Willi Bremi, 26 December 1953, Jung writes: "I was once again struck by the discrepancy between the perpetual talk about fulfilling God's will and reality: when God appeared to him in the shape of 'Reginas' he took to his heals. It was too terrible for him to

have to subordinate his autocratism to the love of another person" (*Letters* 2:145). The essence of Kierkegaard's neurosis, Jung believed, was inability to submit autocratic egotism to the love of another.

56. Jung, *The Development of Personality,* in *Collected Works* 17:174-75, writes: "The development of personality [the individuation process] . . . means fidelity to the law of one's own being." For the word "fidelity" I should prefer, in this context, the word used in the New Testament, *pistis,* which is erroneously translated "faith." It really means "trust," "trustful loyalty." Fidelity to the law of one's own being is a trust in this law, a loyal perseverance and confident hope; in short, an attitude such as a religious man should have toward God.

57. Jung, *Answer to Job,* 372.

58. Ibid, 405.

59. Jung observes in *Answer to Job:* "If Job gains knowledge of God, then God must also learn to know himself. It just could not be that Yahweh's dual nature should become public property and remain hidden from himself alone. Whoever knows God has an effect on him. The failure of the attempt to corrupt Job has changed Yahweh's nature" (391).

60. Cf. Philp, *Jung and the Problem of Evil,* 236-37; and Jung, *Answer to Job,* 419.

61. Jung, *Answer to Job,* 419. Nicholas of Cusa also saw God as the *coincidentia oppositorum.* Unlike Jung, he stopped short of making God both good and evil. Russell remarks on Nicholas of Cusa in *Lucifer:* "Nicholas was on the verge of taking the final step and perceiving evil as part of the deity. If God includes both light and darkness, greatness and smallness, time and timelessness, and all opposites, then he also can be said to include both good and evil. But Nicholas could not face this logical consequence of his theory. He looked at it, flinched, and turned away, and his treatment of evil is therefore thin and blandly traditional" (280). Thus, Nicholas left it for Jung to confront the implications of *coincidentia oppositorum.* The magnitude of the spiritual and intellectual courage Jung displayed may find a measure in the fact that most of Jung's followers have, like Cusa, flinched and turned back to a blandly traditional treatment of evil.

62. For an examination of the psychological process by which betrayal or injustice advances consciousness see James Hillman, "Betrayal," in *Loose Ends* (Zurich: Spring, 1975), 63-81. Hillman observes: "It would seem that the message of love, the Eros mission of Jesus, carries its final force only through the betrayal and crucifixion. For at the moment when God lets him down, Jesus becomes truly human, suffering human tragedy" (70).

63. Walter Kaufmann, *Nietzsche* (Princeton: Princeton Univ. Press, 1950), discusses Nietzsche's basically Aristotlean ethics. See also Arthur C. Danto, *Nietzsche as Philosopher* (New York: Macmillan, 1965), 130-94.

64. Nietzsche's idea of balanced Dionysian and Apollonian forces is in effect a vision of wholeness. Nietzsche, like Jung, believed that the dark shadow, Dionysian-Zarathrustra parts of the self were missing in the psyche of modern man and sought to integrate them so that we could become more complete like the Greeks. Like Jung also, Neitzsche blamed Christianity for the modern one-sidedness.

65. Barbara Walker, *The Crone* (New York: Harper and Row, 1985), 99-122, explores the mythic context of the uroboric cauldron.

66. See Marija Gimbutas, *The Goddesses and Gods of Old Europe: Myths and Cult Images* (Berkeley: Univ. of California Press, 1974); and Norma L. Goodrich, *Medieval Myths* (New York: New American Library, 1972).

67. Francis Huxley, *The Dragon* (New York: Macmillan, 1979), provides a collection of pictoral representations of the negative uroboros.

68. Theologians traditionally attributed Satan's rebellion to two motives: pride and envy. Stella P. Revard, *The War in Heaven* (Ithaca: Cornell Univ. Press, 1980), reviews the

theological treatment of Satan's pride, envy, and malice. Milton refers to all three motives but relies more heavily upon envy and malice than upon pride.

69. St. Thomas Aquinas, *Summa Contra Gentiles*, book 3, chapter 71.

70. See Lovejoy, *Great Chain of Being*. The notion of a chain of being seems to have entered Christian thought through Clement of Alexandria's theory of *privatio boni*, which he derived from the platonists. Milton's peculiar vision of a divine uroboros parodied by Satan's uroboric evil does not repudiate so much as supercede the idea of a hierarchical creation and a chain of being.

71. Lewis, *Preface*, 94-103, argues that Satan is Milton's most successful character because he is the worst and therefore the easiest to draw. Character creation, like character itself, is much more complex and unpredictable than Lewis assumes. Characters are not difficult to draw or memorable as they are good or bad. Hamlet, Shakespeare's greatest and most memorable character, is not bad; Goneril, his most wicked character, is not among his most memorable. In the case of Milton's Satan, his greatness is in large part because of the fascination his archetypal energies hold.

72. Milton's peculiar conception of evil has an analogue in Eastern Orthodox notions deriving from Pseudo-Dionysus the Areopagite and from Maximus the confessor, which stresses both the total emptiness of the devil and his terrible destructive power. In *Lucifer*, 28-51, Russell surveys Byzantine thought on the devil, observing that his evil is seen as "like the low pressure in the center of a tornado." While the analogue is clear, there's no evidence that Milton's idea of evil was influenced by Byzantine thought.

73. Arnold Stein, *Answerable Style* (Seattle: Univ. of Washington Press, 1953), 48-49.

74. Helen Gardner, "Milton's 'Satan' and the Theme of Damnation in Elizabethan Tragedy," *English Studies*, 1 (1948): 46-66, compares Satan, Faustus, and Macbeth.

75. We put psychotics in mental wards for their rehabilitation and to protect both them and society. Such is the modern theory. The practice is often less noble.

76. Eminent among those who hold that Christians must accept on faith the orthodox position on Satan is John Calvin. See *Institutes of the Christian Religion*, trans. Ford Lewis Battles (London: Library of Christian Classics, 1961), book 1, chapter 14.

77. Marie Louise Von Franz, *Projection and Recollection in Jungian Psychology*, trans. William H. Kennedy (London: Open Court, 1980), 119-20, gives the following interpretation to Jung's thoughts on absolute evil: "The integration of conscious and unconscious contents through active imagination seems to function, however, only when it is a question of the lesser daimons, of the 'little devils' that go to make up the personal shadow, but not when it is a question of the principle of evil (the *archetype* of evil). Jung makes a special point of this: '. . . it is quite within the bounds of possibility for a man to recognize the relative evil of his nature, but it is a rare and shattering experience for him to gaze into the face of absolute evil.' Jung's allusion is to the *archetypal* aspect of evil, the dark side of the God-image or of the Self, whose unfathomable depths exceed by far the evil of the human shadow. This inner power, like all archetypal powers of the unconscious, cannot be integrated by the ego. That is why Jung took issue so sharply in *Aion* with the theological doctrine of the *privatio boni*." Von Franz further observes that the doctrine of *privatio boni*'s denial of evil in Godhead, by locating evil in the human soul, leads to a tremendous negative inflation that activates in human affairs the absolute evil it seeks to deny in God.

78. Michael Lieb, "Milton and the *Odium Dei*," *ELH* 53 (Fall 1986): 519-40, investigates what I call divine scapegoating in terms of the theological traditions of *odium dei*. While Lieb's critical conclusions are not always in accord with a Jungian interpretation of the Christian (or Milton's) God, the scholarship he gathers does illumine the divine darkness that Jung analyzes in *Answer to Job*.

79. Russell, *Satan*, 138-48, notes that apocatastasis was formally condemned as hereti-

cal by Justinian in 543 and by the Second Council of Constantinople in 553. While Milton's phrase "God shall be All in All" (*Paradise Lost*, III.379) hints of apocatastasis, nowhere does he openly espouse Origen's heresy that the salvation of Satan is possible.

80. M. Scott Peck, *People of the Lie* (New York: Simon and Schuster, 1983), 69.

81. In *Projection and Recollection in Jungian Psychology*, Von Franz offers observations on evil people that reinforce those of Peck: "Evil often hides behind idealism—and behind -isms in general, which are as often as not simply labels disguising a very unspiritual doctrinairism. . . . The dangers involved in taking this road are very great. It starts with lying, that is, the projection of the shadow" (120).

82. Peck, *People of the Lie*, 124, 177.

83. Peck observes, "The central defect of the evil is not the sin but the refusal to acknowledge it" (69).

84. See Helmut Schoeck, *Envy: A Theory of Social Behavior*, trans. Michael Glenny and Betty Ross (New York: Harcourt, Brace & World, 1970).

85. Jung remarks in *Answer to Job*: "He clearly sees that God is at odds with himself—so totally at odds that he, Job, is quite certain of finding in God a helper and an "advocate" against God. As certain as he is of the evil in Yahweh, he is equally certain of the good" (369).

86. To understand the psychological meaning of myths and fairy tales, Jung taught, we must view them as dreams and see their characters not as real persons but as archetypes constellated by a single psyche. For classic examples of Jungian interpretation of myth and fairy tales see Marie Louise Von Franz, *Interpretation of Fairy Tales* (Zurich: Spring, 1973); *Shadow and Evil*; and *The Feminine in Fairy Tales* (Zurich: Spring, 1972).

87. Jung's own views on Milton's Satan, which appear in "Foreword to Werblowsky's 'Lucifer and Prometheus,'" in *Psychology and Religion* (Princeton: Princeton Univ. Press, 1969), 311-15, are less developed than the Jungian interpretation presented in this work. Jung, not a literary critic, acknowledges, "I do not feel altogether competent to express an opinion on the matter." While he does not see the supernal characters in *Paradise Lost* as archetypes of a single psyche, some of what he says parallels and confirms positions I take. Here are two examples: "I would mention only Jakob Bohme, who sketched a picture of evil which leaves the *privatio boni* pale by comparison. The same can be said of Milton. He inhabits the same mental climate. . . . Satan, who was exalted to a cosmic figure of first rank in Milton, even emancipating himself from his subordinate role at the left hand of God (the role assigned to him by Clement). Milton goes even further than Bohme and apostrophizes the devil as the true *principle individuationis*" (313-14). "The Satan-Prometheus parallel shows clearly enough that Milton's devil stands for the essence of human individuation and thus comes within the scope of psychology" (314).

88. Revard, *War in Heaven*, 198-263, points out that Renaissance poets often represented the Son and Satan as like two warring generals.

89. Eugene Monick, *Phallos: Sacred Image of the Masculine* (Toronto: Inner City, 1987), 101-107, examines the type of masculine "solar phallic" inflation evident in the Father.

90. Ricoeur, *Symbolism of Evil*, 23-46.

91. Jung, "Psychological Approach to the Trinity," 179.

92. It is often erroneously assumed that the Old Testament, like *Paradise Lost*, presents Satan's revolt and the war in heaven as taking place before the fall in Eden. The only Old Testament reference to Satan's revolt is a very late insertion into the book of Isaiah: "How art thou fallen from heaven, O Lucifer, son of the Morning! How art thou cut down to the ground who didst weaken the nations! For thou hast said in thine heart, I will ascend into heaven, I will exalt my throne above the stars of God: I will sit upon the mount of the congregation, and the sides of the north: I will be like the most High" (Isaiah 14:12-13). This reference is not based upon authentic Jewish traditions. It is borrowed from the Canaanites

who fancied their morning star god envying the sun and trying to seize his throne. In the seventh century B.C., long before the Jews adopted the myth, a Canaanite bard wrote: "How thou hast fallen from heaven, Helel's son Shaher! Thou didst say in thy heart, I will ascend to heaven, above the circumpolar stars I will raise my throne, and I will dwell on the Mount of Council in the back of the north; I will mount on the back of a cloud, I will be like Elyon." Cited from William Powell Albright, *Yahweh and the Gods of Canaan* (New York: Doubleday, 1968), 232. Also see Walker, *Crone*, 153-61, for a development of the problem's mythic context.

93. The idea of Satan being an alienated son of God surfaces in certain apocryphal sources from the first century of the Christian era. Concerning his role in the Books of Adam and Eve, Russell, *Devil*, remarks: "This version of the myth presents Satan as one of the greatest and earliest creations of God, a creature who falls through envy and pride from his high estate, a creature whose love of God is turned to hatred by the God's preference for his younger offspring. The Devil appears less as an *urprinzip* of evil than as a being hurt by and alienated from his parent. Once having rebelled, however, he is thrust by the sheer weight of his power further into enmity against the Lord. The division between the two steadily widens. The Devil threatens to raise up his throne against the God, and he attempts to divide the universe with him, informing Adam that 'Mine are the things of earth, the things of heaven are God's'; when the God in anger casts him and his followers down to earth he continues to work his wiles against man and against him in whose likeness man was created" (209).

94. Among the critics, N. Frye, *Great Code*, has shown clear sensitivity to the hostile brothers archetype, remarking: "In this connection there is one theme that recurs frequently in the early books of the Bible: the passing over of the firstborn son, who normally has the legal right of primogeniture, in favor of a younger one. . . . In later literature the theme is carried much further back: if we look at the fifth book of *Paradise Lost*, for instance, we see an archetype of the jealousy of an older son, Lucifer or Satan, at the preference shown to the younger Christ" (180-81).

95. William B. Hunter, *Bright Essence* (Salt Lake City: Univ. of Utah Press, 1973), 116, identifies Psalm 2 as the major proof text of the begetting and the immediate source for Book V. 600ff. Hunter does not, however, excavate the two hostile brothers archetype from the psalm. He assumes, as scholarly critics often do, that the only meanings of interest are conscious meanings. Maurice Kelley, *This Great Argument* (Princeton: Princeton Univ. Press, 1941), 100, notes that in these lines Milton diverges from the theology of *De Doctrina* to move the begetting and exaltation from the resurrection to the time of Satan's revolt in order to motivate that revolt.

96. In the Jacob-Esau story the brothers are actual twins; but Esau is the first born and thus the rightful heir to the birthright and blessing of the father Isaac. With the aid of their mother, Rebekah, whose favorite he was, Jacob (the name means supplanter in Hebrew) stole both the birthright and the blessing from Esau.

97. Much of the Arian controversy concerned the meaning of "sons of God." See Robert C. Gregg and Dennis E. Groh, *Early Arianism: A View of Salvation* (Philadelphia: Fortress, 1981). Hartwell, *Lactantius and Milton*, points out that Lactantius appears to be one of Milton's sources for Satan's rebellion: "In the eighth chapter of the second book of *Divine Institutes* Lactantius gives his decidedly Arian version of the creation of the Son by the Father, the subsequent creation of 'another being in whom the disposition of the divine origin did not remain' and the envy entertained by this second spirit for the Son, an envy which is declared to be the source of all evils" (59).

98. Among the most famous of those heretics who held to the fraternity of Christ and Satan were the Bogomils. See Russell, *Lucifer*, 43-49; also Steven Runciman, *The Medieval*

Manichee (Viking 195) 84-92 notes that some Bogomils believed that God created Satan out of his shadow, while others believed that they were comrades.

99. K. Holl, ed., *Epiphanius: Amoratus und Panarion*, 3 vols (Leipzig: 1915-1933). Milton mentions Epiphanius in *Areopagitica*. See Merritt Y. Hughes., ed. *John Milton: Complete Poems and Major Prose* (New York: Odyssey, 1957), 729. Hughes comments in a footnote: "Milton may have been interested in the *Panarion* or general refutation of heresies which was written by Epiphanius."

100. Revard, *War in Heaven*, 235-63, notes that Milton attributed to the Son many of the characteristics previous Renaissance poets had given Michael.

101. In Psalm 2, according to the *Interpreter's One Volume Commentary On the Bible* (New York: Abingdon, 1971), 261, the word "begot" refers to the coronation of the Judaic king.

102. Michael Lieb, *The Dialectics of Creation* (Amherst: Univ. of Massachusetts Press, 1970) examines the dialectical dynamic between the Son's creativity and Satan's destructiveness.

103. R.J. Zwi Werblowsky's *Lucifer and Prometheus* (London: Routledge, 1952), for which Jung wrote an introduction, deals with Satan and Prometheus in *Paradise Lost*. Werblowsky's book suffers from romanticization of Satan and overstressing the devil's very limited Promethean qualities. We admire Satan, Werblowsky maintains, because he absorbs the Promethean archetype. The objection here, as countless critics have pointed out, is that if we read *Paradise Lost* carefully we will not admire Satan. Moreover, Milton attempted to preclude identifying Satan and Prometheus by attributing creative, Promethean qualities to the Son.

104. Elias Canetti, *Crowds and Power*, trans. Carol Stewart (New York: Continuum, 1962), 332-33.

105. Isabel Gamble MacCaffrey, *Paradise Lost as Myth* (Cambridge: Harvard Univ. Press, 1959) catalogues the similarities between Satan and heroes of legend. A quite different perspective upon Satan's heroism, one that traces his roots in the villain heroes of Jacobean drama, is presented by Helen Gardner, *A Reading of "Paradise Lost"* (Oxford: Clarendon, 1965), 99-120.

106. Revard, *War in Heaven*, 198-234, reviews the specifically Renaissance antecedents of Satan's epic heroism.

107. Milton, "An Apology for a Pamphlet," in *Complete Prose Works of John Milton*, ed. Don Wolfe, et al., vol. 1 (New Haven: Yale Univ. Press, 1953), 916.

108. Satan was believed to be an extremely powerful and pervasive force during those ages when he was commonly represented as a the comic devil. Here, as in Milton's idea of tragic satire, one sees the comic compensating for the menace of evil.

109. See Edward F. Edinger, *Anatomy of the Psyche* (La Salle, Ill.: Open Court, 1985), 47-81, for a study of *solutio* in alchemy and psychotherapy.

110. For discussions of Milton's mortalist heresy see Patrides, *Milton and Christian Doctrine*, 264-66; and George Williamson, "Milton and the Mortalist Heresy," *Studies in Philology* 32 (1935): 553-79.

111. Walker, *Crone*, observes that the ideas of the soul's immortality and of reincarnation, with their assumption of recycling, derive from matriarchal religions. By contrast, strict mortalism, the idea of one life, one birth, and one death followed by a final judgment, is a distinctly patriarchal notion: "The cauldron concept of eternally recycling life was inevitably opposed to the patriarchal linear concept, evinced by such male dominated groups as Jain Buddhists, Mithraic Persians, Essenic Jews, and orthodox Christians. According to the visions shared by such groups, each life passed only once from birth to death, and, if human, must face a postmortem judgment by which to be saved or damned. The pious would go to heaven (Nirvana) and remain forever in a changeless state. The wicked would go to eternal

punishment. As it evolved into the sadistic Christian hell, this infinite punishment seemed rather excessive for the trivial sins of one brief lifetime; but the theologians nevertheless insisted that the results of the final judgment would never be rescinded. There could be no recycling, no reincarnation, no turning of the karmic wheel, no resorption of the soul into the inchoate mass of the universal soul stuff" (112).

112. Russell, *Lucifer,* 216-32, shows how Dante, along with medieval theology, followed Augustinian *privatio boni* to define the devil as essentially nonbeing. Consequently, Russell maintains, Dante would have thought Milton's Satan far too active and effective. Russell observes: "The lack of dramatic action on the part of Dante's Lucifer is a deliberate statement about his essential lack of being. Satan's true being is his lack of being, his futility and nothingness . . . Satan, the symbol of this nothingness, can have no real character except negation, and so his futile immobility is precisely what Dante wished to portray" 226-27.

113. Henri Bergson presents his ideas on mechanism and the comic in *Le Rire* (Paris: Presses Universitaires de France, 1961).

114. Michael Lieb, *Poetics of the Holy* (Champaign-Urbana: Univ. of Illinois Press, 1986), catalogues and investigates the imagery of squares and mountains prevalent in *Paradise Lost.* Like the eschaton, Lieb points out, squares and mountains are all limited— they have ends; circles, by contrast, are endless. The spiral, which resembles a circle yet has a beginning, middle, and end, combines with the idea of an end the notion of process.

115. From the concluding lines of *Paradise Lost*: "The world was all before them, where to choose / Thir place of rest, and Providence thir guide; / They hand in hand with wandring steps and slow, / Through Eden took their solitarie way" (12. 646-49). Shawcross, *With Mortal Voice*, 119-38, presents a suggestive study linking exodus imagery with birth.

116. Anthony Stevens, *Archetypes: A Natural History of the Self* (London: Routledge & Kegan, 1982) considers how archetypes set the tone for whole civilizations.

117. Jeffrey Burton Russell, *Dissent and Reform in the Early Middle Ages* (Berkeley: Univ. of California Press, 1965) provides examples.

118. Inductive science and empiricist philosophy stem from the Satan archetype with its implied flux universe. However, like a rival brother, deductive, mathematical science along with rationalist philosophy, stem from the Christ-logos archetype with its implicit stasis universe.

119. These trends have been the subject of countless books. Two of the books notably pertinent to this study are: Richard Popkin, *The History of Skepticism* (New York: Harper and Row, 1962); and Jonathan Dollimore, *Radical Tragedy* (Chicago: Univ. of Chicago Press, 1986).

CHAPTER 3. DECISIVE IDENTITY

1. Irenaeus, Clement of Alexandria, Origen, Justin Martyr, Tertullian, Augustine, and Ambrose are perhaps the most famous examples of this trend. For some recent studies of the Hellenization of Christian myth see: Henry Chadwick, *Early Christian Thought and the Classical Tradition* (Oxford: Oxford Univ. Press, 1966); Martin Hengel, *The Son of God: The Origin of Christology and the History of Jewish-Hellenistic Religion* (Philadelphia: Fortress, 1976); William J. Hill, *The Three-Personed God* (Washington, D.C.: Catholic Univ. of America Press, 1982); Eric Osborn, *The Beginnings of Christian Philosophy* (Cambridge: Cambridge Univ. Press, 1981) and *Ethical Patterns of Early Christian Thought* (Cambridge: Cambridge Univ. Press, 1976); Jaroslav Pelikan, *Development of Christian Doctrine: Some Historical Prolegomena* (New Haven: Yale Univ. Press, 1969) and *Jesus Through the Ages* (New Haven: Yale Univ. Press, 1985); Hugo Rahner, *Greek Myths and Christian Mystery,* trans. Brian Battershaw (New

York: Harper and Row, 1963); Harry Wolfson, *The Philosophy of the Church Fathers: Faith, Trinity, Incarnation* (Cambridge: Harvard Univ. Press, 1956).

2. This assumption underlies the notion of the great Platonic year. There are exceptions to it of course, the most notable being Heraclitus and Democritus.

3. See G. Van Der Leeuw, "Primordial Time and Final Time"; Erich Neumann, "Art and Time"; Giles Quispel, "Time and History in Patristic Christianity"; and Helmith Plessner, "On the Relation of Time to Death"; in *Man and Time,* Joseph Campbell, ed. (New York: Pantheon, 1957). Moreover, Russell, *Devil,* 152-54, points out the parallel of Christianity with Mithraism where, according to its central myth, the principle of the world is Aion or everlasting time, who engenders the ruling good and evil spirits Ahriman and Ohrmazd; their struggle creates history. See also Hannah Arendt, *Willing* (New York: Harcourt, Brace, Jovanovich, 1978), 11-19, for a discussion of time and will.

4. See William Chase Greene, *Moira: Fate, Good and Evil in Greek Thought* (New York: Harper and Row, 1963).

5. Aristotle's notion of God as the unmoved mover is perhaps the clearest instance of rationalism depriving God of freedom.

6. The Greek influence appears consistently only in Paul and the Johannine Gospel. But there are other glimpses of Greek philosophical ideas, for example 1 John 1:5: "God is light and in Him is no darkness at all." This verse prefigures the doctrine of *summum bonum* and the all light God Jung sharply criticized.

7. Christopher Dawson, *The Dynamics of World History* (New York: New American Library, 1962) gives a Catholic perspective on the dynamic impact of Christianity on Western civilization and history.

8. Hill, *Milton and the English Revolution* (London: Penguin, 1977), 93-144; and *The Experience of Defeat* (London: Penguin, 1984) provide detailed accounts of Milton's complex relationship to radical Protestantism.

9. For Jung Adam and Eve's crucial act was their original *conjunctio.* The fall was almost incidental, since God planned it anyway; but by conjunctio Adam and Eve set the archetype for all human pairings, the archetype that keeps the race going. In some theological views the Father and the Son beget the Holy Spirit out of their love for each other. Jung did not consider this a valid archetype of *conjunctio* because, while the Son does assume certain ambiguously feminine qualities, the Father and the Son remain essentially masculine.

10. Jung, *Answer to Job,* 400.

11. See, for example: Susan Cady, Marian Ronan, and Hal Taussig, *Sophia* (San Francisco: Harper and Row, 1987); Mary Daly, *Beyond God the Father* (Boston: Beacon, 1973); Joan Engelsman, *Feminine Dimension of the Divine* (Wilmette, Ill.: Chiron, 1987); Elizabeth Schussler Fiorenza, *In Memory of Her* (New York: Crossroad, 1987); Virginia Ramsey Mollenkott, *The Divine Feminine* (New York: Crossroad, 1986); Rosemary Radford Ruether, *Sexism and God-Talk,* (Boston: Beacon, 1983).

12. For example, Mollenkott, *Divine Feminine,* 96-104, discusses various Biblical references to Wisdom. Of the Shekinah, she remarks: "The word *Shekinah* derives from the Hebrew root *shkn,* meaning "to dwell." The term *Shekinah* was used by Jewish Rabbis in the first or second century B.C.E. to indicate God's presence among the children of Israel—and the term was feminine in gender. Like the feminine gender terms for Holy Spirit (*Ruach Hakodesh*), voice (*Bath-Kol*), teaching (*Torah*), compassion or womb-love (*racham*), Wisdom (*Hokhma*), and Community of Israel (*Knesseth Yisrael*), *Shekinah* depicts the visible expression or residence of God's glory within the creation" (36). Mollenkott also notes that the spirit that impregnated Mary is associated with the Shekinah in Luke's account: "Luke's story of Christ's birth uses language associated with the Shekinah. Gabriel announces to Mary, 'The

Holy Spirit will come upon you . . . and the power of the Most High will cover you with its shadow' (Luke 1:35). The word for *overshadow* or *cover with shadow* is the same word used in the Septuagint to designate Yahweh's Shekinah glory in the tabernacle (Exodus 40:35)" (39).

13. Jung neglected to develop the relationship of anima to Sophia and the Holy Ghost. Nonetheless, he was not unaware of it. In *Answer to Job* he observes of Sophia: "This feature is already implied in the relationship of Mary to Sophia, and especially in his genesis by the Holy Ghost, whose feminine nature is personified by Sophia, . . . who is symbolized by the dove" (407). That Jung understood the crucial role of Wisdom is seen in *Aurora Consurgens*, ed. Marie Louise Von Franz, trans. R.F.C. Hull (New York: Pantheon, 1966), a late work started by Jung and completed by Marie Louise Von Franz. Here he connects Wisdom to *anima mundi* or the matrix that maintains interconnections among all things: "She [Wisdom] was also considered the *archetypus mundus*, "that archetypal world after whose likeness this sensible world was made," and through which God becomes conscious of himself. *Sapientia Dei* is thus the sum of archetypal images in the mind of God" (155f). Similarly, Jung himself writes of Wisdom in *Answer to Job*: "At about the same time, or a little later it is rumored what has happened: he [Yahweh] has remembered a feminine being who is not less agreeable to him than to man, a friend and playmate from the beginning of the world, the first born of all God's creatures, . . . There must be some dire necessity responsible for this anamnesis of Sophia: things simply could not go on as before, the "just" God could not go on committing injustices, and the "omniscient" could not behave any longer like a clueless and thoughtless human being. Self-reflection becomes an imperative necessity and for this Wisdom is needed" (391).

14. A whole series of New Testament texts, according to Cady et al., *Sophia*, 38ff, present Jesus as Sophia. The Church Fathers saw these texts as masculinizing Sophia, whereas modern feminists see them as feminizing Jesus.

15. See Engelsman, *Feminine Dimension*, 74-120, 140-48, for a cogent discussion of the repression and masculinization of Sophia. Engelsman's treatment of the implications for Christology is particularly helpful.

16. Wisdom or Hokhmah was an attribute of Yahweh while the Shekhina had some of the qualities of a separate goddess. Raphael Patai, *The Hebrew Goddess* (Philadelphia: KTAV, 1967), offers a scholarly account of the feminine companions and attributes of Yahweh. Of the Shekhina Patai observes: "*Shekhina* is the frequently used Talmudic term denoting the visible and audible manifestation of God's presence on earth. In its ultimate development as it appears in the late Midrash literature, the Shekhina concept stood for an independent, feminine divine entity" (137). The Shekhina, therefore, has in Judaism the functions Christianity attributed to the Holy Spirit or Paraclete and to some extent to the Virgin Mary. Of Wisdom or Hokhmah Patai observes: "The term *Shekhina* does not occur in the Bible. However, in the late Biblical period a theological tendency made its appearance which prepared the ground for the emergence of the Talmudic Shekhina. The trend referred to is that of interposed personified mediating entities between God and man. . . . The most frequently appearing of these intermediaries, or *hypostases* (as they are called), is *Hokhma* or Wisdom. In the *Book of Job*, Wisdom is described as a personage whose way is understood and place is known only by God himself, while the *Book of Proverbs* asserts that Wisdom was the earliest creation of God, and that ever since those primeval days she (Wisdom) has been God's playmate" (138-39).

17. James M. Robinson, ed. *The Nag Hammadi Library in English* (San Francisco: Harper & Row, 1977), 175-77.

18. Cady, et al., *Sophia*, 16-37, surveys Sophia in the Hebrew scriptures. Neumann, *Great Mother*, 325-36, speculates that Hebrew monotheism aborted her development.

19. Pagels, *Adam, Eve and the Serpent*, 74-75.

20. Elaine Pagels, *The Gnostic Gospels* (New York: Vintage, 1981), 64-65. Of the theological problem of determining the sex of the Holy Spirit Pagels remarks: "The Greek terminology for the Trinity, which includes the neuter term for spirit (*pneuma*), virtually requires that the third person of the Trinity be asexual. But the author of the *Secret Book* has in mind the Hebrew term for spirit, *ruah*, a feminine word" (61-62).

21. June Singer, "Jung's Gnosticism and Contemporary Gnosis," in *Jung's Challenge to Contemporary Religion*, Murray Stein and Robert L. Moore, eds. (Wilmette, Ill.: Chiron, 1987), 88. Also, in *Androgyny* (Garden City: Doubleday, 1976), Singer notes that the Gnostics identified Sophia with the Holy Spirit's creative power and gave it the form of a dove: "In another version of the Gnostic tale of creation, Sophia, in the form of a dove, descends into the waters below the firmament and begets 'Saturn, who is identical with Yahweh'" (132).

22. Jung's disciple Neumann, it should be noted, comes somewhat closer than Jung to recognizing the Holy Spirit's feminine function. In *Great Mother*, he notes: "Over the figure of the spirit with its outspread arms flies the upper bird, the Great Mother, the dove of the Holy Ghost—the supreme spiritual principle. . . . The feminine vessel as vessel of rebirth and higher transformation becomes Sophia and the Holy Ghost" (327-29).

23. See Ann Ulanov, *The Feminine in Jungian Psychology and in Christian Theology* (Evanston, Ill.: Northwestern Univ. Press, 1971); and Edward C. Whitmont, *The Symbolic Quest* (New York: Putnam, 1969), for a development of the basic female archetypes; and Damaris Wehr, *Feminism and Jung* (Boston: Beacon Press, 1987) for a criticism thereof. While the basic feminine archetypes I've cited bear certain similarities to those of Ulanov and Whitmont, I do not fully accept their descriptions of them. Moreover, I believe that Wehr's criticism, that they elevate patriarchally defined social roles to the level of symbol, is valid. In *The Psychology of Transfer* in *Collected Works* 16:174, Jung speaks of "four stages of eroticism," which he correlates with four grades of anima: Eve, Helen, Mary, and Sophia. Jung's grades of anima, I suspect, are inspired more by personal chauvinism than archetypal realities. The chauvinism is evident in his choice of passive feminine figures (Eve, Helen, and Mary) for his first three grades or stages. Certainly, these do not reflect the primary feminine archetypes, which I see as mother-wife (Mary-Eve), daughter-virgin, mistress-harlot, and the wisewoman. This schema has the advantage of correlating with the male archetypes in a way that shows how consciousness develops in men and women along a similar progression.

24. Near Eastern religions did use other feminine archetypes as goddesses. For a detailed treatment of the feminine medium archetype as it runs through many mythologies, see Walker, *Crone*, 43-68. For a Jungian perspective developed through active imagination, see Rix Weaver, *The Wise Old Woman* (New York: Putnam, 1973).

25. See Jung, *Two Essays on Analytic Psychology* and *Aion*; James Hillman's *Anima: An Anatomy of a Personified Notion* (Dallas: Spring, 1985).

26. Syzygy is a Gnostic term. Jung's most extensive treatment of it is in *Aion*, 11-22. See also Hillman, *Anima*, 167-83.

27. Jacob Boehme, *The Way of Christ*, trans. Peter Erb (New York: Paulist, 1978), 57-62.

28. Hillman, *Anima*, 88-91.

29. Jung, "Psychotherapists or the Clergy," in *Collected Works* 11:345.

30. See Hillman, *Anima*, 71-97. Singer, "Jung's Gnosticism," notes: "We can recognize the archetype of the *anima* in the figure of Sophia, the wilful, creative, compassionate, suffering redemptive feminine principle" (81).

31. See Stein, *Jung's Treatment of Christianity*, 111-94.

32. Hillman, *Anima*, 129-46, indicates that anima's protean nature stems from her mediatrix role. Jung, Hillman maintains, identified anima's wisdom with the undifferentiated wise old man (139).

33. Edinger, *Anatomy of the Psyche*, 211-32, observes that *conjunctio* or unification of opposites is the culmination of the alchemical opus. Augustine, Edinger notes, established the identity of the *conjunctio* and the crucifixion (218).

34. For Gnostic and apocryphal sources for Sophia as the bride of God, see Pagels, *Gnostic Gospels*, 60-80.

35. Though Paul Tillich does not recognize the Holy Spirit's feminine anima nature, he does recognize that the Spirit brings about integration of opposites in the Godhead. Dourley treats Jung and Tillich's shared notion that the Holy Spirit functions to unite opposites in *Psyche as Sacrament*, 79-90.

36. Engelsman maintains that the Gospel Jesus displays many aspects of archetypal androgyny, particularly in the Johannine Gospel, of which she writes: "John continually portrays Jesus as a caring, nurturing person in a way that is evocative of the great virgin goddesses Demeter and Isis. . . . It is immediately evident in his relationship to women: his mother (at Cana and the crucifixion); Mary (at the tomb); the Samaritan woman at the well; the woman taken in adultery; and Mary and Martha, the sisters of Lazarus. His care of them is characterized by respect, awareness, sensitivity, compassion and love. . . . It can be seen by this analysis that the Gospel of John identifies Christ with the archetypal feminine in three ways. First by means of the Prologue, Jesus is defined as the incarnate Logos, which is a masculine substitute for Sophia. Second the 'I am' statements and their symbols—e.g., light, water, vine—evoke the 'I am' statements of Wisdom and, therefore, support the Evangelist's understanding of Jesus as incarnate Wisdom. Third, the picture of Jesus as a divine figure who is particularly nurturing and caring endows him with at least some of the great virgin goddesses of that day" (117-19).

37. Erich Fromm, *The Dogma of Christ and Other Essays on Religion, Psychology and Culture* (New York: Holt, Rinehart & Winston, 1963), offers a Freudian analysis of this change.

38. Ernest Jones, *Essays in Applied Psycho-Analysis* (London: Hogarth, 1951), 2:367.

39. Boswell, *Christianity, Social Tolerance and Homosexuality*; Robin Scroggs, *The New Testament and Homosexuality* (Philadelphia: Fortress, 1986); and Vern L. Bullough and James Brundage, *Sexual Practices and the Medieval Church* (Buffalo: Prometheus, 1982), shed the light of modern scholarship on these changes.

40. See Boswell, *Christianity, Social Tolerance and Homosexuality*, 269-302.

41. For example, Jung identifies with Joaichem di Flora, a twelfth century visionary who foresaw an age of the Paraclete. Jung to Father White, 24 November 1953, *Letters* 2: 133-38; also *Aion*, 83-90.

42. See Paul Johnson, *A History of Christianity* (New York: Atheneum, 1979), 191-264; and Russell, *Dissent and Reform*.

43. See E. Jung, *Anima and Animus*; and Wehr *Jung and Feminism*, 103-26, for criticism of these traditional Jungian concepts. While animus may be an outmoded concept for explaining woman's psyche, as some feminists argue, it is still useful for explaining how patriarchal men, such as Milton, view women, and for that reason I have used it in modified form to explain Eve's behavior in *Paradise Lost*.

44. Here, as elsewhere, I do not speak of Milton the man in his real identity but of the writer in his persona as Christian apologist. The question of what Milton the man really believed I leave to the biographers. I am aware of the line of criticism that stresses modern and liberal trends in Milton's thoughts on women. While I believe that these trends greatly influenced Milton the artist, resulting in a sympathetic and relatively balanced portrait of Eve, I do not agree with those who use these elements of Milton's thought to deny that the stance of Milton the apologist is by and large patriarchal. Such a line of argument, sometimes used by Islamic scholars who point to the many feminine attributes of Allah as evidence that their religion and its God are not really patriarchal, reduces all examples of patriarchalism to

instances of feminist paranoia. For the recent feminist controversy over Milton, see Sandra Gilbert, "Patriarchal Poetry and Women Readers: Reflections on Milton's Bogey," *PMLA* 93 (1978): 368-82; Joan M. Webber, "The Politics of Poetry: Feminism and *Paradise Lost,*" *Milton Studies* 14 (1980): 3-24; Christine Froula, "Pechter's Specter: Milton's Bogey Writ Small; or, Why Is He Afraid of Virginia Woolf?" *Critical Inquiry* 2 (1984): 171-78; Diane Kelsey McColley, *Milton's Eve* (Urbana: Univ. of Illinois Press, 1983); William Shullenberger, "Wrestling with the Angel: *Paradise Lost* and Feminist Criticism," *Milton Quarterly* 20 (1986): 69-84; and Stevie Davies, *The Feminine Redeemed: The Idea of Woman in Spenser, Shakespeare, and Milton* (Lexington: Univ. Press of Kentucky, 1986). Also, Wittreich, *Feminist Milton*, argues that Milton subtly subverts misogynistic stereotypes in his portrait of Eve.

45. Joseph Summers, *The Muses Method* (London: Chatto and Windus, 1960), 87-111, presents a balanced view of Milton's own attitudes on the two great sexes. He concludes: "However much Adam and many masculine readers may wish to distort the issues, there is no justification in the poem for serious misogyny: it is man's, not woman's weakness, which is responsible for the Fall" (111).

46. Russell Smith, Jr., "Adam's Fall" (*ELH* 35, no. 4 (Dec. 1968): 44-56) develops an analogous approach as he argues that Adam is, for want of a better term, a split personality consisting of the "Adam in Adam" (Adam's masculine ego) and the "Eve in Adam" (his feminine anima). Smith shows that well before the fall, in Adam's conversations with Raphael, the "Eve in Adam" seeks angelhood.

47. J.M. Evans, *"Paradise Lost" and the Genesis Tradition* (Oxford: Oxford Univ. Press, 1968), 272-80, contends that Eve's speech is symptomatic, in the words of St. Augustine, of "a certain proud, self-presumption." This view places her moral defection at her decision to leave Adam.

48. Dennis Burden, *Milton's Logical Epic* (Cambridge: Harvard Univ. Press, 1967), 60-77, is a notable exception. Burden, sacrificing the logic of dramatic emotion to the logic of Miltonic doctrine, argues that Adam's mistake was not to divorce Eve.

49. For a standard scholarly account of Milton's use of Genesis see Evans, *"Paradise Lost" and the Genesis Tradition.*

50. The idea that Milton's art stands at odds with his theology was promulgated by Waldock, *Paradise Lost and its Critics*; E.N.W. Tillyard, *Studies in Milton* (London: Chatto, 1951); Empson, *Milton's God*; and Millicent Bell, "The Fallacy of the Fall in *Paradise Lost*" *PMLA* 68 (1953): 863-83. Numerous works have appeared to counter this notion, among them: H.V.S. Ogden, "The Crisis of Paradise Lost Reconsidered," *Philological Quarterly* 36 (1957): 1-19; Burden, Milton's *Logical Epic*; Fish, *Surprised by Sin*; Barbara K. Lewalski, "Innocence and Experience in Milton's Eden," *New Essays on "Paradise Lost,"* ed. Thomas Kranidas (Berkeley: Univ. of California Press, 1971), 86-117; and Diane McColley, "Free Will and Obedience in the Separation Scene of *Paradise Lost,*" *Studies in English Literature* 12 (1972): 103-20.

51. Patrides, *Bright Essence*, remarks: "Milton differentiates between the Father and the Son only during their verbal exchanges in the various councils that took place in heaven, but as soon as these councils end and the Godhead acts beyond the confines of heaven, the distinction between the two persons is abruptly dropped. . . . During the council after the Fall of Man the Father and the Son are clearly differentiated (10.21ff), but once the Judge leaves heaven for the Garden of Eden he is once again termed 'God,' even 'the Lord God' (10.163)" (12). So who judges Adam in Eden? It would be a mistake to conclude that God the Father or God as all Three Persons of the Trinity judge man. After all, the Father has sent the Son, and while the Son is called "God" and "the Lord God," as Patrides notes, the narrator also refers to Him as "both Judge and Savior sent" (10.209) and "the mild Judge and Intercessor" (10.96), which Patrides fails to note. I find it hard to imagine how the "Judge

and Savior" and "Intercessor" could be anyone other than the Son in view of the paucity of references in Milton or any other Christian writer to the Father or the Holy Ghost as "Savior" or "Intercessor."

52. John Reichert, "'Against his Better Knowledge': A Case for Adam," *ELH* 48 (1981): 83-109, suggests that Adam may fall because he makes an intellectual mistake about the severity of God's judgment. This view ignores sequence. Clearly, Adam makes and announces his decision in IX.900-16. Having made the decision on impulse of love, he reflects upon and reconfirms it to himself: "So Having said, as one from sad dismay/ Recomforted, and after thoughts disturb'd/Submitting to what seemd remediless/Thus in calm mood his Words to Eve he turnd" (IX.917-20). His reflections are followed by (1) the "fallen" rationalizations of 921-50; (2) a restatement of his love and initial decision, 952-58; (3) Eve's praise of his decision and rationalization of hers, 961-89; and (4) Adam's eating of the fruit.

53. Milton's neo-orthodox expositors seem unaware that commands, training, and discipline are inextricably bound together. Danielson, *Milton's Good God*, for example, writes: "But the point is that all Adam apparently need do in order to prevent Eve's wandering off by herself is to forbid it. And because it is constraint, not command, that negates freedom, he *can* forbid it. He would not thereby violate Eve's freedom to go if she so chose, any more than God's commanding them not to eat of the forbidden fruit prevents their freely doing so" (127). What Danielson overlooks is that constraint must be used to train people to obey command. We only learn to obey by internalizing through training what was originally an external constraint. Far from negating freedom, constraint teaches the discipline that alone can free us from slavery to our passions and impulses. Furthermore, while freedom is the fruit of inner discipline taught through external constraint, arbitrary commands instituted as a symbolic act of submission to external authority are inimical to freedom.

54. Matthew 7:16.

55. Jung, *Alchemical Studies*, in *Collected Works* 13:302.

56. Jung details them in "The Philosophical Tree," in *Alchemical Studies*, 251-349.

57. Here the tree represents the earth and matter from which the alchemists tried to free Mercurius, the fiery spirit, and put him into their service. Jung, *Alchemical Studies*, 195-230.

58. Ibid, 283, for Jung's remarks on the synonymity of Christ, Logos, and Mercurious.

59. Theodor Reik, *Myth and Guilt* (New York: George Braziller, 1957), 138-43.

60. Ibid, 360.

61. Ibid, 32.

62. Jungians are likely to disagree with Reik since in *Answer to Job* Jung's central point is that the crime atoned for on the cross is not man's crime against God but God's crime against man. The orthodox will probably view Jung's theory and Reik's with equal horror. Once that horror has subsided, they are left with their own failure to so much as venture a psychologically satisfactory explanation.

63. Reik, *Myth and Guilt*, 377.

64. Ibid, 396.

65. See Alice Miller, *Thou Shalt Not Be Aware*, trans. Hildegarde Hannum and Hunter Hannum (New York: Farrar, Straus and Giroux, 1984); and *For Your Own Good*, trans. Hildegarde Hannum and Hunter Hannum (New York: Farrar, Straus and Giroux, 1983).

66. In respect to Milton, the Millerite position has to some extent been adumbrated by Empson.

67. Miller, *Thou Shalt Not be Aware*, 219-28, asserts that Freud's personal fear of the tyrant father God led to his drive theory with its oedipal complex.

68. Ibid, 221.

69. Hillman, "Betrayal," argues, quite contrary to Miller, that the tree, far from being the exemplar of the first child abuse, symbolizes the father's positive role in initiating the child into the world. The father, Hillman contends, deliberately betrays the child to train him to deal with a hostile world.

70. Reik, *Myth and Guilt*, 399-415.

71. For philosophical background on the subject of free will as it relates to the fall in *Paradise Lost*, see Arendt, *Willing*; Paul Ricoeur's phenomenological study, *Freedom and Nature: The Voluntary and Involuntary*, (Evanston, Ill.: Northwestern Univ. Press, 1966); and Bergmann, *On Being Free*.

72. Ironically, the concept of free will moves closest to the surface of consciousness in passages that charge the Israelites to "choose" between servitudes—Yahweh's or that of some other god. Cf. Joshua 24:15, "Choose ye this day whom ye will serve" and 1 Kings 18:21, "How long halt ye between two opinions." See also Leviticus 22:18, 21, 23, 38; Numbers 15:3, 29:39; Deuteronomy 12:6, 12; 16:10; 2 Chronicles 31:14; Psalms 119:108.

73. Pagels, *Gnostic Gospels*, 57-77, reviews the Gnostic interpretations of Genesis, including Valentinius's view that the power of free will is extremely limited. Russell, *Satan*, 80-88, notes that Irenaeus, Tertulian, and the Montanists were among the earliest to use free will to justify the ways of God to men.

74. See Peter Brown, *Augustine of Hippo* (Univ. of California Press, 1971), 372ff, for a summary of Augustine's views on freedom.

75. Pelagius's stance reflects the orthodox belief common in the second and third centuries that God created men with a moral freedom that, empowered by Baptism, could enable them to live transformed lives. Thus, on free will Pelagius and Milton are both closer to primitive Christianity than is Augustine. Moreover, Pelagius and Milton, Britons each, embraced an empirical outlook that contrasted with Augustine's rationalism. Pagels, *Adam, Eve, and the Serpent*, 126-50, presents a concise, up-to-date scholarly account of the Pelagian controversy. In uncovering the controversy's political roots, Pagels makes clear Pelagius's and Julian of Eclanum's similarity to Milton. John Ferguson, *Pelagius: A Historical and Theological Study* (Cambridge: Cambridge Univ. Press, 1966), also presents a Pelagius whose ideas on free will closely resemble those of Milton in *Paradise Lost*. Milton denied association with the branded heretic Pelagius. However, he didn't really know what Pelagius taught because all his writings were destroyed, and what we know comes from enemies, chief among them Augustine, who was never known for fairness to opponents. Contemporary scholars present Pelagius more objectively and indicate the similarity of his ideas to those of the Arminians and Milton. See also Danielson, *Milton's Good God*, 58-91; and Patrides *Milton and Christian Doctrine*, 121-52. For a fulsome example of Miltonic optimism, see his *Tractate on Education*.

76. Drawing on *De Civitate Dei* 13:21, Elaine Pagels argues in *Adams, Eve and the Serpent*, that Augustine believed that humanity was never meant to be free: "Augustine, on the contrary, having denied that human beings possess any capacity whatever for free will, accepts a definition of liberty far more agreeable to the powerful and influential . . . It is the serpent who tempts Adam with the seductive lure of liberty. . . . So, as we noted above, Augustine concludes that humanity never was really meant to be, in any sense, truly free. God allowed us to sin in order to prove to us from our own experience that 'our true good is slavery'" (120).

77. Historians often attribute Augustine's pessimism to the dark times and specifically to the despair induced by the fall of Rome. However, Pelagius himself may refute those who blame the times. Augustine's contemporary, he developed opposing views as optimistic as anything advanced in the exuberant Renaissance.

78. Tanner, "'Say First What Cause'," shows that Milton fluctuates between a Pelagian and an Augustian view on the etiology of sin.

79. Arnold Toynbee, *A Study of History,* revised and abridged (New York: Weathervane, 1974), 169.

80. "Thou hast made us for thyself [*fecisti nos ad te*] and our hearts are restless until they rest in thee"—so runs the famous and untranslatable phrase in the *Confessions.* Ireneus, concerned with the alienation of humanity from God, first developed the concept of alienation as the source of original sin. It soon became a common patristic notion and, like so many common patristic notions, eventually found its abiding form in Augustine.

81. In *Dei Civitate,* book 14, chap. 13, 25-26, Augustine calls the falling away spontaneous. By this he means it flows spontaneously from the will, not that it was without causal explanation. That the fall has an internal cause in man's alienation from God becomes evident when Augustine explains that the will would not have sought satisfaction in itself had it remained steadfast in its love: "Our first parents fell into open disobedience because already they were secretly corrupted; for the evil act had never been done had not an evil will preceded it. . . . This falling away is spontaneous; for if the will had remained steadfast in the love of that higher changeless good by which it was illumined to intelligence and kindled into love, it would not have turned away to satisfaction in itself, and so become frigid and benighted; the woman would not have believed the serpent spoke the truth, nor would the man have preferred the request of his wife to the command of god."

82. To sin in Genesis is simply to anger or displease Yahweh. From Moses onward sin becomes either impurity or transgression of Yahweh's laws, which is a form of rebellion against him. With the prophets it begins to take on meanings closer to alienation. For Jung and much of modern psychology, sin violates the self by choosing the part over the whole—the paradigmatic sin is thus idolatry.

83. Accordingly, Pagels, *Adam, Eve and the Serpent,* 120, argues that Augustine taught, "Slavery to God in the first place and, in the second, to his agent, the emperor."

84. In attempting to eliminate the sense of sin and guilt, Nietzsche, like Spinoza, strives to liberate us from the only bondage that ultimately matters, spiritual bondage.

85. In *De Doctrina,* 298, Milton assures us that the Holy Spirit stands far below the Son, who is subordinate to the Father: "The Holy Spirit . . . was created . . . maybe before the foundations of the world were laid, but after the Son, to whom he is far inferior." Milton further informs us that "the brightness of God's glory and the image of his divine subsistence are said to have been impressed on the Son but not on the Holy Spirit."

86. Hugh Richmond, *The Christian Revolutionary: John Milton* (Berkeley: Univ. of California Press, 1974), 54-55, comments upon Milton's early ode on "The Passion": "Milton admits that his mind cannot cope with the horrifying challenge of the crucifixion: 'This Subject the Author finding to be above the years he had, when he wrote it, and nothing satisfied with what was begun, left it unfinished.' This early incapacity to cope with tragic suffering is typical of the other failures induced by over-optimism . . . It is also characteristic of the ambitious spirit of the age which increasingly avoids the tragic view of life."

87. I shall use the term "Messiah" for the protagonist of *Paradise Regained* rather than "Christ," because for Milton he is not Christ until the crucifixion, a distinction about which Milton is very careful throughout his writings.

88. While the view that the temptation in Milton centers on the two hostile brothers archetype is Jungian, it is not a view posited by Jung himself. Jung, who rarely deals with Milton, interpreted the temptation in the Gospel myth as a collision between Jesus as ego and the power of the objective psyche. Jung writes of the temptation: "The story of the Temptation clearly reveals the nature of the psychic power with which Jesus came into collision: it was the power intoxicated devil of the prevailing Caesarean psychology that led him into dire temptation in the wilderness. This devil was the objective psyche that held all peoples of the Roman Empire under its sway, . . . Jesus voluntarily exposed himself to the

assaults of the imperialistic madness that filled everyone, conqueror and conquered alike. In this way he recognized the nature of the objective psyche which had plunged the whole world into misery and had begotten a yearning for salvation that found expression even in the pagan poets. Far from suppressing or allowing himself to be suppressed by this psychic onslaught, he let it act on him consciously, and assimilated it. Thus was world conquering Caesarism transformed into spiritual kingship, and the Roman empire into the universal Kingdom of God that was not of this world" *Development of Personality*, 180.

89. See Blake's watercolor #2, The First Temptation, and watercolor #7, The Second Temptation. Edinger, *Encounter with Self*, offers a specifically Jungian commentary of Blake's illustrations. Joseph Anthony Wittreich, *Angel of Apocalypse* (Madison: Univ. of Wisconsin Press, 1975), 104-42, weighs the critical import of the illustrations.

90. The classic scholarly treatment of the Book of Job's influence on *Paradise Regained* remains Barbara J. Lewalski, *Milton's Brief Epic* (Providence: Brown Univ. Press, 1966).

91. Marvin Pope, introduction to the *Anchor Bible Book of Job*, (Garden City, Doubleday, 1965), XV.

92. Stephen Mitchell, *The Book of Job* (San Francisco: North Point, 1987), presents a lively modern translation. For a survey of various modern perspectives on Job, see *The Dimensions of Job*, ed. Nahum N. Glatzer (New York: Schocken, 1969). The following verses from Mitchell's translation illustrate Job's Promethean stance:

"I swear by God, who has wronged me/and filled my cup with despair,/that while there is life in this body/and as long as I can breathe/I will never let you convict me,/I will never give up my claim,/I will hold tight to my innocence;/my mind will never submit" (64).

93. Antaeus is the son of Gaiia, the primal mother earth, and Poseidon, the sea god. Poseidon is an Olympian and a brother to Zeus Alcides the heavenly father. Thus, Antaeus and Alcides are cousins, or brothers once removed.

94. For a Jungian analysis of initiation, see Joseph L. Henderson *Thresholds of Initiation* (Middletown, Conn.: Wesleyan Univ. Press, 1967).

95. By saying that the Oedipus-Sphinx motif has the Jungian meaning of the trickster tricked I do not mean that this is either the only Jungian meaning or Jung's personal interpretation, which was rather different. Jung, *Symbols of Transformation, Collected Works* 5:181-82, writes: "Oedipus thinking he had overcome the Sphinx sent by the mother-goddess merely because he had solved her childishly simple riddle, fell a victim to matriarchal incest. . . . This had all those tragic consequences which could easily have been avoided if only Oedipus had been sufficiently intimidated by her frightening appearance of the "terrible" or "devouring" Mother whom the Sphinx personified . . . It is evident that a factor of such magnitude cannot be disposed of by solving a childish riddle. . . . Over-estimating his intellect in a typically masculine way, Oedipus walked right into it, and all unknowingly committed the crime of incest. The riddle of the Sphinx was herself—the terrible mother-imago, which Oedipus would not take as a warning." The above observations also apply to Messiah and Satan. Satan, representing the devouring Mother, cannot be dispelled in a masculine, rational way. Though he falls, he is not dispelled but returns, disguised in the inflated, rationalistic theology that makes God all powerful and all good.

96. Neumann, "Mystical Man," 198.

97. Ibid, 398.

98. N. Frye, *Five Essays*, notes: "Christ's main scriptural ally in rejecting this temptation is Ecclesiastes, with its doctrine that there is a time for all things" (146).

99. Lieb, *Dialectics of Creation*, presents the Son as a representive of creativity in *Paradise Lost*. See also Kierkegaard, *Philosophical Fragments* and *Concluding Unscientific Postscript*, for discussions of how in the Christian world view creativity works through time and in history.

100. Neumann, "Mystical Man," 401.

101. Ibid., 402.

102. James Driscoll, "Hamlet's Quest for Self-Knowledge," in *Identity in Shakespearean Drama*, 50-69, develops the dragon fight in *Hamlet* in terms of Jung's psychology.

103. The uroboros devours itself while Sin's offspring feed upon her without ever devouring her (*Paradise Lost*, 2.746-814). But since these offspring (e.g. Death) are aspects of Sin, in feeding on her they complete the uroboric circle.

104. Milton intends Satan, Death, and Sin to be an evil Trinity parodying Father, Son, and Holy Spirit. The fact that he portrayed Sin as unmistakably feminine is further evidence of the poet's unconscious recognition of the femininity of her divine counterpart, the Holy Spirit. Milton's conscious position, developed in *De Doctrina*, where the Holy Spirit is neuter, is of course quite different. Sin as the Unholy Spirit is a clear instance of the poet's unconscious compensating conscious errors and imbalances.

105. See Lee S. Cox, "Food-Word Images in *PR*," *ELH* 28 (1961): 225-43.

106. Breugel, El Greco, Bosch, and numerous other Renaissance painters represented the opening of hell as a devouring mouth.

107. Certain dualist heretics made that complicity an article belief. Some Bogomils, for example, held that God and Satan were comrades, brothers, or associates from eternity. See Runciman, *Medieval Manichee*, 73-87.

108. Dostoevski develops this point in *The Brothers Karamazov* with the characters of Father Zossima and Alyosha Karamazov.

109. Lewalski, *Milton: Brief Epic*, 133.

110. Jung, *Answer to Job* writes: "There is no evidence that Christ ever wondered about himself, or that he ever confronted himself. To this rule there is only one significant exception—the despairing cry from the cross: 'My God, my God, why hast thou forsaken me?' Here his human nature attains divinity; at that moment God experiences what it means to be a mortal man and drinks to the dregs what he made his faithful servant Job suffer. Here is given the answer to Job, and clearly, this supreme moment is as divine as it is human, as 'eschatological' as it is 'psychological'" (408).

111. The notion that Messiah does not learn or change challenges the critical consensus on *Paradise Regained*. Speaking for the consensus, Lewalski states: "Satan appears to do all the acting . . . Yet it is in Christ's consciousness, not Satan's, that the real development and change take place" (162).

112. See, for example, Lewalski, *Milton: Brief Epic*, 310.

113. William Butler Yeats, *The Autobiography of W.B. Yeats*, (New York: Macmillan, 1971), 128.

114. *De Doctrina*, 589.

115. David Masson, *The Life of John Milton*, 7 vols (Cambridge: Macmillan, 1859-1894), 6:746.

116. W. B. Hunter "Milton's Muse," in *Bright Essence*, 149-56. By contrast, Shawcross, *With Mortal Voice*, proposes that the Muse is the spirit of God and defines the Holy Spirit by love, which links it to the eros function of anima: "The spirit of God, at least, is invoked, regardless of which specific person of the Trinity is intended. The Holy Spirit is explained by the love of the Father and the Son, however, which has thus created the third person of the Trinity. The Spirit of God (his virtus) is therefore an aspect of God while implying the presence of the other two aspects" (14). See also Nathaniel H. Henry, "The Mystery of Milton's Muse," *Renaissance Papers 1967* (1968), 69-83.

117. Somewhat unexpectedly, Kerrigan, in his Freudian reading of *Paradise Lost*, *The Sacred Complex*, also assumes Milton's putative conscious intentions are the standard for interpreting the identity Milton's muse: "The third and oldest interpretation, revived

periodically, equates the light addressed with the Holy Spirit. This reading demands subtle dialectics or staunch faith to explain away Milton's flat statement in *Christian Doctrine* that the Spirit, if there is a Spirit, 'cannot be a God nor an object of invocation' (CP VI, 295)" (150).

118. Jung, "Psychology and Literature," 90.

119. Neumann, *Great Mother,* 330.

120. Stevie Davies and William B. Hunter, "Milton's Urania: 'The meaning, not the name I call,'" *SEL* 28 (Winter 1988): 101-102.

121. Ibid, 105.

CHAPTER 4. YAHWEH AGONISTES

1. See John T. Shawcross, "The Chronology of Milton's Major Poems," *PMLA* 76 (1960): 345-58; Alan H. Gilbert, "Is *Samson Agonistes* Unfinished?" *PQ* 28 (1949): 98-106; and William Riley Parker, "The Date of *Samson Agonistes*," *PQ* 28 (1949): 145-66.

2. See William Riley Parker, *Milton: A Biography,* 2 vols (Oxford: Clarendon, 1968).

3. The most exhaustive treatment of this notion is Mary Ann Radzinowicz, *Toward "Samson Agonistes,"* (Princeton: Princeton Univ. Press, 1978). See also James Holly Hanford, *"Samson Agonistes* and Milton in Old Age," *Studies in Shakespeare, Milton and Donne* (New York: Macmillan, 1925), 167-89.

4. The monarchists considered executing Milton at the beginning of the Restoration, decided not to, and thereafter ignored him.

5. In sonnet 22 Milton attributes his blindness to work done on *Defensio prima,* although this probably only hastened the inevitable. He lost the sight in the left eye in 1647, had troubles before, and may have inherited weak vision from his mother.

6. The subject of sonnet 23, Milton's "late espoused Saint," could be Mary Powell, but that would not alter my point that the sonnet reflects a more mature view of woman than does *Samson Agonistes.* Furthermore, if the sonnet's subject if Mary Powell, it must reflect Milton's fonder recollections of her whereas the portrait of Dalila would reflect his bitter experiences with her.

7. While I am the first to note the resemblance between Yahweh and Lear (see my *Identity in Shakespearean Drama*), I am not the first to perceive the Yahweh archetype behind Samson. Edinger discusses it, albeit briefly, in *Bible and Psyche*: "The story of Samson (Judges 13-16) is that of a conjunctio gone wrong. It begins with a wedding between Samson the Israelite and the daughter of a Philistine. In the midst of the wedding feast Samson poses a riddle. 'Out of the eater came what is eaten, and out of the strong came what is sweet' (Judges 14:5-8) This refers to the honeycomb Samson found in the carcass of the lion he had killed. . . . What does it mean that out of a dead lion comes sweet honey? It signifies the transformation of the power principle. The 'spirit of Yahweh' dwelled in Samson, allowing him to do great deeds of valor and vengeance when under the influence of intense affect (e.g., Judges 14:19). . . . The synchronistic event of finding a honeycomb in the body of the lion he had killed was meant to inform Samson the nazirite and man of God that it was his task to contribute to the transformation of God. From this perspective, the lion's death and Samson's defeat and death are symbolically equivalent. They both picture the transformation of the archetypal power principle . . . Samson personifies the torturous process of transformation of the power motive: Lion→Honey, Yahweh→Christ" (72-73).

8. Irene Samuel, "*Samson Agonistes* as Tragedy," in *Calm of Mind,* ed. Joseph Anthony Wittreich (Cleveland: Case Western Reserve Univ. Press, 1971), 235-57.

9. Samuel observes in "*Samson Agonistes* as Tragedy": "That he is garrulous still, even a theater-going audience inured to Beckett and Albee must grant. He easily outtalks the Chorus (their lyrical passages of course excepted). He similarly outtalks Manoa, though old

age is generally reckoned garrulous. He answers all but one of Dalila's speeches (if we except her parting speech which he has no chance to answer) with speeches yet longer, though he makes the common accusation against female longwindedness (II. 905-906)" (246).

10. For a Freudian view of Dalila's shaving Samson that interprets shaving as a symbolic castration see Herman Rappoport, *Milton and the Post-Modern* (Lincoln: Univ. of Nebraska Press), 141-55. A shaved head can doubtless symbolize emasculation. Whether because of his rejection of Freud or because of patriarchal and Protestant inhibitions, Jung failed to recognize that one of the characteristic impulses of repressed anima was to emasculate men. Dalilah's shaving Samson is the prime mythic enactment of this destructive anima impulse.

11. See Jung, *Transformation Symbolism in the Mass*, in *Collected Works* 11:228-29; and *Alchemical Studies* 12:338-339.

12. Shawcross, "Irony as Tragic Effect," in Samuel, *Calm of Mind*, observes: "Samson should be viewed ironically as one who acting entirely out of his faith, commits an act whose meaning and consequences he does not understand—an act that achieves what he desired and what he would have done consciously had he been able" (291).

13. A restrained version of this position is offered in A.S.P. Woodhouse, "The Tragic Effect of *Samson Agonistes*," *University of Toronto Quarterly* 28 (1958-1959): 205-22. Less restrained is the argument for Samson's regeneration in William Riley Parker, *Milton's Debt to Greek Tragedy in "Samson Agonistes,"* (Baltimore: Johns Hopkins, 1937).

14. Don Cameron Allen, *The Harmonious Vision: Studies in Milton's Poetry* (Baltimore: Johns Hopkins Univ. Press, 1954), 71-94. Allen may well be the only major critic to have risen to the Philistine lady's defense. Although he has a point of view worth exploring, his conclusions are extreme.

15. For detailed accounts of anima's role in male psychology see Jung, *Two Essays*, and *Aion*; James Hillman, *Anima: An Anatomy of a Personified Notion*, (Dallas: Spring, 1985) as well as E. Jung, *Animus and Anima* (Zurich: Spring, 1972).

16. In his *Anima*, Hillman lists four grades of anima: (1) Eve; (2) Helen; (3) Mary; (4) Sophia. Mary spiritualizes Eve, and Sophia spiritualizes Helen. Milton's Dalila, I believe, can be seen as Helen's dark, entirely sensual side. Samson-Yahweh, thus, instead of joining with the spiritualized Helen to attain wisdom, joins with the sensual Helen to consummate folly and self-degradation.

17. Bradley A. Te Paske, *Rape and Ritual* (Toronto: Inner City, 1982), observes: "A condition in which the anima is consciously unrealized, and thus left submerged in or contaminated with the whole of the unconscious, constitutes the foundation of all misogynous attitudes. Precisely this blindness sustains as well the collective prejudice which considers woman as the responsible party in sexual assault" (80).

18. Part of the answer doubtless also lies in Milton's own personal vulnerabilities. For perceptive studies of these vulnerabilities see John T. Shawcross, "Milton and Diodati: An Essay in Psychodynamic Meaning," *Milton Studies* 7 (1975): 127-63, and William Kerrigan, *Sacred Complex*, 21-72.

19. Jung, *Answer to Job*, 391. Since Jung wrote *Answer to Job* considerable historical scholarship has appeared that sheds more light on the feminine companions to the Hebrew deity, if not directly upon the anima of Yahweh in the Book of Job. See, for example, Englesman, *Feminine Dimension*; Rosemary Ruether, ed., *Religion and Sexism: Images of Woman in the Jewish and Christian Traditions* (New York: Simon Schuster, 1974); Patai, *Hebrew Goddess*; and Phyllis Trible, "Depatriarchalizing in Biblical Interpretation," *The Jewish Woman: New Perspectives* (New York: Schocken, 1972), 73-114.

20. Patai, *Hebrew Goddess*, summarizes Lilith's career as follows: "No she-demon has ever achieved as fantastic a career as Lilith who started out from the lowliest of origins, was a

failure as Adam's intended wife, became the paramour of lascivious spirits, rose to be the bride of Samuel the demon King, ruled as the Queen of Zemargad and Sheba, and finally ended up as the consort of God himself. The main features of Lilith's mythical biography first appear in Sumerian culture about the middle of the 3rd millennium B. C. What she meant for the Biblical Hebrews can only be surmised, but by the Talmudic period (2nd to 5th centuries A. D.) she was a fully developed evil she-demon, and during the kabbalistic age she rose to the high position of queenly consort at God's side" (207). Milton, who knew the Zohar and the Kabbala, would of course have been familiar with Lilith's career. She is mentioned, moreover, in Isaiah 34:14: "The wild cat shall meet with the jackals, and the satyr shall cry to his fellow, Yea, Lilith shall repose there and find her place of rest."

    21. Samuel, *Calm of Mind*, 247.

    22. See William G. Madsen, *From Shadowy Types to Truth: Studies in Milton's Symbolism* (New Haven: Yale Univ. Press, 1968).

    23. Some may object that Milton's intent in *De Doctrina* is educative rather than theological, that he is explaining doctrine rather than arguing it. While this may be his conscious intent, his departure from orthodoxy on the Trinity, a dogma that stands at the very heart of Christian doctrine, and his elaborate scriptural justifications for that departure indicate, at the very least, desire to play theologian and argue doctrine.

    24. For a discussion of Aristotle and the Preface see John M. Steadman, "'Passions Well Imitated': Rhetoric and Poetics in the Preface to *Samson Agonistes*," in Samuel, *Calm of Mind*, 175-207; and Radzinowicz, *Toward Samson Agonistes*, 8-14.

    25. R.C. Jebb, "*Samson Agonistes* and the Hellenic Drama," *Proceedings of the British Academy* 3 (1908): 1-8.

    26. George Steiner, *The Death of Tragedy* (New York: Oxford Univ. Press, 1980), poses this pregnant question while discussing the Preface to *Samson Agonistes*: "Could a man write the word "tragedy" across a blank page without hearing at his back the immense presence of the *Oresteia*, of *Oedipus*, of *Hamlet*, and of *King Lear*?" (35).

    27. At an early date Milton set down some possible topics for development in the life of Christ, and he wrote a brief outline of *Christus Patiens*: these efforts indicate early interest in the tragedy of Godhead. The preface to the dramatic poem may have been written in 1670. But being written in 1670 does not mean that its concerns were exclusively those of the day, for Milton may have taken the occasion of writing the preface to reflect on his concerns when he first began the project. Moreover, regardless of when it was written, the preface refects his intuitions about the *Samson Agonistes*'s controlling archetypes.

Index

Note: g following a page number signifies a glossary entry

DATE DUE

~~MAR 19 1999~~	~~MAR 24 2005~~	
~~MAY 3 2005~~		
	~~SEP~~	

Demco, Inc. 38-293